Interface Circuits for Microsensor Integrated Systems

Interface Circuits for Microsensor Integrated Systems

Special Issue Editors

Giuseppe Ferri
Vincenzo Stornelli

MDPI • Basel • Beijing • Wuhan • Barcelona • Belgrade

Special Issue Editors
Giuseppe Ferri
University of L'Aquila
Italy

Vincenzo Stornelli
Università degli Studi dell'Aquila
Italy

Editorial Office
MDPI
St. Alban-Anlage 66
4052 Basel, Switzerland

This is a reprint of articles from the Special Issue published online in the open access journal *Micromachines* (ISSN 2072-666X) in 2018 (available at: https://www.mdpi.com/journal/micromachines/special_issues/Interface_Circuit_Microsensor_Integrated_Systems)

For citation purposes, cite each article independently as indicated on the article page online and as indicated below:

LastName, A.A.; LastName, B.B.; LastName, C.C. Article Title. *Journal Name* **Year**, *Article Number,* Page Range.

ISBN 978-3-03897-376-8 (Pbk)
ISBN 978-3-03897-377-5 (PDF)

Contents

About the Special Issue Editors ix

Giuseppe Ferri and Vincenzo Stornelli
Editorial for the Special Issue on Interface Circuits for Microsensor Integrated Systems
Reprinted from: *Micromachines* **2018**, *9*, 527, doi:10.3390/mi9100527 1

Leonardo Pantoli, Gianluca Barile, Alfiero Leoni, Mirco Muttillo and Vincenzo Stornelli
A Novel Electronic Interface for Micromachined Si-Based Photomultipliers
Reprinted from: *Micromachines* **2018**, *9*, 507, doi:10.3390/mi9100507 3

Zhiliang Qiao, Boris A. Boom, Anne-Johan Annema, Remco J. Wiegerink and Bram Nauta
On Frequency-Based Interface Circuits
for Capacitive MEMS Accelerometers
Reprinted from: *Micromachines* **2018**, *9*, 488, doi:10.3390/mi9100488 17

Marco Demori, Marco Baù, Marco Ferrari and Vittorio Ferrari
Interrogation Techniques and Interface Circuits for Coil-Coupled Passive Sensors
Reprinted from: *Micromachines* **2018**, *9*, 449, doi:10.3390/mi9090449 38

Hyungseup Kim, Byeoncheol Lee, Yeongjin Mun, Jaesung Kim, Kwonsang Han,
Youngtaek Roh, Dongkyu Song, Seounghoon Huh and Hyoungho Ko
Reconfigurable Sensor Analog Front-End Using Low-Noise Chopper-Stabilized Delta-Sigma
Capacitance-to-Digital Converter
Reprinted from: *Micromachines* **2018**, *9*, 347, doi:10.3390/mi9070347 61

Arnaldo D'Amico, Marco Santonico, Giorgio Pennazza, Alessandro Zompanti,
Emma Scipioni, Giuseppe Ferri, Vincenzo Stornelli, Marcello Salmeri and Roberto Lojacono
Resonant Directly Coupled Inductors–Capacitors Ladder Network Shows a New, Interesting
Property Useful for Application in the Sensor Field, Down to Micrometric Dimensions
Reprinted from: *Micromachines* **2018**, *9*, 343, doi:10.3390/mi9070343 77

Piero Malcovati and Andrea Baschirotto
The Evolution of Integrated Interfaces for MEMS Microphones
Reprinted from: *Micromachines* **2018**, *9*, 323, doi:10.3390/mi9070323 89

Chen-Mao Wu, Hsiao-Chin Chen, Ming-Yu Yen and San-Ching Yang
Chopper-Stabilized Instrumentation Amplifier with Automatic Frequency Tuning Loop
Reprinted from: *Micromachines* **2018**, *9*, 289, doi:10.3390/mi9060289 109

Rongshan Wei and Xiaotian Bao
A Low Power Energy-Efficient Precision CMOS Temperature Sensor
Reprinted from: *Micromachines* **2018**, *9*, 257, doi:10.3390/mi9060257 122

Yongshan Hu, Qiuqin Yue, Shan Lu, Dongchen Yang, Shuxin Shi, Xiaokun Zhang and
Hua Yu
An Adaptable Interface Conditioning Circuit Based on Triboelectric Nanogenerators for
Self-Powered Sensors
Reprinted from: *Micromachines* **2018**, *9*, 105, doi:10.3390/mi9030105 132

Wei Liu, Rong An, Chunqing Wang, Zhen Zheng, Yanhong Tian, Ronglin Xu and Zhongtao Wang
Recent Progress in Rapid Sintering of Nanosilver for Electronics Applications
Reprinted from: *Micromachines* **2018**, *9*, 346, doi:10.3390/mi9070346 . . . . **140**

About the Special Issue Editors

Giuseppe Ferri was born in L'Aquila, Italy. He received the "Laurea" degree (cum laude) in electronic engineering in 1988. In 1991, he joined the Department of Electronic Engineering, University of L'Aquila, L'Aquila, Italy, where he is actually a full professor of Electronics and Microelectronics at the University of L'Aquila, Italy. His research activity mainly concerns the design of analog electronic circuits for integrated sensor applications both in voltage and in current-mode. In this field of research, he is author or coauthor of 6 patents, 3 international books, one book chapter and more than 380 publications in international journals and conference proceedings. He is an IEEE senior member and Editor of Sensors and of Journal of Circuits, Computers and Systems.

Vincenzo Stornelli was born in Avezzano, Italy. He received the "Laurea" degree (cum laude) in electronic engineering in 2004. In October 2004, he joined the Department of Electronic Engineering, University of L'Aquila, L'Aquila, Italy, where he is involved as Associate Professor. His research interests include several topics in computational electromagnetics, including microwave antenna analysis for outdoor ultrawideband applications. He serves as a reviewer for several international journals and Editor of the Journal of Circuits, Computers and Systems.

Editorial

Editorial for the Special Issue on Interface Circuits for Microsensor Integrated Systems

Giuseppe Ferri * and Vincenzo Stornelli *

Department of Industrial and Information Engineering and Economics, University of L'Aquila, 67100 L'Aquila, Italy
* Correspondence: giuseppe.ferri@univaq.it (G.F.); vincenzo.stornelli@univaq.it (V.S.)

Received: 15 October 2018; Accepted: 15 October 2018; Published: 17 October 2018

Recent advances in sensing technologies, especially those for Microsensor Integrated Systems, have led to several new commercial applications. Among these, low voltage and low power circuit architectures are a focus of growing interest, being suitable for portable long battery life devices. The aim is to improve the performances of actual interface circuits and systems, both in terms of voltage mode and current mode, in order to overcome the potential problems due to technology scaling and different technology integrations. Related problems, especially those concerning parasitics, lead to a strong interest in interface design; particularly, analog front-end and novel and smart architecture must be explored and tested, both at simulation and prototype level. Moreover, the growing demand for autonomous systems is more difficult to meet in the interface design due to the need for energy-aware cost-effective circuit interfaces integration and, where possible, energy harvesting solutions. The objective of this Special Issue has been to explore the potential solutions to overcome actual limitations in sensor interface circuits and systems, especially those for low voltage and low power Microsensor Integrated Systems. The present Special Issue presents and highlights the advances and the latest novel and emergent results on this topic, showing best practices, implementations, and applications.

There are 10 papers published in this Special Issue, covering micromachined sensors interfacing circuits [1–4], techniques for sensor interrogation and conditioning circuits [5–7], and sensors and systems design [8–10].

In particular, Malcovati et al. presented an overview of MEMS microphones evolution interfacing based on actual design examples, focusing on the latest cutting-edge solutions [1]. Kim et al. proposed a reconfigurable sensor analog front-end using low-noise chopper-stabilized delta-sigma capacitance-to-digital converter (CDC) for capacitive microsensors [2]. Qiao et al. addressed an alternative to capacitive MEMS accelerometers interface circuits, conventionally based on charge-based approaches, based on frequency-based readout techniques that have demonstrated they have some unique advantages [3]. Pantoli et al. proposed a novel interface circuits for micromachined silicon photomultipliers based on a second-generation voltage conveyor as an active element, performing as a transimpedance amplifier [4]. On the interrogation and conditioning circuits side, Hu et al., in order to match the high output impedance of Tribo-electric-Nano-generator (TENG) and increase the output power, presented an adaptable interface conditioning circuit, which is composed of an impedance matching circuit, a synchronous rectifier bridge, a control circuit, and an energy storage device [5]. D'Amico et al. presented the study of useful electrical properties of directly coupled L–C cells forming a discrete ladder network (L–C L.N.) to be applied to the sensor field up to be applied on a large scale down to micrometric dimensions in agreement with the technologic ability to shrink the capacitive sensor dimensions [6]. Demori et al. proposed an interrogation techniques and interface circuits for coil-coupled passive sensors: the interrogation of sensor units is based on resonance, denoted as resonant sensor units, in which the readout signals are the resonant frequency and, possibly, the quality factor [7]. On the sensors and systems design, Wei and Bao presented a low power, energy-efficient precision CMOS temperature sensor based on bipolar junction transistors and a pre-bias circuit and bipolar core [8]. Wu et al. presented an A variable-gain chopper-stabilized instrumentation amplifier (chopper IA), which employs a low pass filter (LPF) to attenuate the up-converted noise at the chopping frequency for micromachined sensors applications [9]. Liu et al. presented a review of recent progress in the rapid sintering of nanosilver pastes: preparation of nanosilver particles and pastes, mechanisms of nanopastes sintering, and different rapid sintering processes were discussed [10].

The guest Editors would like to take this opportunity to thank all the authors for submitting their papers to this special issue and also want to thank all the reviewers for dedicating their time and helping to improve the quality of the submitted papers.

Conflicts of Interest: The authors declare no conflict of interest.

References

1. Malcovati, P.; Baschirotto, A. The Evolution of Integrated Interfaces for MEMS Microphones. *Micromachines* **2018**, *9*, 323. [CrossRef]
2. Kim, H.; Lee, B.; Mun, Y.; Kim, J.; Han, K.; Roh, Y.; Song, D.; Huh, S.; Ko, H. Reconfigurable Sensor Analog Front-End Using Low-Noise Chopper-Stabilized Delta-Sigma Capacitance-to-Digital Converter. *Micromachines* **2018**, *9*, 347. [CrossRef]
3. Qiao, Z.; Boom, B.; Annema, A.; Wiegerink, R.; Nauta, B. On Frequency-Based Interface Circuits for Capacitive MEMS Accelerometers. *Micromachines* **2018**, *9*, 488. [CrossRef]
4. Pantoli, L.; Barile, G.; Leoni, A.; Muttillo, M.; Stornelli, V. A Novel Electronic Interface for Micromachined Si-Based Photomultipliers. *Micromachines* **2018**, *9*, 507. [CrossRef]
5. Hu, Y.; Yue, Q.; Lu, S.; Yang, D.; Shi, S.; Zhang, X.; Yu, H. An Adaptable Interface Conditioning Circuit Based on Triboelectric Nanogenerators for Self-Powered Sensors. *Micromachines* **2018**, *9*, 105. [CrossRef]
6. D'Amico, A.; Santonico, M.; Pennazza, G.; Zompanti, A.; Scipioni, E.; Ferri, G.; Stornelli, V.; Salmeri, M.; Lojacono, R. Resonant Directly Coupled Inductors–Capacitors Ladder Network Shows a New, Interesting Property Useful for Application in the Sensor Field, Down to Micrometric Dimensions. *Micromachines* **2018**, *9*, 343. [CrossRef]
7. Demori, M.; Baù, M.; Ferrari, M.; Ferrari, V. Interrogation Techniques and Interface Circuits for Coil-Coupled Passive Sensors. *Micromachines* **2018**, *9*, 449. [CrossRef]
8. Wei, R.; Bao, X. A Low Power Energy-Efficient Precision CMOS Temperature Sensor. *Micromachines* **2018**, *9*, 257. [CrossRef]
9. Wu, C.; Chen, H.; Yen, M.; Yang, S. Chopper-Stabilized Instrumentation Amplifier with Automatic Frequency Tuning Loop. *Micromachines* **2018**, *9*, 289. [CrossRef]
10. Liu, W.; An, R.; Wang, C.; Zheng, Z.; Tian, Y.; Xu, R.; Wang, Z. Recent Progress in Rapid Sintering of Nanosilver for Electronics Applications. *Micromachines* **2018**, *9*, 346. [CrossRef]

Article

A Novel Electronic Interface for Micromachined Si-Based Photomultipliers

Leonardo Pantoli *, Gianluca Barile, Alfiero Leoni, Mirco Muttillo and Vincenzo Stornelli

Department of Industrial and Information Engineering and Economics, Università degli Studi dell'Aquila, 67100 L'Aquila, Italy; gianluca.barile@graduate.univaq.it (G.B.); alfiero.leoni@graduate.univaq.it (A.L.); mirco.muttillo@graduate.univaq.it (M.M.); vincenzo.stornelli@univaq.it (V.S.)
* Correspondence: leonardo.pantoli@univaq.it; Tel.: +39-0862-434440

Received: 18 September 2018; Accepted: 1 October 2018; Published: 8 October 2018

Abstract: In this manuscript, the authors propose a novel interface for silicon photomultipliers based on a second-generation voltage conveyor as an active element, performing as a transimpedance amplifier. Due to the absence of internal feedback, this solution offers a static bandwidth regardless of the tunable gain level. The simulation results have shown good performances, confirming the possibility of the proposed interface being effectively used in different scenarios. A preliminary hybrid solution has also been developed using second-generation current conveyors and measurements conducted on an equivalent discrete-elements board, which is promising.

Keywords: silicon photomultipliers (SiPMs); analog interfacing; second-generation voltage conveyor (VCII) interfaces; second-generation current conveyor (CCII) interfaces; integrated circuits

---

1. Introduction

Silicon photomultipliers (SiPMs) are becoming a highly attractive alternative to traditional photomultiplier tubes (PMTs) because they are an affordable solution, able to combine high sensitivity and detection capabilities towards low-emission phenomena, together with advantages relative to the use of integrated sensors and circuits. In addition, they have a compact and robust structure, which also makes them suitable for portable applications considering the low-power consumption of the integrated solutions. A variety of SiPMs have been developed and made commercially available in order to satisfy several applications [1,2]. Given that the SiPM is based on the use of single photon avalanche diodes (SPADs), performance can be defined and changed in terms of sensitivity, resolution, response time and driving capability [3–6]. A fast output allows, for instance, the sensor to resolve high-repetition, fast pulses. In other words, a wider active area enhances the detection capability as more SPADs detect photons identically and independently. In general, the SiPMs characteristics are mainly dependent on technology and the physical architecture of the sensor, while, on the other hand, the achievable performance of the SiPM stresses the subsequent electronic circuits that are responsible for the detection and identification of the photons.

In recent years, a great effort has been devoted to the definition of new circuital solutions for the design of suitable sensor interfaces for SiPMs. These sensors demand strict performance from the electronics, in particular those which concern the response time, the resolution, and the driving capability. This means that an agile electronic interface with a large bandwidth, low noise performance and a low input impedance is desirable in order to take advantage of the use of photomultipliers. In the literature, many solutions have already been presented [7–14]. A typical choice in particle physics design consists of the use of voltage-mode amplifiers with feedback networks, which are useful for decreasing both the input impedance and noise contribution. In general, a current-mode design approach is usually discouraged because it is useful to provide a higher speed with respect to voltage-mode solutions but also higher noise performance in experiments. Recently, a mixed-mode solution has also been presented by the same authors [15], which represented a good compromise between the achievable performances and also demonstrated a capability to be used with fast SiPMs.

In this paper, this design approach has been further investigated. It is based on a second-generation voltage conveyor (VCII) [16,17] that is able to drive very large input capacitive loads as usually happens with large SiPMs or SiPMs arrays, providing a fast response. This solution is further explored here, demonstrating even better performance and its capacity to be used for practical applications in realizing a compact integrated interface. A major point of novelty presented here, is that this voltage-current approach offers variable gain without affecting the bandwidth of the interface circuit differently from other, already published solutions.

In addition, a preliminary prototype board has also been developed with commercial components, for the purpose of testing the proposed design approach. It makes use of the AD844 operational amplifiers from Analog Devices (Norwood, MA, USA) adopted to develop current conveyors [18,19]. The unique advantage of the integrated solution, apart from the novel electronic scheme, is the absence of an internal feedback. This offers a static bandwidth regardless of the tunable gain level, together with very low voltage, and therefore, portable operation capability. This is generally true for most integrated circuit (IC) solutions accomplished by low voltage and low power battery operation and also therefore, portable capability. The Hamamatsu S13360 series SiPM characteristics have been considered for simulations and to emulate the sensors current peaks during our test sessions. The results have clearly shown that even if performance of the hybrid solution cannot be compared to those of the integrated interface simulated with a standard 0.35 um complementary metal–oxide semiconductor (CMOS) technology process from AMS Foundry, the discrete version is able to provide a good response with a reasonable delay time, given the multi-peak input signal simulating multiple-photon detection.

2. CMOS Integrable Solution

The equivalent block diagram of a generic VCII is reported in Figure 1, where parasitic components have also been included and highlighted in the dashed areas. As evident, a VCII is a three-port device which exploits the dual concept of the better known second-generation current conveyor (CCII). The complete input–output relationship between each port can be extracted from the Equation (1) matrix:

$$
\begin{bmatrix} i_x \\ v_y \\ v_z \end{bmatrix} = \begin{bmatrix} \frac{1}{(r_x\|1/sC_x)} & \pm\beta & 0 \\ 0 & Z_y(r_y+sL_y) & 0 \\ \alpha & 0 & (r_z+sL_z) \end{bmatrix} \cdot \begin{bmatrix} v_x \\ i_y \\ i_z \end{bmatrix} \tag{1}
$$

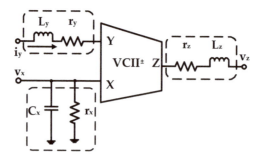

Figure 1. Second-generation voltage conveyor (VCII) equivalent representation. Dashed boxes highlight the parasitic components at each terminal.

Analyzing Equation (1), α is the voltage gain between X input and Z output, which according to the CCII parallelism, should be designed as close to unity as possible. β is the current gain between Y input and X output and similarly to α, it should be designed as equal to unity. Moreover, based on the

Y–X current senses, we can have a VCII$^+$ (if both the currents are pointing inwards or outwards) or a VCII$^-$ (if currents are pointing in opposite directions). The parameters r_y, L_y, r_x, C_x, r_z and L_z are the parasitic impedances related to each terminal. They should ideally be equal to zero except for r_x, which should be equal to infinity. Given these considerations, we can simplify Equation (1) to Equation (2):

$$I_x = \pm \beta I_y, \quad V_z = \alpha V_x, \quad V_y = 0 \tag{2}$$

We can then conclude that the X terminal can be considered as a current output and hence, it should ideally have an infinite input impedance. The Y terminal is a current input and therefore it should be designed with zero input impedance, similarly to the Z terminal, which on the other hand can be considered as a voltage output. The main VCII$^+$ building block used in the SiPM interface is shown in Figure 2. The transistor dimensions are reported in the same schematic. Its design was created using a standard Austria micro systems (AMS) 350 nm CMOS technology with a supply voltage of ± 1.65 V. As highlighted, it consists of a current buffer and a voltage buffer. In particular, M_{c4}, $M_{in1,2}$, and $M_{c1,2}$ employ a gain boosted common gate amplifier, which together with the current mirror $M_{c3,4}$, conveys the Y input current to the X node, implementing the $I_x = \beta I_y$ relationship. On the other hand, $M_{v2,3}$ forms a flipped-voltage-follower buffer, mirroring the X input voltage (suitably shifted by M_{v1}) to the Z node ($V_z = \alpha V_x$).

Figure 3 shows the simulated terminal impedances. As evident, the X, Y, and Z nodes demonstrated a resistive behavior with a wide bandwidth and a value of 800 kΩ, 49 Ω, and 79 Ω, respectively. Figure 4 shows the α and β parameter trends in the frequency domain. Again, we can see an almost unitary value for both of them with a bandwidth greater than 100 MHz and 10 MHz, respectively.

The actual SiPM interface is shown in Figure 5. As mentioned in the introduction, we considered the equivalent electrical characteristics of the Hamamatsu S13360 series SiPM (Hamamatsu Photonics, Hamamatsu, Japan). They are multi-pixel photon counters, specially made for precision measurements such as flow cytometry, DNA sequencing, laser microscopy, and fluorescence measurements. The Hamamatsu S13360-3025CS was used as a reference for our design. It has 14,400 pixels and an effective photosensitive area of 3.0 mm $\times$ 3.0 mm, with an equivalent parasitic capacitance of 320 pF. For bandwidth performance evaluation, we measured the capacitance range of the Hamamatsu S13360 family, which was 60–1280 pF. All of these parameters contributed to the definition of the equivalent input signal used for both the simulations and measurements. From the circuit front-end point of view, one of the most important SiPM parameters was the equivalent total parasitic capacitance, as observed at the output terminals of the photomultiplier array. This affects the bandwidth, and thus the time response of the front-end circuit. Particular attention must therefore be paid to the design of the input stage. In addition, because the considered current peaks are quite low in amplitude, the circuit should be designed so as to have a very low noise feature. The equivalent model of a single SiPM which has suitable regard for these design constraints is shown in Figure 5a. As can be seen, the core of the multiplier is composed of a current source and a 'diode capacitance' emulating the behavior of the single photon avalanche diode (SPAD). To allow the device to shut down after an event, a quenching resistor was added in series with the SPAD. Finally, a parallel capacitor C_{p_N} was placed to account for the total single-core parasitics. The SiPM was then obtained as an array of N repetitions of this basic structure. A switch (see Figure 5b) was also added in series with the SiPM in order to be able to decide the exact time of an occurrence. The actual interface is shown in Figure 5b. It consists of a single VCII performing as a transimpedance amplifier (TIA). The photomultiplier (or array of photomultipliers) output is connected to the Y terminal. By analyzing the X terminal and using the first relationship of Equation (1), we can write:

$$V_x = I_x R_{gain} \approx \pm \beta I_{in} R_{gain} \tag{3}$$

5

Knowing that $V_z = \alpha V_x = V_{out}$ we can conclude that:

$$V_{out} = \alpha V_x \approx \pm \alpha \beta R_{gain} I_{in} \approx R_{gain} I_{in} \qquad (4)$$

The main results of the simulation conducted on the transimpedance amplifier are reported in Figure 6. Figure 6a shows the transfer function of the amplifier, which confirms Equation (4). By varying the gain resistor it is possible to achieve a transimpedance gain of up to 90 dB while keeping noise levels almost constant, as shown in Figure 6b.

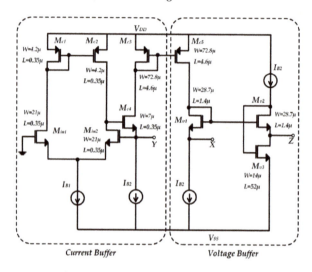

Figure 2. VCII transistor level implementation.

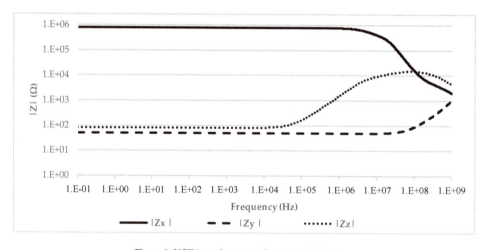

Figure 3. VCII impedances vs. frequency behavior.

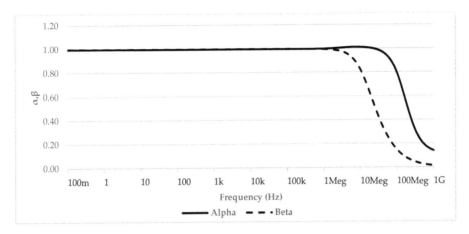

Figure 4. VCII α and β vs. frequency behavior.

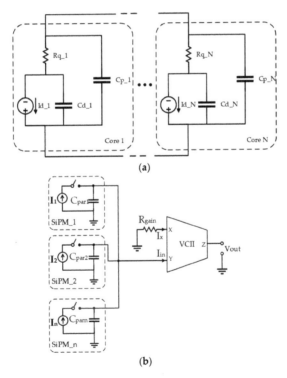

Figure 5. (**a**) Silicon photomultipliers (SiPM) equivalent model; (**b**) the proposed VCII-based SiPM array interface where $C_{par\_i} = \Sigma\, C_{p\_N}$.

The gain limitation resides in the value of the gain resistor. It has to remain well below the VCII X node input resistance in order for Equation (4) to be valid. A remarkable behavior of the VCII that we present is the fact that increasing the gain does not affect the output bandwidth. This is because the transfer function zero crossing frequency varies according to the gain level.

The response of the interface to the SiPM output was obtained by emulating the photomultiplier current pulse in response to one or more photons hitting its surface. The results are shown in Figure 7. As can be seen, the TIA can detect a short series of pulses effectively converting them into voltage pulses. From the same figure it is also clear that the interfacing circuit is able to detect situations where multiple photons hit a SiPM or when different photons hit different SiPMs at the same time in a SiPM array, without saturating its output (i.e., while still being capable of 'counting' the number of photons that reached the sensors).

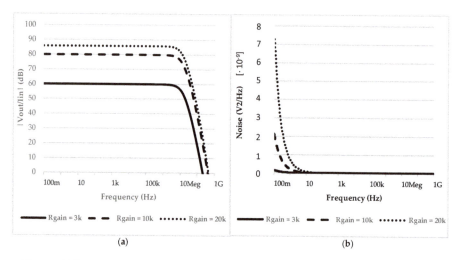

Figure 6. (a) Transimpedance amplifier (TIA) transfer function at different gain levels; (b) TIA output equivalent noise at different noise levels.

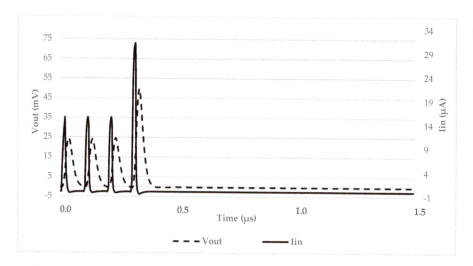

Figure 7. Time domain response of the interface to a train of SiPM current pulses at different amplitude levels.

Figure 8 shows an ensemble of different working conditions. Figure 8a confirms the feasibility for the interface to be used with an array of photomultipliers, as its output voltage is not critically distorted by variations in the SiPMs parasitic capacitance. Figure 8b shows the temperature variations of the interface output voltage, whereby differences from −10 °C to 80 °C are negligible, making the interface suitable to work in different environments. Figure 8c shows the same TIA output magnitude at different capacitive load levels; from 1 pF to 6 pF. Again, we can see minimal differences, meaning that the interface output stage is capable of driving further processing stages, as well as being connected directly to a chip output pad. Figure 8d shows that the interface output does not vary for a ±5% supply voltage variation, reinforcing what was previously stated about the versatility of our proposal. Finally, statistical (corner) simulations considering the utilized CMOS technology parameters were also performed, showing a 10% variation in the performances in terms of amplitude reproductivity, confirming the feasibility of the proposed solution.

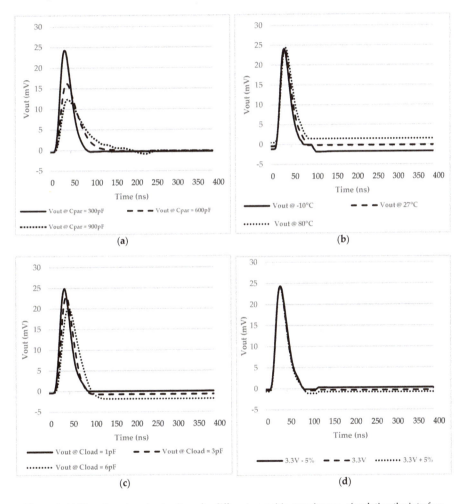

Figure 8. (**a**) Time domain output voltage for different parasitic capacitances, simulating the interface to be used with an array of SiPMs; (**b**) interface output voltage variations at different temperatures; (**c**) interface output voltage for three different capacitive loads connected to the VCII Z node; (**d**) interface output voltage for ±5% supply voltage variations.

3. Hybrid Solution, Simulations and Test

Since the VCII is not available as a commercial component, the proposed design approach has been tested with a preliminary hybrid prototype by using high speed monolithic operational amplifiers (OP-AMPs)—the AD844 from Analog Device (Analog Devices, Inc., Norwood, MA, USA), and implementing a voltage buffer and current buffer. In References [18,19] it has been demonstrated that this OP-AMP can be successfully applied to create a CCII in practical applications and so it can be adopted to obtain a transimpedance gain as in the integrated solution, already proposed in Section 2. In Figure 9, a simplified schematic of the discrete interface is reported. Two AD844 were used. The first one is devoted to the current-to-voltage conversion, while the second one is used as a traditional operational amplifier, taking advantage of the high slew rate provided by this component.

The SiPM source is simulated with a self-defined exponential current source with a very large parallel capacitor simulating the output capacitive load provided by the sensors. The output of the first stage is received on the output current terminal of the AD844 and it is connected to the input stage of the following OP-AMP, which can be used to create an inverting or non-inverting gain stage without significantly affecting the overall performance.

In order to investigate the performance that can be achieved with this simple architecture, a current pulse with an amplitude of 16 μA and a duration up to the minimum value of 30 ns was used as the input source. Figure 10 clearly shows that the proposed solution, even considering fast SiPM signals, is able to preserve almost the same shape factor of the input current pulse, with a minimum delay of about 15 ns. This is reasonable in our opinion considering the technological limits of a discrete prototype.

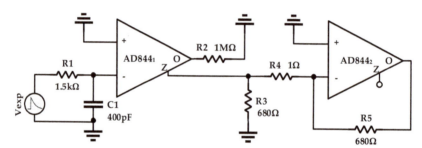

Figure 9. Simplified schematic of the discrete interface.

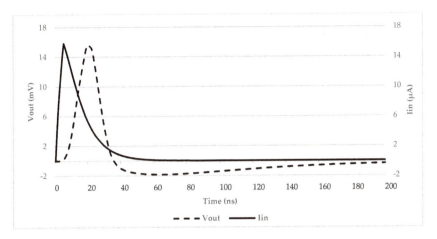

Figure 10. Simulation results on the prototype board: input current and output voltage of the discrete interface.

A prototype board was also fabricated on a low-losses perfboard FR4 substrate with our facilities. In Figure 11a, the final hybrid prototype board is presented. The input signal was generated with the Keysight 33600A (Keysight Technologies, Santa Rosa, CA, USA) signal generator in order to have a fully characterized input source, which is useful to analyze the circuit behavior. The board has been tested in several conditions and both time and frequency domain measurements have been performed. Examples of the test bench are shown in Figure 11b,c. In the time domain, a single current pulse with different amplitudes and durations, followed by a multi-pulse signal of both fixed and variable amplitudes, was considered in order to evaluate the circuit performance with respect to an agile, time-varying incoming signal. A couple of examples are reported in Figures 12 and 13. In detail, Figure 12 shows the measured output signal of the described interface when a periodic input signal is applied, consisting of a pulse train with fixed amplitude and duration while in Figure 13, the input pulse train shows variable amplitude. It is important to notice that in both cases the designed interface is able to track any changes of amplitude or repetition time with a small delay time but without significantly affecting the shape of the output pulse, even when considering very short input pulses with a minimum duration of 30 ns. Some results in the frequency domain are also reported in Figure 14. The AC voltage transfer function of the proposed circuit was measured with the Keysight N9915A FieldFox Microwave Analyzer (Keysight Technologies, Santa Rosa, CA, USA). The measured results demonstrate the very large bandwidth that can be achieved with the proposed solution. The analysis was carried out for different values of the input resistance R1, and the results are congruent with the expected behavior. The voltage gain decreased for the largest values of R1, meaning that the transimpedance gain increased accordingly, as expected from Equation (4).

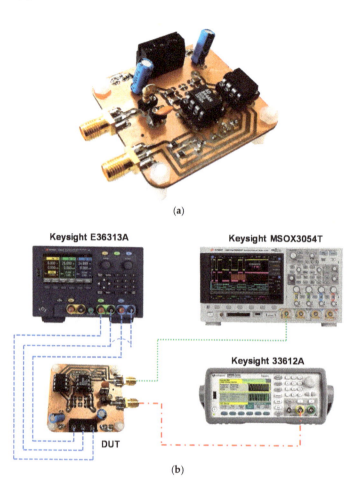

(a)

Keysight E36313A   **Keysight MSOX3054T**

Keysight 33612A

DUT

(b)

Figure 11. *Cont.*

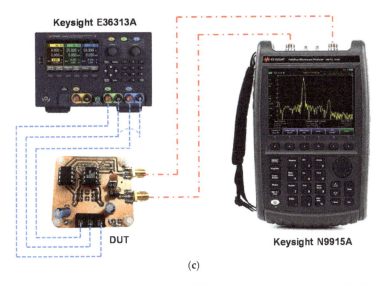

Keysight E36313A

DUT

Keysight N9915A

(**c**)

Figure 11. (**a**) Final prototype board; test benches: (**b**) for time domain measurements; (**c**) for frequency domain measurements.

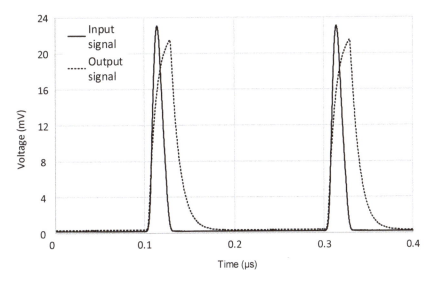

Figure 12. Multi-pulse input signal (continuous line) and measured output response (dotted line) of the discrete interface.

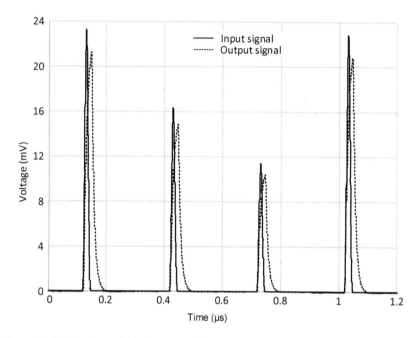

Figure 13. Multi-pulse variable input signal (continuous line) and measured output response (dotted line) of the discrete interface.

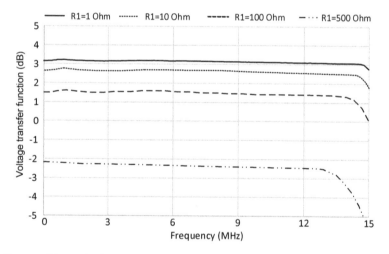

Figure 14. Measured voltage transfer function for different values of the input resistance R1.

4. Conclusions

In this manuscript a novel interface for SiPMs is proposed and addressed with circuitry details. The proposed solution used a transimpedance amplifier in order to convert the incoming current pulses from the SiPMs into corresponding voltage pulses by means of a VCII. This design approach has shown promising results, offering a compact and integrated solution in CMOS technology. A preliminary hybrid solution was also developed and evaluated using AD844 components (Analog Devices),

Micromachines **2018**, *9*, 507

OP-AMPs suitable for implementing CCIIs. The results have demonstrated the feasibility of the proposed solution.

Author Contributions: Conceptualization, L.P. and V.S.; Investigation, L.P. and G.B.; Data Curation, A.L. and M.M.; Writing-Original Draft Preparation, L.P. and G.B.; Supervision, V.S.

Funding: This research received no external funding

Acknowledgments: The authors want to thank the technician of the electronic laboratory of the University of L'Aquila, Stefano Ricci and Andrea Pelliccione for the precious support during the prototype's implementation and measurements.

Conflicts of Interest: The authors declare no conflict of interest.

References

1. Low Noise, Blue-Sensitive Silicon Photomultipliers. Available online: http://sensl.com/downloads/ds/DS-MicroCseries.pdf (accessed on 26 July 2018).
2. Hamamatsu Products. Available online: http://www.hamamatsu.com/eu/en/4004.html (accessed on 26 July 2018).
3. Powolny, F.; Auffray, E.; Brunner, S.; Garutti, E.; Goettlich, M.; Hillemanns, H.; Jarron, P.; Lecoq, P.; Meyer, T.; Schultz-Coulon, H.; et al. Time-based readout of a silicon photomultiplier (SiPM) for time of flight positron emission tomography (TOF-PET). *IEEE Trans. Nucl. Sci.* **2011**, *58*, 597–604. [CrossRef]
4. Marano, D.; Bonanno, G.; Garozzo, S.; Grillo, A.; Romeo, G. A new simple and effective procedure for SIPM electrical parameter extraction. *IEEE Sens. J.* **2016**, *16*, 3620–3626. [CrossRef]
5. Bérubé, B.L.; Rhéaume, V.P.; Parent, S.; Maurais, L.; Therrien, A.C.; Charette, P.G.; Charlebois, S.A.; Fontaine, R.; Pratte, J.F. Implementation study of single photon avalanche diodes (SPAD) in 0.8 μm HV CMOS technology. *IEEE Trans. Nucl. Sci.* **2015**, *62*, 710–718. [CrossRef]
6. Garutti, E. Silicon photomultipliers for high energy physics detectors. *J. Instrum.* **2011**, *6*, C10003. [CrossRef]
7. Huizenga, J.; Seifert, S.; Schreuder, F.; van Dam, H.; Dendooven, P.; Löhner, H.; Vinke, R.; Schaart, D. A fast preamplifier concept for SiPM-based time-of-flight PET detectors. *Nucl. Instrum. Method Phys. Res. Sect. A Accel. Spectrom. Detect. Assoc. Equip.* **2012**, *695*, 379–384. [CrossRef]
8. Albuquerque, E.; Bexiga, V.; Bugalho, R.; Carriço, B.; Ferreira, C.; Ferreira, M.; Godinho, J.; Gonçalves, F.; Leong, C.; Lousã, P.; et al. Experimental characterization of the 192 channel Clear-PEM frontend ASIC coupled to a multi-pixel APD readout of LYSO:Ce crystals. *Nucl. Instrum. Method Phys. Res. Sect. A Accel. Spectrom. Detect. Assoc. Equip.* **2009**, *598*, 802–814. [CrossRef]
9. Silva, M.; Oliveira, L. Regulated common-gate transimpedance amplifier designed to operate with a silicon photo-multiplier at the input. *IEEE Trans. Circ. Syst. I Regul. Pap.* **2014**, *61*, 725–735. [CrossRef]
10. Comerma, A.; Gascón, D.; Garrido, L.; Delgado, C.; Marín, J.; Pérez, J.; Martínez, G.; Freixas, L. Front end ASIC design for SiPM readout. *J. Instrum.* **2013**, *8*, C01048. [CrossRef]
11. Dinu, N.; Imando, T.; Nagai, A.; Pinot, L.; Puill, V.; Callier, S.; Janvier, B.; Esnault, C.; Verdier, M.; Raux, L.; et al. SiPM arrays and miniaturized readout electronics for compact gamma camera. *Nucl. Instrum. Method Phys. Res. Sect. A Accel. Spectrom. Detect. Assoc. Equip.* **2015**, *787*, 367–372. [CrossRef]
12. Zhu, X.; Deng, Z.; Chen, Y.; Liu, Y.; Liu, Y. Development of a 64-channel readout ASIC for an SSPM array for PET and TOF-PET applications. *IEEE Trans. Nucl. Sci.* **2016**, *63*, 1327–1334. [CrossRef]
13. Corsi, F.; Marzocca, C.; Foresta, M.; Matarrese, G.; Del Guerra, A.; Marcatili, S.; Piemonte, C. Preliminary results from a current mode CMOS front-end circuit for silicon photomultiplier detectors. *IEEE Nucl. Sci. Symp. Conf. Rec.* **2007**. [CrossRef]
14. Orita, T.; Koyama, A.; Yoshino, M.; Kamada, K.; Yoshikawa, A.; Shimazoe, K.; Sugawara, H. The current mode Time-over-Threshold ASIC for a MPPC module in a TOF-PET system. *Nucl. Instrum. Method Phys. Res. Sect. A Accel. Spectrom. Detect. Assoc. Equip.* **2017**. [CrossRef]
15. Pantoli, L.; Barile, G.; Leoni, A.; Safari, L.; Stornelli, V. A New VCII based low-power low-voltage front-end for silicon photomultipliers. In Proceedings of the SpliTech2018–3rd International Conference on Smart and Sustainable Technologies, Split, Croatia, 26–29 June 2018.

16. Filanovsky, I. CMOS voltage conveyors. In Proceedings of the 44th IEEE 2001 Midwest Symposium on Circuits and Systems, Dayton, OH, USA, 14–17 August 2001; pp. 318–321.
17. Čajka, J.; Vrba, K. The voltage conveyor may have in fact found its way into circuit theory. *AEU Int. J. Electron. Commun.* **2004**, *58*, 244–248. [CrossRef]
18. Wan, L.; Natarajan, S. Experimental verification of variable gain CCII-K circuits and modeling of AD844. In Proceedings of the Twenty-Ninth Southeastern Symposium on System Theory, Cookeville, TN, USA, 9–11 March 1997; pp. 168–172.
19. Svoboda, J.; McGory, L.; Webb, S. Applications of a commercially available current conveyor. *Int. J. Electron.* **1991**, *70*, 159–164. [CrossRef]

 *micromachines*

Article

On Frequency-Based Interface Circuits for Capacitive MEMS Accelerometers

Zhiliang Qiao [1],*, Boris A. Boom [2], Anne-Johan Annema [1], Remco J. Wiegerink [3] and Bram Nauta [1]

[1] IC Design Group, Faculty of Electrical Engineering, Mathematics and Computer Science, University of Twente, P.O. Box 217, 7500 AE Enschede, The Netherlands; A.J.Annema@utwente.nl (A.-J.A.); B.Nauta@utwente.nl (B.N.)
[2] Nikhef, P.O. Box 41882, 1009 DB Amsterdam, The Netherlands; borisb@nikhef.nl
[3] Integrated Devices and Systems Group, Faculty of Electrical Engineering, Mathematics and Computer Science, University of Twente, P.O. Box 217, 7500 AE Enschede, The Netherlands; r.j.wiegerink@utwente.nl
* Correspondence: z.qiao@utwente.nl; Tel.: +31-53-489-5194

Received: 17 August 2018; Accepted: 24 September 2018; Published: 25 September 2018

Abstract: Interface circuits for capacitive MEMS accelerometers are conventionally based on charge-based approaches. A promising alternative to these is provided by frequency-based readout techniques that have some unique advantages as well as a few challenges associated with them. This paper addresses these techniques and presents a derivation of the fundamental resolution limits that are imposed on them by phase noise. Starting with an overview of basic operating principles, associated properties and challenges, the discussions then focus on the fundamental trade-offs between noise, power dissipation and signal bandwidth (BW) for the LC-oscillator-based frequency readout and for the conventional charge-based switched-capacitor (SC) readout. Closed-form analytical formulas are derived to facilitate a fair comparison between the two approaches. Benchmarking results indicate that, with the same bandwidth requirement, charge-based readout circuits are more suitable when optimizing for noise performance, while there is still some room for frequency-based techniques when optimizing for power consumption, especially when flicker phase noise can be mitigated.

Keywords: oscillator; frequency; interface; readout; MEMS; capacitive; accelerometer; noise; power; bandwidth

1. Introduction

MEMS accelerometers have found their way into various applications, ranging from consumer, automotive, industrial to biomedical [1–3]. The alluring prospect of Internet of Things and Services (IoTs) is expected to enable a huge growth of MEMS accelerometer's applications [3], thereby also requiring more stringent specifications on accuracy, power consumption (P) and bandwidth (BW). Close cooperation and co-optimization between MEMS sensors and interface circuits are always necessary and desired to achieve low-power performance for a specific accuracy and dynamic range.

In general, an accelerometer's accuracy is limited by both linearity and noise. This results in a dynamic range that is given by the ratio of the smallest detectable signal set by noise, and the largest usable signal set by the system's linearity, including clipping. Improving the linearity can be achieved in many ways, for example by using force feedback [4], or by postprocessing the data. These measures usually do not dominate the power consumption in high accuracy systems, as is similarly the case in conventional analog circuitry. Therefore, this paper focuses on the lower end of the dynamic range, which is where the noise and bandwidth requirements determine the power consumption.

Among the different kinds of transduction mechanisms, such as piezo-resistive, electromagnetic, thermal, resonant and so on, capacitive MEMS accelerometers have been widely used due to their combined advantages of high-sensitivity, good compatibility with IC technology, low cost, relatively simple structure, high reliability, low temperature sensitivity and low-power potential [1].

The basic architecture of a capacitive accelerometer consists of a proof mass suspended via mechanical springs and capacitors that act as sensor elements. Acceleration induces a displacement Δx of the proof mass and thereby yields a capacitance change $\Delta C(\Delta x)$ that can be detected by readout circuits. For these capacitive MEMS accelerometers, the main task of the interface circuits is to measure the capacitance change ΔC accurately. From a physical point of view, ΔC can be measured by means of detecting a change of current, voltage, charge or frequency. A good deal of literature has been published on voltage, current and charge-based interface techniques [5–16]. In particular, the switched-capacitor (SC) charge-based method is commonly applied to the capacitive MEMS accelerometers [7–16] and a noise floor as low as 200 ng/$\sqrt{Hz}$ is already reported in [16]. Systems using this method typically collect a charge imbalance from a capacitive bridge onto a set of integration capacitors and use a switching scheme to implement correlated double sampling to effectively suppress flicker noise.

Frequency-based interface techniques can be found in a large variety of sensor readout systems, such as microwave chemical sensors [17,18], dielectric spectroscopy [19,20], Wheatstone-bridge resistive sensors [21,22], eddy-current sensors [23], magnetic sensors [24], and so forth. In the context of MEMS accelerometers, frequency-based methods can be realized using either mechanical or electrical resonators. For electrically resonating readout circuitry using capacitive MEMS accelerometers, the information of $\Delta C(x)$ is transformed to a frequency difference ($\Delta f(x)$) by employing oscillators in which a capacitance (partly) sets the oscillation frequency. These types of oscillators include relaxation oscillators, ring oscillators and LC oscillators, etc.

Compared to other approaches, intuitively, continuous-time frequency-based readout circuits (like ring oscillators and LC oscillators) have a number of advantages compared to conventional charge-based SC readout circuitry. Firstly, continuous-time frequency-based readouts avoid noise folding that is associated with SC charge-based readouts, and avoid the necessity of power-hungry high-gain low-noise operational amplifiers in current-based and voltage-based techniques. Consequently, frequency-based readouts may appear to have the potential to achieve low-noise low-power performance. Secondly, frequency-based readouts are less sensitive to MEMS mismatch and circuit offset. Mismatch and offset in SC based readouts can easily overload the amplifiers because of the high gain used to get good resolution. Both usually must be mitigated by non-trivial efforts such as calibration [6], trimming [9], and electrostatic spring constant modulation [14]. In contrast, frequency based readouts will show just a static, possibly large, frequency shift, which does not need to result in overload or clipping. Thirdly, the quasi-digital output and the possibility of using a digital-intensive circuit implementation offer the chance to be compatible with low supply voltages in advanced CMOS technologies.

There are unique properties and challenges for frequency-based sensor readout systems in general. Some of these have been addressed in literature [24–29]. For example, Reference [25] gives a general discussion about time-based circuits. The works in [26–29] mainly focus on the topic of ring-oscillator-based sensor interfaces. However, LC oscillators can typically achieve better performance in terms of the phase noise and jitter for a given power budget [30–33]. Some analysis results about LC-oscillator-based magnetic sensors have been shown in [24].

This paper discusses frequency-based interface circuits using LC oscillators for capacitive MEMS accelerometers. Before going to the detailed analyses, Section 2 presents an overview of basic operating principles, properties and challenges for frequency-based capacitive MEMS accelerometer readout approaches. Next, in order to compare the frequency-based readout to conventional switched-capacitor (SC) charge-based techniques, closed-form analytical formulas including noise, power and BW are derived in Sections 3 and 4. Section 5 provides the comparison results. Finally, the most important findings are summarized in Section 6.

2. Basic Operating Principles, Properties and Challenges of Frequency-Based Interface Circuits

2.1. Sensor-Controlled Oscillators

Electronic oscillators can be built using a number of different approaches [25,31]. Theoretically, replacing any capacitor in electronic oscillators by a capacitance sensor yields a sensor-controlled oscillator whose frequency depends on the sensed signal. Figure 1 shows three main types of these: a relaxation-oscillator type (Figure 1a) [4,34–39], a ring-oscillator type (Figure 1b) [19,26–29] and an LC oscillator type (Figure 1c) [17,18,40,41]. In these, the information measured from the sensors is transformed to frequency and then it is further digitized by simple counters [19,29,34,39,41], time-to-digital converters (TDC) [26,37,38] or by the combination of frequency-to-voltage converters (F2Vs) and normal analog-to-digital converters (ADCs) [17,18,27,28,35,36,40].

In the relaxation-oscillator type of capacitive MEMS readout circuits as shown in Figure 1a, the frequency is related to the charge/discharge current (I_c), hysteresis voltages (V_H and V_L) and MEMS capacitors (C_M) as:

$$f = \frac{I_c}{2(V_H - V_L)C_M} \tag{1}$$

Similarly, the frequency of ring-oscillator type sensor-controlled oscillators, shown in Figure 1b, can be expressed as:

$$f = \frac{1}{2\pi R C_{load}}\sqrt{1 + \frac{2C_{load}}{C_M}} \tag{2}$$

where R is the output resistance of the inverters, C_M is the MEMS capacitor and C_{load} is the loading capacitor. When $C_M \gg C_{load}$ or $C_M \ll C_{load}$, its operating principle actually shifts to that of a relaxation oscillator.

In frequency-based MEMS readouts, the signal noise floor is ultimately determined by the phase noise and jitter of the oscillator. An important parameter in any oscillator is its quality factor Q, which corresponds to (2π times) the ratio of energy stored in the resonator and energy loss per cycle. It appears that the phase noise/jitter performance of oscillators is related to the Q of the oscillator, where a higher Q results in a lower phase noise, at a constant power budget.

As derived in e.g., [30–33], the phase noise/jitter performance of LC oscillators is typically much better than that of relaxation oscillators and ring oscillators, for the same power budget, due to their high Q. An in-depth analysis of the power-accuracy-bandwidth trade-offs is shown in Section 3. It follows that, for the same power budget, the LC oscillator outperforms the relaxation oscillator and ring oscillator, for frequency-based MEMS readout. For this reason, the remainder of the discussions on frequency-based MEMS readout techniques assumes LC-type oscillators. See, e.g., Figure 1c for an example. The oscillation frequency for this type of oscillator as function of MEMS capacitance C_M is:

$$f = \frac{1}{2\pi\sqrt{LC_M}} \tag{3}$$

Assuming $C_M(a_{cc}) = C_0 + C_p \pm \Delta C(a_{cc})$ and $C_0 \gg \Delta C(a_{cc})$ (i.e., for relatively small displacement), where C_0 is the static capacitance without input acceleration (a_{cc}), C_p is the parasitic capacitance and $\pm\Delta C(a_{cc})$ is the change of capacitance induced by a_{cc}, the relationship between $\pm\Delta C(a_{cc})$ and f in first order is:

$$f(a_{cc}) \approx \frac{1}{2\pi\sqrt{L(C_0 + C_p)}}[1 \mp \frac{1}{2}\frac{\Delta C(a_{cc})}{C_0 + C_p}] \tag{4}$$

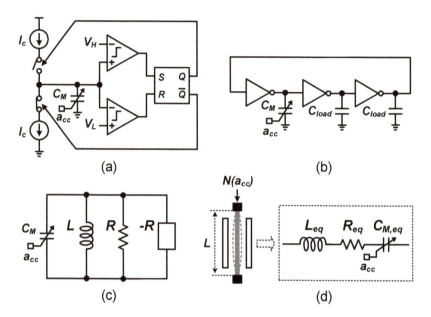

Figure 1. Examples of MEMS controlled oscillators: (**a**) a relaxation-oscillator type [38], (**b**) a ring-oscillator type [26], (**c**) an LC oscillator type, and (**d**) a mechanical resonator and its electrical equivalent model [42,43], where C_M denotes the changeable MEMS capacitor controlled by external acceleration a_{cc}.

2.1.1. MEMS Resonators vs. LC Oscillators

It is instructive to compare electrical LC oscillators to MEMS resonators (see Figure 1d). Mechanical resonators typically can achieve much higher quality factors than electrical LC oscillators. However, the frequency excursions ($\Delta f(a_{cc})$) of a MEMS resonant accelerometer,

$$\Delta f(a_{cc}) = f_{0,r}\sqrt{1 + \alpha_r \frac{N(a_{cc})L^2}{EI}} - f_{0,r}\sqrt{1 - \alpha_r \frac{N(a_{cc})L^2}{EI}}$$
$$\approx \frac{f_{0,r}\alpha_r N(a_{cc})L^2}{EI},$$

(5)

are limited due to the typically small mechanical resonance frequencies, $f_{0,r}$ [42,43]. In this equation, E is Young's modulus, I is the 2nd moment of area, L is the beam length, $N(a_{cc})$ is the axial force induced by input acceleration a_{cc} on the beam and α_r is a coefficient that depends on the boundary conditions [42,43].

2.1.2. Signal Bandwidth vs. Oscillation Frequency Deviations

The acceleration signal information is translated into a shift in the oscillation frequency. To get this frequency-domain signal into e.g., digital data, some kinds of frequency analysis must be done. Fundamentally, to resolve a frequency difference Δf, the observation window in the time domain should be of the order of $1/\Delta f$. This means that detecting small frequency excursions requires a relatively long time (see e.g., [44]). This also implies that the mechanical resonator is not suitable to detect signals with a relatively large signal BW at high resolutions (i.e., at also relatively small frequency deviations). In contrast, electrical LC oscillators can operate at much higher (GHz range) oscillating frequencies, and then relatively small frequency excursions—related to the oscillation frequency itself—may still be sufficiently large for high accuracy across a sufficiently large signal BW.

For this reason, the remainder of this paper focuses on electrically resonating frequency-based readout systems.

2.2. Closed-Loop Operations of Sensor-Controlled Oscillators

Apart from open-loop applications of sensor-controlled oscillators, there are also two kinds of closed-loop operations for frequency-based MEMS readout: force balance [4,35,38] and phase-locked loop (PLL) [17–19,36]. As shown in Figure 2a for the first option, the output information is converted to force and then fed back to balance the displacement due to input acceleration (a_{cc}). Thereby, the linearity of the readout system is now determined by the data-to-force transfer, which is usually more well behaved than the open loop behavior in Equation (4). However, similar to the situation in any closed-loop amplifier [45], the noise requirement for the front-end oscillator is not relaxed, meaning that the power consumption will still be dominated by the readout front-end.

A sensor-controlled oscillator can also be embedded into a PLL, as illustrated in Figure 2b. In this kind of architecture, the output frequency is locked to a multiple of reference frequency (f_{ref}) with the help of a varactor (inside *OSC*), divider ($\div N$), phase frequency detector (*PFD*), charge pump (*CP*) and low-pass loop filter (*LF*). Accordingly, the sensor information is converted to the control voltage (*V*) of the oscillator, which is quantized by an ADC. The overall linearity is a mix of the relation from acceleration to frequency of the MEMS-controlled oscillator and of the voltage-to-frequency relation of the voltage-controlled oscillator (*VCO*). One of the benefits of using PLLs is that temperature-dependent and supply-dependent variations can be mitigated, especially for relaxation and ring oscillators [36]. In addition, in some microwave sensing applications, the PLL stabilizes the oscillator frequencies so that the sensor properties may be characterized more precisely [17–19]. Note that even though PLLs are considered as the circuit topologies by which the noise from *VCOs* are high-pass filtered and thereby produce accurate frequency outputs, embedding sensor-controlled oscillators into PLLs results in a readout noise penalty. This is because the transfer function from noise of sensor-controlled oscillators, i.e., noisy frequency to output voltage is not a high-pass filter and the reference frequency does not reduce the in-band noise. Instead, additional noise is introduced from the divider and *PFD/CP* [46].

In summary, closed-loop operations of frequency-based readout for capacitive MEMS accelerometers may be able to provide some advantages regarding linearity, but do not improve noise performance. Therefore, this paper will only focus on the noise analysis of free-running sensor-controlled oscillating circuits (see Section 3).

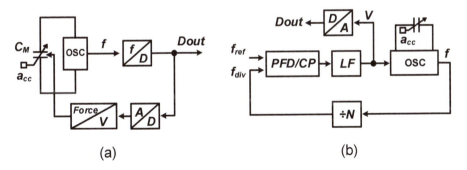

(a)   (b)

Figure 2. Closed-loop operations of sensor-controlled oscillators: (**a**) force balance; (**b**) PLL.

2.3. Other Properties and Challenges of Frequency-Based Techniques

2.3.1. Tolerance to Offset and Mismatch

In conventional high-gain interface circuits, like SC charge sensing amplifiers (CSAs), the amplifier offset and any capacitance mismatches may saturate the output voltages even if the standard remedy techniques [47], such as correlated double sampling (CDS) and chopper stabilization (CHS), are applied. In contrast to this, for frequency-based readouts, offset and mismatch are easily absorbed into a constant frequency offset, which usually is not a problem.

2.3.2. Frequency Pulling Problem

Two sensor-based oscillators may be used in frequency-based readouts. In that case, either one of them behaves as the reference frequency generator or the two work in a "differential" mode if the sensor has differentially changing capacitors. Two free-running oscillators will experience undesirable mutual pulling due to the coupling through the supply, substrate, package and mutual inductance between two oscillator inductors [48,49]. As the basic principle of frequency-based readout is to detect a frequency difference, it might be disastrous for the two oscillators to undergo frequency mutual pulling.

This effect can be mitigated by distancing the two inductors, by designing 8-shaped inductors, by using separate supply regulators [49] or by time-interleaved operation of the two oscillators [24]. In addition, the issue of frequency mutual pulling is significantly alleviated if the difference between the initial oscillating frequencies is sufficiently large [49]. In this regard, a constant frequency offset as discussed above is beneficial.

2.3.3. Proof Mass Connection in Micromechanical LC oscillators

As shown in Figure 3, when the proof mass consists of a conductive material, the proof mass connection is inevitably shared when a capacitive MEMS accelerometer is connected to two cross-coupled LC oscillators. This may induce or enhance frequency pulling (see Section 2.3.2), which can be reduced by electrical isolation. Using a multi-layered technology allows for electrically separating different parts of the proof mass, with the drawback of complicating device fabrication. For example, if the MEMS is fabricated out of a silicon-on-insulator (SOI) wafer and the handle layer is designed as the part of proof-mass, then electrical separation can be achieved by splitting the device layer while keeping the mechanical connection via the handle layer [50,51], illustrated in Figure 4.

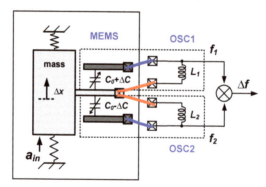

Figure 3. Illustration of proof mass connection in micromechanical LC oscillators.

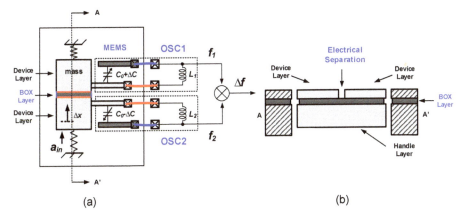

Figure 4. Electrical separation of MEMS proof mass: (**a**) top view; (**b**) cross-section of (**a**) at AA'.

2.3.4. Q Factor Issues for MEMS-Controlled Oscillators

The Q factor of an LC tank is determined by the parasitic resistances of both the inductor and the capacitor. Typically, the parasitic resistance of an electrical inductor is much larger than that of an electrical capacitor. However, due to the usually long and high-resistance connections of MEMS capacitors, their parasitic resistances might be larger than inductors and thus dominate the Q factors in MEMS-controlled oscillators. The detailed effect of Q factor on noise will be discussed in Section 3.2.

3. Noise Analysis of Frequency-Based Interface Circuits

The most important specifications for sensor interface circuits are the power dissipation, the signal BW and the dynamic range (DR). This DR is limited from above by handling capabilities of large signals which may manifest as clipping in readout circuits and/or MEMS sensors. On the other side, the DR is usually limited from below by noise, which sets the signal detection accuracy limit. In this paper, we focus on this noise, together with power dissipation and signal BW. To compare the noise performance of a frequency-based readout method with that of a conventional SC charge-based counterpart, theoretical noise relations are derived below. For the frequency-based readout, the analyses assume two cross-coupled MEMS-controlled LC oscillators that show an opposite frequency deviation for the same acceleration (see Figure 5).

The frequency difference of the two oscillators in Figure 5 is a measure for the MEMS capacitance change ($\pm\Delta C$) even in the presence of mismatches of MEMS static capacitors (C_1 and C_2), electrical inductors (L_1 and L_2), parasitic resistances (R_1 and R_2) and the parasitic capacitances (C_{p1} and C_{p2}). All these mismatched parameters can be absorbed in a static mismatch in the oscillators' initial frequencies (f_{01} and f_{02}). Without loss of generality, the architecture of this LC-oscillator-based front-end circuit can be simplified to the system configuration in Figure 6 by assuming the same parameters for the two oscillators except for increased ($C_0 + \Delta C$) and decreased ($C_0 - \Delta C$) MEMS capacitors, and assuming that the loss of the LC-tank is dominated by MEMS series parasitic resistance R_M (see Sections 2.3.4 and 3.2).

From Equation (4), for the configurations in Figures 5 and 6, the frequency difference between the two oscillators due to a change of the MEMS capacitances (ΔC) is:

$$\Delta f \approx \frac{\Delta C}{C_0 + C_p} f_0 \qquad (6)$$

in which $f_0 = \frac{1}{2\pi\sqrt{L(C_0+C_p)}}$ denotes the initial oscillation frequencies of two oscillators. These initial frequencies for zero external acceleration are assumed to be identical for simplicity reasons only. C_0 is the static capacitor in the MEMS; C_p denotes the total parasitic capacitance from both the MEMS and the readout circuit.

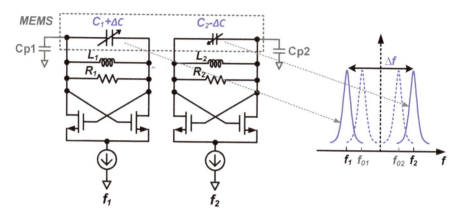

Figure 5. Simplified principle of an LC-oscillator-based interface circuit for MEMS accelerometers. Due to the change of MEMS capacitances (±ΔC), f_1 decreases and f_2 increases from their initial frequencies f_{01} and f_{02}, respectively.

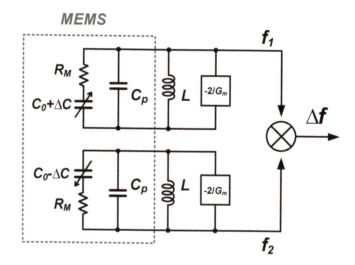

Figure 6. Simplified LC-oscillator-based front-end circuit for noise analysis. Here, G_m is the transconductance of one of the cross-coupled NMOS transistors in Figure 5.

Defining S_{a2C} as the sensitivity of acceleration to capacitance conversion (in unit of F/g) and σ_{f_n} as the root-mean-square (RMS) frequency noise, the minimum MEMS acceleration measurement accuracy (σ_{a_n}, in unit of g, $1g = 9.8$ m/s^2) is:

$$\sigma_{a_n} = \frac{1}{S_{a2C}} \frac{C_0 + C_p}{f_0} \cdot \sigma_{f_n} \qquad (7)$$

In oscillators, the frequency variance σ_{f_n} is limited by the phase noise (or jitter) of these oscillators. Since a relatively long-measurement time—compared to the period of a single oscillation—is usually employed in frequency-based readout circuits, σ_{f_n} is related to long-time jitter performance. In [24], the relative frequency resolution is written as:

$$\frac{\sigma_{f_n}^2}{f_0^2} = \frac{2\sigma_{J,tot}^2(\Delta t)}{\Delta t^2} = \frac{2\kappa^2}{\Delta t} + 2\zeta^2 \tag{8}$$

where Δt is the measurement time and $\sigma_{J,tot}(\Delta t)$ is the total RMS jitter over Δt: $\sigma_{J,tot}(\Delta t) = \sqrt{\kappa^2 \Delta t + \zeta^2 \Delta t^2}$. Here, κ and ζ characterize the jitters contributed from white phase noise and flicker phase noise, respectively [24,52]. Note that an extra factor of two is added because two sensing oscillators are used (see Figures 5 and 6).

Thanks to the utilization of sufficiently long measurement time, the jitter contributed from white phase noise can be averaged out and jitter from flicker phase noise dominates the noise floor in frequency-based readouts. Hence, the expression of σ_{f_n} can be reduced to:

$$\sigma_{f_n} = \sqrt{2} f_0 \cdot \zeta \tag{9}$$

Combining Equations (7) and (9), the RMS acceleration noise (σ_{a_n}) of frequency-based readout is linked to the oscillators' flicker phase noise as:

$$\sigma_{a_n} = \sqrt{2}\frac{C_0 + C_p}{S_{a2C}} \cdot \zeta \quad [g] \tag{10}$$

3.1. Estimation of ζ

According to Equation (10), the characterization parameter for the jitter contributed from flicker phase noise, ζ, must be known to be able to make an estimation for the RMS acceleration noise floor σ_{a_n}. In this section, we will derive an estimate of ζ in terms of system parameters.

3.1.1. Estimation of ζ Based on White Phase Noise and Noise Corner Frequency

Equation (8) includes two jitter characterization parameters, κ and ζ, which model the white noise and flicker noise contributions to oscillator phase noise, respectively [31,52,53]. White phase noise is relatively well modelled as it is related to thermal noise phenomena. This white noise characterizing parameter κ is [52,53]:

$$\kappa = \frac{\Delta f_1}{f_0} 10^{\mathcal{L}(\Delta f_1)/20} \tag{11}$$

where Δf_1 is the offset frequency from the oscillation frequency (f_0) and $\mathcal{L}(\Delta f_1)$ (in unit of dBc/Hz) is the white phase noise at Δf_1. The relation between κ and ζ is [52]:

$$\zeta = \alpha \sqrt{f_c} \kappa \tag{12}$$

in which f_c is the corner frequency of flicker phase noise and α is a constant factor that can be approximated by 5 [52]. This corner frequency is the frequency offset from the oscillation frequency where the contribution of white noise and flicker noise to the total phase noise is equal. Substituting Equation (11) into (12), ζ is related to white phase noise as:

$$\zeta = \alpha \sqrt{f_c} \frac{\Delta f_1}{f_0} 10^{\mathcal{L}(\Delta f_1)/20} \tag{13}$$

Now, further estimation of ζ depends mainly on the white phase noise $\mathcal{L}(\Delta f_1)$ and the corner frequency f_c. Typically, f_c is determined by transistor technologies and design topologies. Since flicker phase noise and white phase noise ($\mathcal{L}(\Delta f_1)$) scale together as a function of the oscillators' power dissipation (P), f_c can be assumed to be independent from $\mathcal{L}(\Delta f_1)$ and P in a first-order approximation.

3.1.2. Estimation of White Phase Noise Based on Leeson's Empirical Model

Leeson's empirical model [54] provides a good approximation for $\mathcal{L}(\Delta f_1)$ in the white phase noise region, linking thermal noise, power dissipation and the oscillator's Q factor:

$$\mathcal{L}(\Delta f_1) = 10 \log_{10} \left[\frac{2 F k_B T}{P_{tank}} \frac{f_0^2}{4Q^2 \Delta f_1^2} \right] \qquad \qquad \cdot (14)$$

In this relation, k_B is the Boltzmann constant, T is the absolute temperature, P_{tank} is the power consumption of LC tank, Q is the quality factor of the LC tank and F is a noise factor. With γ, the channel noise coefficient of the MOS transistors used in the oscillator, the minimum for F is [55]:

$$F_{min} = 1 + \gamma \qquad \qquad (15)$$

The oscillator power dissipation is related to P_{tank} by the efficiency η_P [56,57]:

$$\eta_P = \frac{P_{tank}}{P} \qquad \qquad (16)$$

Leeson's model is only valid for high-Q oscillators; we, however, use it as a fair approximation for $Q \geq 1$.

Combining Equations (13)–(16), ζ can be rewritten into:

$$\zeta = \frac{1}{\sqrt{2}} \cdot \alpha \cdot \sqrt{f_c} \cdot \sqrt{(1+\gamma) k_B T} \cdot \frac{1}{\sqrt{\eta_P P} \, Q} \qquad \qquad (17)$$

Using Equation (17), the effect of Q factors on ζ is shown in Figure 7, with $\alpha = 5$, $\gamma = \frac{2}{3}$, $k_B = 1.38 \times 10^{-23}$, $T = 300$ and $\eta_P = 2/\pi \approx 0.64$ (for ideal standard class-B oscillators [56,57]). It shows that ζ significantly increases with decreasing Q at certain f_c.

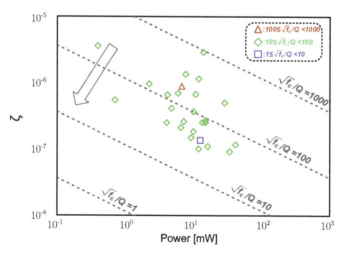

Figure 7. Relation between ζ and P based on Equation (17) for various $\sqrt{f_c}/Q$. For reference, the markers indicate calculated results (Equation (13)) of ζ based on measured phase-noise and f_c data from 27 JSSC/ISSCC papers about electrical LC oscillators published since 1997 (link: https: //ieeexplore.ieee.org/).

3.2. The MEMS Q Factor

As discussed above, the Q factor of the LC tank plays a crucial role in the estimation of ζ which in turn is crucial for the accuracy limits in frequency-based MEMS readouts. For many MEMS capacitive accelerometers, the Q factor of an LC oscillator including the MEMS capacitance is limited by the Q factor of this MEMS capacitor due to the relatively large series parasitic resistance R_M (Figure 6) rather than being limited by the Q factor of the inductor as in low-GHz electrical oscillator circuits (see also Section 2.3.4). Then, the Q factor can be estimated to be:

$$Q \approx \frac{1}{2\pi f_0 R_M C_0} \tag{18}$$

Substituting Equations (17) and (18) into Equation (10), the RMS acceleration noise (σ_{a_n}) of frequency-based readout for capacitive MEMS accelerometers is:

$$\sigma_{a_n} = \frac{C_0 + C_p}{S_{a2C}} \left(\pi C_0 \alpha \sqrt{f_c} \right) \sqrt{4 \left(1 + \gamma \right) k_B T \, R_M} \frac{f_0}{\sqrt{\eta_P P}} \quad [g] \tag{19}$$

3.3. Trade-Offs for f_0

As can be seen in Equations (18) and (19), a lower f_0 yields a higher Q for LC oscillators where the Q is limited by the capacitor's series resistance. This lower f_0 and hence higher Q yields a lower RMS noise (σ_{a_n}). However, f_0 cannot be chosen arbitrarily low: it is limited from below by requirements on signal BW and Q factor. Equation (6) shows that a lower f_0 leads to a smaller frequency deviation Δf which requires a longer observation time to detect, thereby possibly compromising the signal BW. The *lower* limit of Δf is hence determined by the highest signal frequency $f_{sig,max}$:

$$f_{sig,max} \leq \frac{1}{r_f} \frac{\sigma_{a_n} S_{a2C}}{C_0 + C_p} f_0 \tag{20}$$

Here, r_f denotes a constant factor which requires $r_f \geq 2$ according to *Nyquist's sampling theorem*. Therefore, we can assume:

$$f_{0,lowest} = r_f \frac{C_0 + C_p}{\sigma_{a_n} S_{a2C}} \cdot f_{sig,max} \tag{21}$$

In Section 3.1.2, we derived Equation (17) that links contributed jitter from flicker phase noise (i.e., ζ) to white phase noise in LC oscillators. As boundary condition, $Q \geq 1$ was assumed. This condition limits the highest f_0 to:

$$f_{0,highest} = \frac{1}{2\pi R_M C_0} \tag{22}$$

Combining Equations (21) and (22) leads to:

$$r_f \frac{C_0 + C_p}{\sigma_{a_n} S_{a2C}} \cdot f_{sig,max} \leq f_0 \leq \frac{1}{2\pi R_M C_0} \tag{23}$$

3.3.1. Minimum Input-Referred Acceleration Noise Density

From Equation (23), we get an inequality,

$$\sigma_{a_n} \geq r_f \frac{C_0 + C_p}{S_{a2C}} 2\pi R_M C_0 f_{sig,max} \quad [g] \tag{24}$$

Assuming that $f_{sig,max} \gg f_{sig,min}$, the signal BW roughly equals the maximum signal frequency, i.e., $BW \approx f_{sig,max}$. Then, dividing $\sqrt{BW}$ on both sides, we obtain an inequality in terms of input-referred acceleration noise density ($\overline{a_{n,f}}$):

$$\overline{a_{n,f}} = \frac{\sigma_{a_n}}{\sqrt{BW}} \geq r_f \frac{C_0 + C_p}{S_{a2C}} 2\pi R_M C_0 \sqrt{BW} \quad [g/\sqrt{Hz}] \tag{25}$$

This shows that $\overline{a_{n,f}}$ cannot be reduced infinitely by purely increasing power in the readout circuits. Instead, it is ultimately limited by the BW requirement and the parameters of MEMS accelerometers, such as sensitivity (S_{a2C}), static capacitor (C_0), parasitic capacitance (C_p) and resistance (R_M). Note that the latter determines the Q factor of the oscillator.

3.4. Estimation of Input-Referred Acceleration Noise Density

Based on above analysis results, now we can derive the estimation formulas for the input-referred acceleration noise density.

3.4.1. Input-Referred Acceleration Noise Density with Flicker Phase Noise

To estimate the best-case acceleration noise density with flicker phase noise, replacing f_0 of Equation (19) by (21) ($f_{0,lowest}$), assuming $BW \approx f_{sig,max}$ and rearranging σ_{a_n}, we get:

$$\sigma_{a_n} = \frac{C_0 + C_p}{S_{a2C}} \sqrt{\pi C_0} \sqrt[4]{\alpha^2 f_c} \sqrt[4]{4(1+\gamma)k_B T R_M^2} \frac{\sqrt{r_f BW}}{\sqrt[4]{\eta_P P}} \quad [g] \tag{26}$$

Thus, the *input-referred acceleration noise density with flicker phase noise* ($\overline{a_{n,f}}$) can be estimated as:

$$\overline{a_{n,f}} = \frac{\sigma_{a_n}}{\sqrt{BW}} = \frac{C_0 + C_p}{S_{a2C}} \sqrt{\pi C_0} \sqrt[4]{\alpha^2 f_c} \sqrt[4]{4(1+\gamma)k_B T R_M^2} \frac{\sqrt{r_f}}{\sqrt[4]{\eta_P P}} \quad [g/\sqrt{Hz}] \tag{27}$$

Note that larger values of the parasitic capacitor (C_p) and the resistance (R_M) increase the noise density and therefore these must be kept small during the MEMS design phase. Interestingly, it also shows a noise-power relation of $\sigma_{a_n} \propto P^{-\frac{1}{4}}$ rather than the customary relation of $\sigma_{a_n} \propto P^{-\frac{1}{2}}$ for non-frequency-based readouts. A possible explanation is given as follows. Assuming f_0 is fixed and $BW \approx f_{sig,max}$ in Equations (19) and (20), we find the power dissipation (P) can affect RMS noise (σ_{a_n}) directly (Equation (19)) and then affect BW indirectly via σ_{a_n} (Equation (20)). In other words, the power dissipation closely links to both noise and BW in frequency-based readouts.

As seen from Equation (27), the effect of flicker phase noise on noise density shows up as $\sqrt[4]{\alpha^2 f_c}$. This is not surprising. Recall that the relative frequency resolution ($\sigma_{f_n}^2/f_0^2$) which is related to acceleration noise as discussed before is expressed by white-phase-noise contributed jitter (κ), flicker-phase-noise contributed jitter (ζ) and measurement time (ΔT) in Equation (8). The corner time (t_c) where white-phase-noise contributed jitter equals to flicker-phase-noise contributed jitter, see Figure 8a, can be derived as $t_c = 1/(\alpha^2 f_c)$ [24,52]. Therefore, it is interesting to see that the effect of flicker phase noise on noise density is actually related to $\sqrt[4]{1/t_c}$. As will be shown in Section 3.4.2, this conclusion is also true in the noise-density relation without flicker phase noise.

3.4.2. Input-Referred Acceleration Noise Density without Flicker Phase Noise

A lot of efforts, such as filtering [58], reduction of current harmonics [59], switching bias [60,61], and so forth have been made to reduce the corner frequency of flicker phase noise in LC oscillators. However, all these techniques require sophisticated analyses and design skills or relatively complicated architectures that might not be suitable for sensor-controlled oscillator applications. Furthermore, system-level ideas, like correlated double counting (CDC) [24] and oscillator-based correlated double sampling (CDS) [62] are also investigated to address this issue. In general, the efficient suppression of flicker phase noise is still an ongoing and popular research topic.

If we assume the flicker phase noise is somehow completely removed in the oscillators, then ideally the frequency noise floor can decrease along with increasing the measurement time. However, the measurement time will be limited by the BW requirement as explained before. Therefore, as shown in Figure 8b, the corner time can be extended to t_{nf}:

$$t_{nf} = \frac{1}{r_f BW} \tag{28}$$

Performing the similar derivations to Equation (27) while using $\sigma_{f_n}^2 / f_0^2 = 2\kappa^2 / t_{nf}$ (see Equation (8)), *input-referred acceleration noise density without flicker phase noise* is modified as:

$$\overline{a_{n,nf}} = \frac{C_0 + C_p}{S_{a2C}} \sqrt{\pi C_0} \sqrt[4]{\frac{1}{t_{nf}}} \sqrt[4]{4(1+\gamma)k_B T R_M^2} \frac{\sqrt{r_f}}{\sqrt[4]{\eta_P P}} \quad [g/\sqrt{Hz}] \tag{29}$$

In fact, this is the ultimate minimum noise density that can be achieved from frequency-based readouts for capacitive MEMS accelerometers.

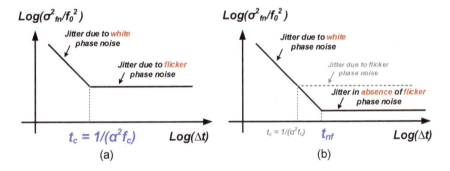

$\log(\sigma^2 {}_{fn}/f_0{}^2)$

Jitter due to *white* phase noise

Jitter due to *flicker* phase noise

$t_c = 1/(\alpha^2 f_c)$ $\log(\Delta t)$

(a)

$\log(\sigma^2 {}_{fn}/f_0{}^2)$

Jitter due to *white* phase noise

Jitter due to *flicker* phase noise

Jitter in *absence* of *flicker* phase noise

$t_c = 1/(\alpha^2 f_c)$ t_{nf} $\log(\Delta t)$

(b)

Figure 8. (a) averaging and flattening characteristic of frequency resolution ($\sigma_{f_n}^2 / f_0^2$) with an increase of measurement time Δt, where the corner time t_c is $1/(\alpha^2 f_c)$ [24,52]; (b) the corner time is extended to t_{nf} without flicker phase noise.

4. Noise Analysis of Conventional SC Charge-Based Interface Circuits

Interface circuits for capacitive MEMS accelerometers conventionally use charge-based approaches. Force feedback is often used to improve linearity and dynamic range, but this does not relax the noise requirements on the front-end amplifier, which as a result typically dominates the power consumption. The following analysis therefore only considers a single-ended front-end amplifier as shown in a simplified schematic in Figure 9, and neglects any power consumption related to other parts of the system, including digitization. Considering CDS and/or chopping techniques are usually employed to effectively reduce 1/f noise [47], *only thermal noise* is analyzed here, originating from the amplifier itself ($V_{n,amp}^2$) and the parasitic resistance at the input ($V_{n,R}^2$). This is different from the oscillator-based readout case where flicker noise cannot be effectively reduced at present.

Under the assumption that a virtual ground is formed at the amplifier's inverting input node, the input acceleration (at frequencies below the mechanical resonant frequency) is calculated from the output voltage as:

$$\Delta a_Q = \frac{C_f}{S_{a2C}} \frac{V_{out}}{2V_s} \tag{30}$$

Here, S_{a2C} is the sensitivity of acceleration to capacitor conversion (in unit of F/g), C_f is the feedback capacitor and V_s is the magnitude of the readout driving voltages.

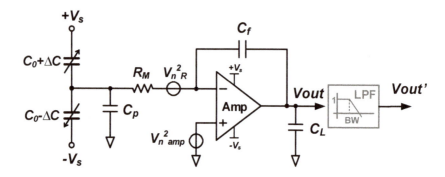

Figure 9. The single-ended simplified schematic for noise analysis of conventional SC readout.

Assuming a single-stage single-pole amplifier and taking noise folding into account, the output-referred noise voltage is [9,12,16]:

$$V_{n,out} = 2\sqrt{\left(\frac{2C_0 + C_p}{C_f}\right)^2 4k_BTR_M + \left(\frac{2C_0 + C_p + C_f}{C_f}\right)^2 \frac{4k_BT\gamma\eta_{amp}}{g_m}\sqrt{\frac{\pi BW_{amp,cl}}{f_s}}} \quad [V/\sqrt{Hz}] \quad (31)$$

where the denotations of C_0, C_p, k_B, T, R_M and γ are the same as for their frequency-based counterparts. Moreover, η_{amp} accounts for the total noise contribution of all the transistors: this depends on the topology and bias conditions of the operational amplifiers. The g_m is the transconductance of input transistors. Additionally, the closed-loop bandwidth of the amplifier and the sampling frequency are indicated as $BW_{amp,cl}$ and f_s, respectively. Finally, a factor of 2 comes from the fact that differential ($\times \sqrt{2}$) instead of single-ended circuits are normally used together with the noise doubling ($\times \sqrt{2}$) due to CDS technique in practical designs.

The power consumption (P) of this amplifier, with $\pm V_s$ supplies (assuming the same as MEMS driving voltages) can be estimated as:

$$P = 2V_s \frac{2I_D}{g_m} g_m \, m_P \tag{32}$$

$$= 2V_s \, V_{ov} \, g_m \, m_P$$

Here, $g_m/I_D = 2/V_{ov}$ for saturated MOS transistors is used. In this, V_{ov} represents the overdrive voltage of the input transistors and I_D is the biasing current for one of them, i.e., the total biasing current for the input differential pair is $2I_D$. Again, a factor m_P accounts for additional power dissipated in other transistors apart from the input pair.

Combining Equations (30)–(32) and rearranging them, the *input-referred acceleration noise density* ($\overline{a_{n,Q}}$) is obtained as:

$$\overline{a_{n,Q}} = \frac{1}{S_{a2C}}\sqrt{(2C_0 + C_p)^2 \frac{4k_BTR_M}{V_s^2} + (2C_0 + C_p + C_f)^2 \frac{8k_BT\gamma\eta_{amp}V_{ov}m_P}{V_s \, P}\sqrt{\frac{\pi BW_{amp,cl}}{f_s}}} \quad [g/\sqrt{Hz}] \quad (33)$$

As a design parameter of amplifier, the $BW_{amp,cl}$ is:

$$BW_{amp,cl} = \beta \frac{g_m}{2\pi C_{L,eff}}$$
$$= \frac{\beta}{4\pi V_s V_{ov} m_P} \frac{P}{C_{L,eff}} \tag{34}$$

where β is the feedback factor, g_m is from Equation (32) and $C_{L,eff}$ is the total effective capacitive load. Settling requirements sets a boundary condition on the amplifiers' BW as:

$$e^{-\frac{2\pi BW_{amp,cl}}{nf_s}} < \frac{1}{2^{N_q+1}} \tag{35}$$

under the assumption that the settling error must be less than half an LSB (N_q-bit resolution). Here, n accounts for the fraction of the sampling periods is used for charge transfer. Equivalently, the bandwidth ratio r_{BW} for acceptable settling error can be defined as:

$$r_{BW} = \frac{BW_{amp,cl}}{f_s} > \frac{n}{2\pi}(N_q + 1)\ln(2) \tag{36}$$

Substituting Equation (36) into (33), the *input referred acceleration noise density* $\overline{a_{n,Q}}$ is finally given by:

$$\overline{a_{n,Q}} = \frac{1}{S_{a2C}}\sqrt{(2C_0+C_p)^2\frac{4k_BTR_M}{V_s^2} + (2C_0+C_p+C_f)^2\frac{8k_BT\gamma\eta_{amp}V_{ov}m_P}{V_sP}}\sqrt{\pi r_{BW}} \quad [g/\sqrt{Hz}] \tag{37}$$

Equation (37) shows that the *thermal noise contributed from R_M* can only be minimized by proper design of the MEMS and increasing readout driving voltage V_s. Ways to improve the MEMS include minimizing sensing and parasitic capacitors and increasing the sensitivity. The driving voltage V_s is usually limited by CMOS technology or mechanical stiffness. The noise contributed by R_M may dominate the noise floor in ultra-sensitive interface circuits if R_M is relatively large.

Moreover, the *thermal noise contributed from the amplifier* can be reduced by increasing power while keeping properties such as sampling frequency (f_s), bandwidth $BW_{amp,cl}$, voltage gain and more. This can most easily be done by impedance level scaling [63] for which all (trans) conductances are scaled inversely proportional to the power level, and where (trans) capacitances are scaled proportionally to the power dissipation level. With impedance scaling, noise and mismatches are decreased at the cost of power dissipation. This is in line with practical experience that noise of SC circuits is essentially proportional to $k_BT/C_{L,eff}$.

5. Performance Comparison

The fundamental trade-offs between noise, power and BW for frequency-based and charge-based techniques are summarized in Equations (25), (27) and (37). To see how these trade-offs compare between the two different readout techniques, we use the typical parameter values in Table 1 referring to a specific capacitive sensor design [51]. Since the derived equations are fully parametric, designers can easily obtain similar trade-offs for their own sensor designs, by using a different set of parameters and checking them against the assumptions made when deriving the relations in Sections 3 and 4. We don't compare the readout techniques regarding linearity and dynamic range. Those parameters can be made independent of the readout front-end by using a force feedback configuration, while the power consumption then still is dominated by the front-end noise requirement.

Figure 10 shows the power dissipation versus acceleration noise density for frequency-based and charge-based readout techniques with $BW = 100$ Hz, $f_c = 1$ MHz and a MEMS series parasitic resistance R_M of $1\,\Omega$, $10\,\Omega$, $100\,\Omega$, respectively. Stemming from the noise-power relation of $\sigma_{a_n} \propto P^{-\frac{1}{4}}$ in frequency-based methods (see Equation (27)) rather than relation of $\sigma_{a_n} \propto P^{-\frac{1}{2}}$ in its charge-based counterpart (see Equation (37)), the power dissipation of frequency-based readouts in medium/relatively high noise density regions drop faster than that of charge-based techniques. This means that, with the same BW requirement, charge-based readout techniques are more suitable for low-noise requirements while oscillator-based approaches could be a more power-efficient solution when noise requirements are relaxed. The break-even points for these two readout principles vary with the MEMS capacitance series resistance R_M.

Table 1. The parameters used for numerical comparison.

C_0	C_p	S_{a2c}	R_M	r_f	α	f_c	η_P	γ
8 pF	16 pF	10 pF/g	10 Ω	2	5	1 MHz	0.64	2/3
C_f	V_s	V_{ov}	η_{amp}	m_p	k_B	T	$r_{BW}(n=8, Nq=3)$	BW
1 pF	3.5 V	0.1 V	1.5	1.5	1.38×10^{-23}	300 K	4	100 Hz

In addition, as shown in Figure 10, the R_M-contributed thermal noise leads to the noise-density "walls" in charge-based readouts (Equation (37)). This is different for frequency-based readouts, where the R_M and BW together (see Equation (25)) set the "walls". According to Equations (25) and (37), these "walls" can only be pushed towards the left (i.e., towards smaller noise density) by proper MEMS designs and increasing readout driving voltages in charge-based readouts (see Section 4), or by proper MEMS designs and narrowing BW in frequency-based readouts (see Section 3.3.1).

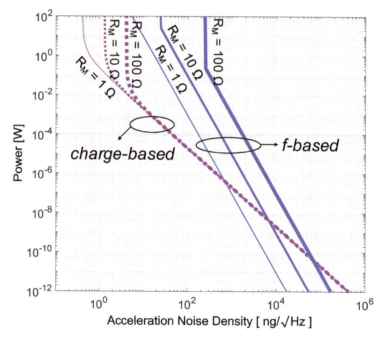

Figure 10. Power dissipation of readout circuits vs. acceleration noise density for charge-based and frequency-based (f) readout techniques with $BW = 100$ Hz, $f_c = 1$ MHz and R_M of 1 Ω, 10 Ω, 100 Ω, respectively.

Note that the power-noise curve of frequency-based readout technique will significantly shift down when flicker phase noise is completely removed, as illustrated in Figure 11. However, suppression of flicker phase noise in oscillators is not a trivial challenge: there is no highly effective reduction technique to date.

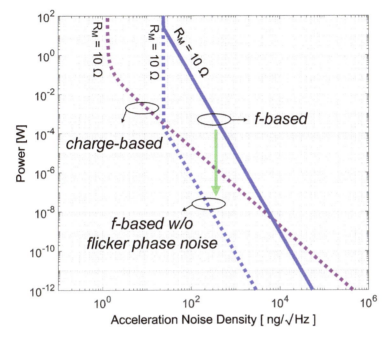

Figure 11. The power-noise curve of frequency-based readout significantly shifts down without flicker phase noise in oscillators. However, there are no techniques to actually accomplish this in real oscillators to date.

6. Conclusions

This paper focuses on frequency-based readout circuits for capacitive MEMS accelerometers. Fundamental limits were analyzed to show that high-Q oscillators and sufficient oscillating frequencies are beneficial to get high readout accuracy across a specific signal bandwidth, consuming relatively low power. Because of this, MEMS-controlled LC oscillators are most likely the best candidates for frequency-based readout systems. With respect to performance, flicker (phase) noise is shown to be the main bottleneck.

For benchmarking purposes against conventional switched-capacitor charged-based capacitive MEMS accelerometer readouts, closed-form relations including power, noise, and signal bandwidth were derived, for both the frequency-based and the charge-based readout techniques. Metrics for linearity and dynamic range were not included because they can be made independent from the employed readout technique and do not dominate the power consumption. From this, it appears that, with the same bandwidth requirement, charge-based readout circuits are more suitable when optimizing for noise performance, while there is still some room for frequency-based techniques when optimizing for power consumption, especially when flicker noise can be mitigated.

Micromachines **2018**, *9*, 488

Author Contributions: Z.Q. made the majority of contributions to this paper. B.A.B. and A.-J.A. provided many ideas to the theoretical analysis and gave detailed comments that improved this paper a lot. R.J.W. and B.N. supervised the research, participated in discussions and polished the paper.

Funding: This research was funded by the Netherlands Organisation for Scientific Research (NWO) (project 13338).

Acknowledgments: The authors would like to thank A.B., D.G., M.S. and N.A.v.B. from Nikhef, the Netherlands for helpful discussions and suggestions. The authors are also thankful to R.E.S. for phase noise/jitter discussions.

Conflicts of Interest: The authors declare no conflict of interest.

References

1. Yazdi, N.; Farrokh, A.; Khalil, N. Micromachined inertial sensors. *Proc. IEEE* **1998**, *86*, 1640–1659. [CrossRef]
2. Partridge, A. Getting In Touch with MEMS: The Electromechanical Interface. In Proceedings of the IEEE International Solid-State Circuits Conference (ISSCC), San Francisco, CA, USA, 19 February 2012.
3. Lammel, G. The future of MEMS sensors in our connected world. In Proceedings of the 28th IEEE Micro Electro Mechanical Systems (MEMS), Estoril, Portugal, 18–22 January 2015; pp. 61–64.
4. Van Drieenhuizen, B.P.; Maluf, N.I.; Opris, I.E.; Kovacs, G.T.A. Force-balanced accelerometer with mG resolution, fabricated using Silicon Fusion Bonding and Deep Reactive Ion Etching. In Proceedings of the International Conference on Solid-State Sensors and Actuators (TRANSDUCERS'97), Chicago, IL, USA, 19 June 1997; pp. 1229–1230.
5. De Marcellis, A.; Ferri, G. *Analog Circuits and Systems for Voltage-Mode and Current-Mode Sensor Interfacing Applications*; Springer: Berlin, Germany, 2011; ISBN 978-90-481-9827-6.
6. Wu, J. Sensing and Control Electronics for Low-Mass Low-Capacitance MEMS Accelerometers. Ph.D. Thesis, Carnegie Mellon University, Pittsburgh, PA, USA, 2002.
7. Yazdi, N.; Kulah, H.; Najafi, K. Precision readout circuits for capacitive microaccelerometers. In Proceedings of the IEEE Sensors, Vienna, Austria, 24–27 October 2004; pp. 28–31.
8. Chen, F.; Li, X.; Kraft, M. Electromechanical Sigma–Delta Modulators (ΣΔM) Force Feedback Interfaces for Capacitive MEMS Inertial Sensors: A Review. *IEEE Sens. J.* **2016**, *16*, 6476–6495. [CrossRef]
9. Lemkin, M.; Boser, B.E. A Three-Axis Micromachined Accelerometer with a CMOS Position-Sense Interface and Digital Offset-Trim Electronics. *IEEE J. Solid-State Circuits* **1999**, *34*, 456–468. [CrossRef]
10. Petkov, V.P.; Boser, B.E. A fourth-order ΔΣ interface for micromachined inertial sensors. *IEEE J. Solid-State Circuits* **2005**, *40*, 1602–1609. [CrossRef]
11. Amini, B.V.; Abdolvand, R.; Ayazi, F. A 4.5-mW Closed-Loop ΔΣ Micro-Gravity CMOS SOI Accelerometer. *IEEE J. Solid-State Circuits* **2006**, *41*, 2983–2991. [CrossRef]
12. Kulah, H.; Chae, J.; Yazdi, N.; Najafi, K. Noise analysis and characterization of a sigma-delta capacitive microaccelerometer. *IEEE J. Solid-State Circuits* **2006**, *41*, 352–361. [CrossRef]
13. Paavola, M.; Kamarainen, M.; Laulainen, E.; Saukoski, M.; Koskinen, L.; Kosunen, M.; Halonen, K.A.I. A Micropower ΔΣ-Based Interface ASIC for a Capacitive 3-Axis Micro-Accelerometer. *IEEE J. Solid-State Circuits* **2009**, *44*, 3193–3210. [CrossRef]
14. Lajevardi, P.; Petkov, V.P.; Murmann, B. A ΔΣ Interface for MEMS Accelerometers Using Electrostatic Spring Constant Modulation for Cancellation of Bondwire Capacitance Drift. *IEEE J. Solid-State Circuits* **2013**, *48*, 265–275. [CrossRef]
15. Petkov, V.P.; Balachandran, G.K.; Beintner, J. A Fully Differential Charge-Balanced Accelerometer for Electronic Stability Control. *IEEE J. Solid-State Circuits* **2014**, *49*, 262–270. [CrossRef]
16. Xu, H.; Liu, X.; Yin, L. A Closed-Loop ΣΔ Interface for a High-Q Micromechanical Capacitive Accelerometer With 200 ng/$\sqrt{Hz}$ Input Noise Density. *IEEE J. Solid-State Circuits* **2015**, *50*, 2101–2112. [CrossRef]
17. Helmy, A.A.; Jeon, H.; Lo, Y.-C.; Larsson, A.J.; Kulkarni, R.; Kim, J.; Silva-Martinez, J.; Entesari, K. A Self-Sustained CMOS Microwave Chemical Sensor Using a Frequency Synthesizer. *IEEE J. Solid-State Circuits* **2012**, *47*, 2467–2483. [CrossRef]
18. Elhadidy, O.; Elkholy, M.; Helmy, A.A.; Palermo, S.; Entesari, K. A CMOS Fractional-N PLL-Based Microwave Chemical Sensor With 1.5% Permittivity Accuracy. *IEEE Trans. Microw. Theory Tech.* **2013**, *61*, 3402–3416. [CrossRef]

19. Elhadidy, O.; Shakib, S.; Krenek, K.; Palermo, S.; Entesari, K. A Wide-Band Fully-Integrated CMOS Ring-Oscillator PLL-Based Complex Dielectric Spectroscopy System. *IEEE Trans. Circuits Syst. I* **2015**, *62*, 1940–1949. [CrossRef]
20. Chien, J.C.; Niknejad, A.M. Oscillator-Based Reactance Sensors With Injection Locking for High-Throughput Flow Cytometry Using Microwave Dielectric Spectroscopy. *IEEE J. Solid-State Circuits* **2016**, *51*, 457–472. [CrossRef]
21. Van Rethy, J.; Danneels, H.; De Smedt, V.; Dehaene, W.; Gielen, G.E. Supply-Noise-Resilient Design of a BBPLL-Based Force-Balanced Wheatstone Bridge Interface in 130-nm CMOS. *IEEE J. Solid-State Circuits* **2013**, *48*, 2618–2627. [CrossRef]
22. Gielen, G.; Van Rethy, J.; Marin, J.; Shulaker, M.M.; Hills, G.; Wong, H.-S.P.; Mitra, S. Time-Based Sensor Interface Circuits in CMOS and Carbon Nanotube Technologies. *IEEE Trans. Circuits Syst. I* **2016**, *63*, 577–586. [CrossRef]
23. Chaturvedi, V.; Nabavi, M.R.; Vogel, J.; Makinwa, K.A.A.; Nihtianov, S. A 0.6 nm resolution 19.8 mW eddy-current displacement sensor interface with 126 MHz excitation. In Proceedings of the IEEE International Solid-State Circuits Conference (ISSCC), San Francisco, CA, USA, 5–9 February 2017; pp. 174–175.
24. Wang, H.; Weng, C.C.; Hajimiri, A. Phase Noise and Fundamental Sensitivity of Oscillator-Based Reactance Sensors. *IEEE Trans. Microw. Theory Tech.* **2013**, *61*, 22152–22229. [CrossRef]
25. Straayer, M. Fundamentals of Time-Based Circuits. In Proceedings of the IEEE International Solid-State Circuits Conference (ISSCC), San Francisco, CA, USA, 5–9 February 2017.
26. Danneels, H.; Coddens, K.; Gielen, G. A fully-digital, 0.3 V, 270 nW capacitive sensor interface without external references. In Proceedings of the IEEE ESSCIRC, Helsinki, Finland, 12–16 September 2011; pp. 287–290.
27. Gaggatur, J.S.; Dixena, P.K.; Banerjee, G. A 3.2 mW 0.13 μm high sensitivity frequency-domain CMOS capacitance interface. In Proceedings of the IEEE International Symposium on Circuits and Systems (ISCAS), Montreal, QC, Canada, 22–25 May 2016; pp. 1070–1073.
28. Gaggatur, J.S.; Banerjee, G. Noise analysis in ring oscillator-based capacitance sensor interface. In Proceedings of the 59th IEEE International Midwest Symposium on Circuits and Systems (MWSCAS), Abu Dhabi, UAE, 16–19 October 2016; pp. 1–4.
29. Cardes, F.; Quintero, A.; Gutierrez, E.; Buffa, C.; Wiesbauer, A.; Hernandez, L. SNDR Limits of Oscillator-Based Sensor Readout Circuits. *Sensors* **2018**, *18*, 445. [CrossRef] [PubMed]
30. Razavi, B. A study of phase noise in CMOS oscillators. *IEEE J. Solid-State Circuits* **1996**, *31*, 331–343. [CrossRef]
31. McNeill, J.A. Jitter in ring oscillators. *IEEE J. Solid-State Circuits* **1997**, *32*, 870–879. [CrossRef]
32. Hajimiri, A.; Lee, T.H. A general theory of phase noise in electrical oscillators. *IEEE J. Solid-State Circuits* **1998**, *33*, 179–194. [CrossRef]
33. Navid, R.; Lee, T.H.; Dutton, R.W. Minimum achievable phase noise of RC oscillators. *IEEE J. Solid-State Circuits* **2005**, *40*, 630–637. [CrossRef]
34. Toth, F.N.; Meijer, G.C.M. A low-cost, smart capacitive position sensor. *IEEE Trans. Instrum. Meas.* **1992**, *41*, 1041–1044. [CrossRef]
35. Matsumoto, Y.; Hong, H.C.; Wu, P.C. Integrated silicon capacitive accelerometer with PLL servo technique. *Sens. Actuators A Phys.* **1993**, *39*, 209–217. [CrossRef]
36. Matsumoto, Y.; Nishimura, M.; Matsuura, M.; Ishida, M. Three-axis SOI capacitive accelerometer with PLL C–V converter. *Sens. Actuators A Phys.* **1999**, *75*, 77–85. [CrossRef]
37. Lee, S.; Lee, M.; Jung, S.; Je, C.; Park, J.; Hwang, G.; Choi, C. A Bidirectional Readout Integrated Circuit (ROIC) with Capacitance-to-Time Conversion Operation for High Performance Capacitive MEMS Accelerometers. In Proceedings of the IEEE Sensors, Atlanta, GA, USA, 28–31 October 2007; pp. 288–291.
38. Michalik, P.; Madrenas, J.; Fernández, D. Sense/drive architecture for CMOS-MEMS accelerometers with relaxation oscillator and TDC. In Proceedings of the 19th IEEE International Conference on Electronics, Circuits, and Systems (ICECS 2012), Seville, Spain, 9–12 December 2012; pp. 937–940.
39. Brookhuis, R.A.; Lammerink, T.S.J.; Wiegerink, R.J. Differential capacitive sensing circuit for a multi-electrode capacitive force sensor. *Sens. Actuators A Phys.* **2015**, *234*, 168–179. [CrossRef]

40. Mineta, T.; Kobayashi, S.; Watanabe, Y.; Kanauchi, S.; Nakagawa, I.; Suganurna, E.; Esashi, M. Three-axis Capacitive Accelerometer With Uniform Axial Sensitivities. In Proceedings of the International Conference on Solid-State Sensors and Actuators (TRANSDUCERS'95), Stockholm, Sweden, 25–29 June 1995; pp. 554–557.

41. Chiu, Y.; Hong, H.C.; Wu, P.C. Development and Characterization of a CMOS-MEMS Accelerometer with Differential LC-Tank Oscillators. *J. Microelectromech. Syst.* **2013**, *22*, 1285–1295. [CrossRef]

42. Langfelder, G.; Caspani, A.; Tocchio, A. Design Criteria of Low-Power Oscillators for Consumer-Grade MEMS Resonant Sensors. *IEEE Trans. Ind. Electron.* **2014**, *61*, 567–574. [CrossRef]

43. Comi, C.; Corigliano, A.; Langfelder, G.; Longoni, A.; Tocchio, A.; Simoni, B. A Resonant Microaccelerometer With High Sensitivity Operating in an Oscillating Circuit. *J. Microelectromech. Syst.* **2010**, *19*, 1140–1152. [CrossRef]

44. Burrer, C.; Esteve, J.; Lora-Tamayo, E. Resonant silicon accelerometers in bulk micromachining technology-an approach. *J. Microelectromech. Syst.* **1996**, *5*, 122–130. [CrossRef]

45. Razavi, B. *Design of Analog CMOS Integrated Circuits*; McGraw-Hill: New York, NY, USA, 2001; ISBN 0-07-238032-2.

46. Gao, X. Low Jitter Low Power Phase Locked Loops Using Sub-Sampling Phase Detection. Ph.D. Thesis, University of Twente, Enschede, The Netherlands, 2010.

47. Enz, C.C.; Temes, G.C. Circuit techniques for reducing the effects of op-amp imperfections: autozeroing, correlated double sampling, and chopper stabilization. *Proc. IEEE* **1996**, *84*, 1584–1614. [CrossRef]

48. Razavi, B. A Study of Injection Locking and Pulling in Oscillators. *IEEE J. Solid-State Circuits* **2004**, *39*, 1415–1424. [CrossRef]

49. Mirzaei, A.; Darabi, H. Mutual Pulling Between Two Oscillators. *IEEE J. Solid-State Circuits* **2014**, *49*, 360–372. [CrossRef]

50. Zhu, W.; Zhang, Y.; Meng, G.; Wallace, C.S.; Yazdi, N. A CMOS-integrated four-quadrant symmetric micro-g accelerometer. In Proceedings of the 29th IEEE Micro Electro Mechanical Systems (MEMS), Shanghai, China, 24–28 January 2016; pp. 926–929.

51. Boom, B.A.; Bertolini, A.; Hennes, E.; Brookhuis, R.A.; Wiegerink, R.J.; van den Brand, J.F.J.; Beker, M.G.; Oner, A.; van Wees, D. Nano-G accelerometer using geometric anti-springs. In Proceedings of the 30th IEEE Micro Electro Mechanical Systems (MEMS), Las Vegas, NV, USA, 22–26 January 2017; pp. 33–36.

52. Liu, C.; McNeill, J.A. Jitter in Oscillators with 1/f Noise Sources. In Proceedings of the IEEE International Symposium on Circuits and Systems (ISCAS), Vancouver, BC, Canada, 23–26 May 2004; pp. I-773–I-776.

53. Hajimiri, A.; Limotyrakis, S.; Lee, T.H. Jitter and phase noise in ring oscillators. *IEEE J. Solid-State Circuits* **1999**, *34*, 790–804. [CrossRef]

54. Leeson, D.B. A simple model of feedback oscillator noise spectrum. *Proc. IEEE* **1966**, *54*, 329–330. [CrossRef]

55. Murphy, D.; Darabi, H.; Wu, H. Implicit Common-Mode Resonance in LC Oscillators. *IEEE J. Solid-State Circuits* **2017**, *52*, 812–821. [CrossRef]

56. Fanori, L.; Andreani, P. Highly Efficient Class-C CMOS VCOs, Including a Comparison With Class-B VCOs. *IEEE J. Solid-State Circuits* **2013**, *48*, 1730–1740. [CrossRef]

57. Garampazzi, M.; Toso, S.D.; Liscidini, A.; Manstretta, D.; Mendez, P.; Romanò, L.; Castello, R. An Intuitive Analysis of Phase Noise Fundamental Limits Suitable for Benchmarking LC Oscillators. *IEEE J. Solid-State Circuits* **2014**, *49*, 635–645. [CrossRef]

58. Hegazi, E.; Sjoland, H.; Abidi, A.A. A filtering technique to lower LC oscillator phase noise. *IEEE J. Solid-State Circuits* **2001**, *36*, 1921–1930. [CrossRef]

59. Shahmohammadi, M.; Babaie, M.; Staszewski, R.B. A 1/f Noise Upconversion Reduction Technique for Voltage-Biased RF CMOS Oscillators. *IEEE J. Solid-State Circuits* **2016**, *51*, 2610–2624. [CrossRef]

60. Klumperink, E.A.M.; Gierkink, S.L.J.; van der Wel, A.P.; Nauta, B. Reducing MOSFET 1/f noise and power consumption by switched biasing. *IEEE J. Solid-State Circuits* **2000**, *35*, 994–1001. [CrossRef]

61. Narayanan, A.T.; Li, N.; Okada, K.; Matsuzawa, A. A pulse-tail-feedback VCO achieving FoM of 195 dBc/Hz with flicker noise corner of 700 Hz. In Proceedings of the IEEE Symposium on VLSI Circuits, Kyoto, Japan, 5–8 June 2017; pp. C124–C125.

62. Du, L.; Zhang, Y.; Liu, C.C.; Tang, A.; Hsiao, F.; Chang, M.C.F. A 2.3-mW 11-cm Range Bootstrapped and Correlated-Double-Sampling Three-Dimensional Touch Sensing Circuit for Mobile Devices. *IEEE Trans. Circuits Syst. II* **2017**, *64*, 96–100. [CrossRef]
63. Bruccoleri, F.; Klumperink, E.A.M.; Nauta, B. Generating all two-MOS-transistor amplifiers leads to new wide-band LNAs. *IEEE J. Solid-State Circuits* **2001**, *36*, 1032–1040. [CrossRef]

Article

Interrogation Techniques and Interface Circuits for Coil-Coupled Passive Sensors

Marco Demori *, Marco Baù, Marco Ferrari and Vittorio Ferrari

Department of Information Engineering, University of Brescia, Via Branze, 38-25123 Brescia, Italy;
marco.bau@unibs.it (M.B.); marco.ferrari@unibs.it (M.F.); vittorio.ferrari@unibs.it (V.F.)
* Correspondence: marco.demori@unibs.it; Tel.: +39-030-371-5897

Received: 17 August 2018; Accepted: 5 September 2018; Published: 9 September 2018

Abstract: Coil-coupled passive sensors can be interrogated without contact, exploiting the magnetic coupling between two coils forming a telemetric proximity link. A primary coil connected to the interface circuit forms the readout unit, while a passive sensor connected to a secondary coil forms the sensor unit. This work is focused on the interrogation of sensor units based on resonance, denoted as resonant sensor units, in which the readout signals are the resonant frequency and, possibly, the quality factor. Specifically, capacitive and electromechanical piezoelectric resonator sensor units are considered. Two interrogation techniques, namely a frequency-domain technique and a time-domain technique, have been analyzed, that are theoretically independent of the coupling between the coils which, in turn, ensure that the sensor readings are not affected by the interrogation distance. However, it is shown that the unavoidable parasitic capacitance in parallel to the readout coil introduces, for both techniques, an undesired dependence of the readings on the interrogation distance. This effect is especially marked for capacitance sensor units. A compensation circuit is innovatively proposed to counteract the effects of the parasitic input capacitance, and advantageously obtain distance-independent readings in real operating conditions. Experimental tests on a coil-coupled capacitance sensor with resonance at 5.45 MHz have shown a deviation within 1.5 kHz, i.e., 300 ppm, for interrogation distances of up to 18 mm. For the same distance range, with a coil-coupled quartz crystal resonator with a mechanical resonant frequency of 4.432 MHz, variations of less than 1.8 Hz, i.e., 0.5 ppm, have been obtained.

Keywords: coil-coupled sensor; passive sensor unit; resonant sensor; telemetric sensor; distance-independent contactless interrogation

---

1. Introduction

The ongoing downscaling of modern sensing devices is facing the main challenges of ensuring adequate power supply sources and removing wired connections. The power supply in wireless sensors has been traditionally provided by batteries that, however, have limited lifetime and need periodic recharge/replacement. Moreover, issues related to their degradation and the environmental impact for their disposal need to be considered.

As an alternative approach, energy harvesting techniques have gained increasing interest and undergone extensive investigations. Energy is harvested from the surroundings in the form of vibrations, motion, thermal energy, or solar energy, just to name a few. Suitable energy converters have been developed to transform the harvested energy into electrical energy using different principles, like piezoelectric [1,2], electromagnetic [3], thermoelectric [4] or pyroelectric [5,6] effects. Depending on the input source, the converted power can be sufficient to supply, continuously or intermittently, one or more sensing devices, which can transmit the measurement information through a radio frequency (RF) link to a receiving and supervising unit, thus creating a completely autonomous system without the need for power supply and cabling [7].

Alternatively, solutions based on the radio frequency identification (RFId) technologies can be adopted to implement sensing solutions exploiting electromagnetic coupling or RF fields to energize and transmit measurement information [8,9]. These solutions are typically based on low power configurations relying on a microcontroller to interface passive sensors, such as capacitive or resistive sensors [10]. Implantable sensors for medical analyses and monitoring are important examples where this solution can be advantageously applied [11–13].

Both energy harvesting and RFId systems use active electronics in the sensor unit which, in specific situations, can be a limitation, like in hostile, high-temperature, and chemically-harsh environments, where traditional silicon-based electronics cannot operate. In this context, the use of coil-coupled passive sensors, i.e., devices which do not need active components and integrated circuits to operate, is attractive. This solution exploits the magnetic coupling between a primary and a secondary coil to read passive sensors. The primary coil, along with the reading circuitry, forms the readout unit, which reads the sensor unit composed of the sensor element connected to the secondary coil [14–17]. This approach offers the promising advantage of reducing the cost of the passive sensor unit, allowing the production of disposable sensors, such as labels, with a passive sensor connected to the embedded coil [18,19].

In this paper, passive coil-coupled sensor units having a resonant behavior will be considered. The resonant behavior allows extracting the measurement information through the reading of the resonant frequency of the sensor unit [14,20]. This approach is robust because it is unaffected by the disturbances, such as noise and electromagnetic interferences, which typically affect the signal amplitude. Specifically, two kinds of sensors are investigated, as introduced in Section 2, namely, capacitive sensors, which form a resonant LC circuit with the secondary coil, and piezoelectric resonators, such as Quartz Crystal Resonators (QCRs) [21] or ceramic Resonant Piezo Layers (RPLs) [22].

One of the challenges of the contactless readout of passive sensors is to adopt reading techniques independent of the coupling between the primary and secondary coils [20,23]. This, in turn, would ensure that the readings are not affected by the interrogation distance. Two readout techniques, that are virtually independent of the coupling, are presented and discussed in detail in Section 3. In particular, a frequency-domain technique based on impedance measurements [20] and a time-domain technique called time-gated technique [21] are discussed. Both techniques suffer from significant accuracy degradation, due to the unavoidable parasitic capacitance in parallel to the readout coil that introduces a dependence of the readings on the interrogation distance. This undesirable effect is investigated in detail. Section 4 illustrates a compensation circuit that is innovatively proposed to counteract the effects of the parasitic input capacitance and advantageously obtain distance-independent readings in real operating conditions. Section 5 reports a set of experimental results on prototypes that successfully demonstrate the validity of the proposed approach and circuit.

2. Coil-Coupled Passive Sensors

A coil-coupled passive sensor is represented in its basic form by the schematic diagram of Figure 1. A primary coil CL_1 with inductance L_1 and series resistance R_1 is magnetically coupled to the secondary coil CL_2 with inductance L_2 and resistance R_2. The magnetic coupling is accounted for by the mutual inductance M, which depends on the geometry of L_1 and L_2 and their spatial arrangement. Alternatively, the magnetic coupling can be described through the coupling factor k, which is a nondimensional parameter defined as $k = M/\sqrt{(L_1 L_2)}$, resulting in $|k| \leq 1$. In the following, the values of L_1, R_1 and L_2, R_2 will be considered as fixed, while the value of M, and hence k, can change due to variations of the distance or orientation between CL_1 and CL_2.

CL_2 is connected to the generic impedance Z_S, which models the sensing element. In the following, the relevant cases will be considered where Z_S either forms, with L_2, a second order network with complex conjugate poles, i.e., Z_S is predominantly capacitive, or Z_S itself includes a second order network with complex conjugate poles, i.e., Z_S comprises an LCR network. In both cases, resonance can occur in the secondary circuit where the quantity to be sensed via Z_S influences the resonant frequency and, possibly, the damping. Therefore, the resulting combination will be termed Resonant Sensor Unit (RSU).

Importantly, for the RSU, the measurement information is carried by the frequency of the readout signal instead of its amplitude. The adoption of the resonant measuring principle has two main advantages with respect to amplitude-based techniques [24,25]. Firstly, the resonant principle is robust against external interferences or nonidealities that affect the signal amplitude. Secondly, as it will be illustrated in the following, the resonant principle, combined with suitable electronic techniques, can ensure that the readout frequency is made independent of the distance between CL_1 and the RSU.

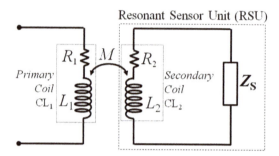

Figure 1. Equivalent circuit of a coil-coupled passive sensor.

The present theory will consider two specific cases for Z_S and the resulting RSU.

In the first case, Z_S is a capacitance sensor of value C_S, forming, with L_2, an LC resonant circuit as shown in Figure 2a. The resonant frequency f_S and quality factor Q_S of the RSU are

$$f_S = \frac{1}{2\pi\sqrt{L_2 C_S}}; \; Q_S = \frac{1}{R_2}\sqrt{\frac{L_2}{C_S}}. \tag{1}$$

In the second case, Z_S is the equivalent impedance of piezoelectric resonant sensors, like QCRs and RPLs. Their electromechanical behavior around resonance can be modelled with the Butterworth–van Dyke (BVD) equivalent lumped-element circuit, as shown in Figure 2b. The BVD circuit is composed of a motional, i.e., mechanical branch, and an electrical branch. The motional branch comprises the series of inductance L_r, capacitance C_r, and resistance R_r, which respectively represent the equivalent mass, compliance, and energy losses of the resonator. The electrical branch is formed by the parallel capacitance C_0, due to the dielectric material of the resonator. Under excitation by a voltage source, the mechanical resonant frequency f_r, i.e., the frequency at which the current in the motional arm is maximum, corresponds to the series resonant frequency of the BVD circuit, i.e., the frequency at which the reactance of the mechanical branch impedance vanishes [26]. Accordingly, f_r and the quality factor Q_r of the electromechanical resonator can be expressed as

$$f_r = \frac{1}{2\pi\sqrt{L_r C_r}}; \; Q_r = \frac{1}{R_r}\sqrt{\frac{L_r}{C_r}}. \tag{2}$$

Typically, when electromechanical piezoelectric resonators are used as sensors, the measurand quantity generates variations of the parameters of the motional branch L_r–C_r–R_r and, as a consequence, of f_r and Q_r.

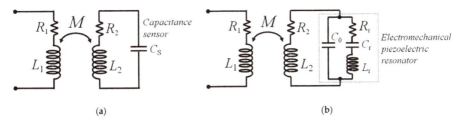

(a) (b)

Figure 2. Equivalent circuits of the two considered cases for a coil-coupled resonant sensor unit (RSU):
(**a**) capacitance sensor C_S; (**b**) electromechanical piezoelectric resonator represented with its equivalent
Butterworth–van Dyke (BVD) model.

3. Analysis of the Interrogation Techniques

3.1. General Considerations

Specific interrogation techniques are required to extract information from the RSU through
electronic measurements at the primary coil, exploiting the advantage of coil-coupled, i.e.,
contactless, operation.

One major issue to consider is the dependence of the mutual inductance M and coupling factor
k of the coils on geometrical parameters, such as their distance, alignment, and relative orientation.
Techniques that are influenced by the value of M, or equivalently k, would require keeping such
geometrical parameters fixed and constant [27,28]. On the other hand, in most practical applications,
keeping the distance and the alignment between coils fixed is unpractical/unfeasible. Therefore, as a
key requirement for out-of-the-lab use of coil-coupled sensors, robust measurement techniques are
demanded that are independent of k.

In the following, two innovative techniques are illustrated to perform k-independent readout of
RSUs of both capacitance and electromechanical piezoelectric resonator types. In particular, the first
is a frequency-domain technique which relies on the measurement of the reflected impedance at
CL_1. The second is a time-domain technique, termed time-gated technique, which considers the free
damped response of the RSU measured at the primary coil after that the RSU has been energized.

3.2. k-Independent Techniques Applied to Coil-Coupled Capacitance Sensors

Figure 3a shows the block diagram of the readout technique based on impedance measurements,
where the readout system consists in an impedance analyzer connected to the primary coil CL_1. From
the equivalent circuit of Figure 3b, the impedance Z_1, as a function of $\omega = 2\pi f$, is

$$Z_1 = R_1 + j\omega L_1 + Z_R = R_1 + j\omega L_1 + \omega^2 k^2 L_1 L_2 \frac{1}{R_2 + j\omega L_2 + \frac{1}{j\omega C_S}}. \tag{3}$$

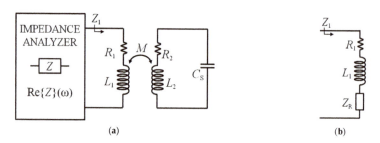

Figure 3. (a) Block diagram of the interrogation system based on impedance measurement from the primary coil; (b) equivalent circuit for the calculation of Z_1.

It can be seen from Equation (3) that the effect of the coupling with the RSU results in a reflected impedance Z_R in series with the primary coil that makes the total impedance Z_1 dependent on the coupling factor k. Nevertheless, the resonant frequency f_S and the quality factor Q_S of the RSU, defined in Equation (1), can be obtained from the real part of Z_1 [20], given by

$$\text{Re}\{Z_1\}(\omega) = R_1 + \omega^2 k^2 L_1 L_2 \frac{R_2}{R_2^2 + \left(\omega L_2 - \frac{1}{\omega C_S}\right)^2}. \tag{4}$$

$\text{Re}\{Z_1\}$ has a local maximum at the frequency $f_m = \omega_m/2\pi$, which can be found by equating to zero the derivative of Equation (4) with respect to ω. Interestingly enough, f_m is independent of k, and it can be related to f_S and Q_S only. Then, combining Equations (1) and (4), the following relations hold:

$$f_m = f|_{\max(\text{Re}\{Z_1\})} = \frac{2Q_S}{\sqrt{4Q_S^2 - 2}} f_S; \quad Q_S \approx \frac{f_S}{\Delta f_m}, \tag{5}$$

where Δf_m is the full width at half maximum (FWHM) of $\text{Re}\{Z_1\}$, around f_m [20]. If Q_S is sufficiently large, then $f_m \approx f_S$, with a relative deviation $|f_m - f_S|/f_S < 100$ ppm for $Q_S > 50$. Equations (4) and (5) demonstrate that from the measurement of f_m and Δf_m in $\text{Re}\{Z_1\}$, the frequency f_S and quality factor Q_S of the capacitive RSU can be advantageously extracted independently from k. Figure 4 shows sample plots of $\text{Re}\{Z_1\}$ calculated for three different values of k, and illustrates the definition of Δf_m. Consistently with Equation (4), k only affects amplitude.

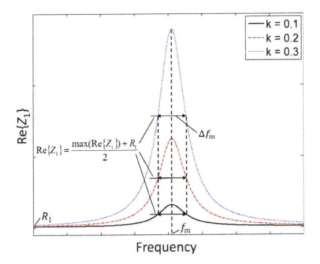

Figure 4. Real part of Z_1 as a function of frequency from Equation (4) for three different values of k.

The operating principle of the time-gated technique is shown in Figure 5a [21]. It comprises two subsequent alternating phases, namely, excitation and detection phases. During the excitation phase, when the switch is in the E position, CL_1 is connected to the sinusoidal signal $v_{exc}(t)$ to excite the RSU through inductive coupling. During the subsequent detection phase, when the switch is in the D position, the excitation signal is disconnected, and CL_1 is connected to a readout circuit with a high-impedance input, resulting in a virtually zero current in CL_1.

The input voltage $v_1(t)$ of the readout circuit during the detection phase D can be derived by taking the inverse Laplace transform of the corresponding voltage $V_1(s)$, where s is the complex frequency. Since the RSU forms a second order LCR network, the voltage $v_1(t)$ is expected to be a damped sinusoid with frequency f_d and a decay time τ_d from which the resonant frequency f_S and the quality factor Q_S of the RSU can be inferred.

Generally, assuming that the detection phase D starts at $t = 0$, the readout voltage $v_1(t)$ depends on the initial conditions at $t = 0$ of all the reactive elements, namely, C_S, L_1, L_2, and M. The effect of the initial conditions on $v_1(t)$ for $t > 0$ is to globally affect only its starting amplitude, while the complex frequencies of the network, that define f_d and τ_d, are unaltered. Therefore, without losing any generality, the single initial condition V_{CS0} defined as the voltage across C_S at $t = 0$ can be considered, neglecting the remaining ones. As an equivalent alternative that does not change the consequences of the present treatment, V_{CS0} can also be seen as an effective initial condition.

As a result, the equivalent circuit of Figure 5b representing the time-gated configuration during the detection phase in the Laplace domain can be considered, and the expression of $V_1(s)$ is

$$V_1(s) = k\sqrt{\frac{L_1}{L_2}} V_{CS0} \frac{s}{s^2 + s\frac{R_2}{L_2} + \frac{1}{L_2 C_S}}. \tag{6}$$

The corresponding time expression $v_1(t)$ can be calculated:

$$v_1(t) = k\sqrt{\frac{L_1}{L_2}}\sqrt{\frac{4Q_S^2}{4Q_S^2 - 1}} V_{CS0} e^{-\frac{t}{\tau_d}} \cos\left[2\pi f_d t - \text{atan}\left(\frac{1}{2\pi f_d \tau_d}\right)\right]. \tag{7}$$

The signal $v_1(t)$ is a damped sinusoid with damped frequency f_d and decay time τ_d that are related to f_S and Q_S of the RSU as

$$f_d = f_S\sqrt{1 - \frac{1}{4Q_S^2}}; \; \tau_d = \frac{Q_S}{\pi f_S}. \tag{8}$$

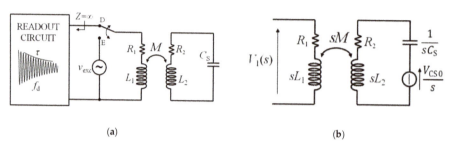

(a)   (b)

Figure 5. (a) Block diagram of the time-gated technique; (b) equivalent circuit of the time-gated technique during the detection phase.

If Q_S is sufficiently large, it results in $f_d \approx f_S$, with a relative deviation $|f_d - f_S|/f_S < 50$ ppm for $Q_S > 50$. Notably, the coupling factor k only acts as an amplitude factor on $v_1(t)$ without influencing either f_d or τ_d. Figure 6 reports sample plots of $v_1(t)$ calculated for three different values of k.

In summary, Equations (7) and (8) demonstrate that, under the assumptions made, the time-gated technique can also allow extraction of the frequency f_S and quality factor Q_S of the capacitive RSU, independently of k.

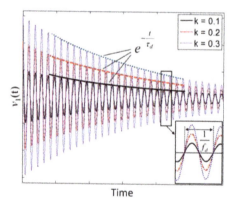

Time

Figure 6. Voltage $v_1(t)$ during the detection phase calculated for three different values of the coupling factor k.

3.3. k-Independent Techniques Applied to Coil-Coupled Electromechanical Piezoelectric Resonators

Considering the technique based on impedance measurements with reference to the equivalent circuit of Figure 2b, the impedance Z_1 measured at the primary coil can be expressed as

$$Z_1 = R_1 + j\omega L_1 + \omega^2 k^2 L_1 L_2 \frac{1}{R_2 + j\omega L_2 + \frac{1}{j\omega C_0} \| \left(j\omega L_r + \frac{1}{j\omega C_r} + R_r \right)}. \tag{9}$$

As it can be observed in Equation (9), the impedance Z_1 depends on the coupling factor k. Nevertheless, also in this case, the frequency f_r can be extracted from the frequency of the maximum of the real part of Z_1.

Close to the angular frequency $\omega_r = 2\pi f_r$, the impedance of the motional arm $Z_r = R_r + j\omega L_r + 1/(j\omega C_r)$ has a magnitude typically much smaller than that of the impedance of C_0, i.e., $|Z_r| \ll 1/\omega C_0$. Then, the presence of C_0 can be neglected, resulting in the simplified equivalent circuit of Figure 7a. Accordingly, $\mathrm{Re}\{Z_1\}$ around ω_r has the following approximated expression:

$$\mathrm{Re}\{Z_1\} \approx R_1 + \omega^2 k^2 L_1 L_2 \frac{R_r + R_2}{(R_r + R_2)^2 + \left[\omega(L_r + L_2) - \frac{1}{\omega C_r}\right]^2}. \tag{10}$$

Equation (10) has the same form as Equation (4) and, hence, $\mathrm{Re}\{Z_1\}$ has a maximum at the frequency f_{m_r} given by

$$f_{m\_r} = f_{r2}\frac{2Q_{r2}}{\sqrt{4Q_{r2}{}^2 - 2}}, \text{ where } f_{r2} = \frac{1}{2\pi\sqrt{(L_r + L_2)C_r}} \text{ and } Q_{r2} = \frac{1}{R_r + R_2}\sqrt{\frac{L_r + L_2}{C_r}}. \tag{11}$$

It can be observed that for large Q_{r2}, $f_{m\_r} \approx f_{r2}$ with a deviation $|f_{m\_r} - f_{r2}|/f_{r2} < 100$ ppm for $Q_{r2} > 50$. In addition, assuming that $L_2 \ll L_r$, the frequency f_{r2} approximates f_r and, hence, $f_{m\_r} \approx f_r$ holds. Similarly, if $R_2 \ll R_r$, Q_{r2} approaches Q_r. Importantly, again, the coupling factor k acts only as an amplitude factor that advantageously does not affect either the frequency or the quality factor of the resonance.

Considering, now, the frequencies $\omega \gg \omega_r$, the impedance magnitude of C_0 is smaller than the impedance magnitude of Z_r, which then can be neglected, obtaining the equivalent circuit of Figure 7b. Consequently, the following approximated expression of $\mathrm{Re}\{Z_1\}$ results:

$$\mathrm{Re}\{Z_1\} \approx R_1 + \omega^2 k^2 L_1 L_2 \frac{R_2}{R_2^2 + \left(\omega L_2 - \frac{1}{\omega C_0}\right)^2}. \tag{12}$$

Also Equation (12) has the same form as Equation (4), and it can be seen that $\mathrm{Re}\{Z_1\}$ now has a maximum at the frequency f_{m_el}:

$$f_{m\_el} = f_{el}\frac{2Q_{el}}{\sqrt{4Q_{el}{}^2 - 2}}, \text{ where } = f_{el} = \frac{1}{2\pi\sqrt{L_2 C_0}} \text{ and } Q_{el} = \frac{1}{R_2}\sqrt{\frac{L_2}{C_0}}. \tag{13}$$

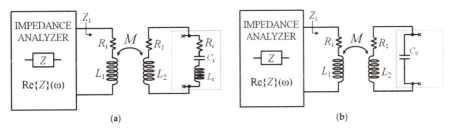

(a)   (b)

Figure 7. (a) Block diagram of the interrogation system with equivalent circuit of electromechanical piezoelectric resonator around f_r; (b) block diagram of the interrogation system with equivalent circuit of electromechanical piezoelectric resonator for $f \gg f_r$.

From the previous analysis, it can be concluded that Re{Z_1} has two peaks: the first is related to the mechanical resonance f_r, the second to the electrical resonance f_{el}. With the previous assumptions on the values of L_r and L_2, and considering that, typically, $C_r \ll C_0$, then it follows that $f_{el} \gg f_r$.

To validate, numerically, the proposed approximations, Figure 8a,b report the comparison of the values of f_{m_r} and f_{m_el} derived respectively from Equations (11) and (13), and the frequency of the maxima derived numerically from Re{Z_1} in Equation (9) as a function of L_2. The following values of the BVD model of a 4.432 MHz AT-cut QCR have been used: $C_0 = 5.72$ pF, $R_r = 10.09$ Ω, $L_r = 77.98$ mH, and $C_r = 16.54$ fF. For CL$_1$ and CL$_2$, the values of the electrical parameters are $L_1 = 8.5$ μH, $R_1 = 5$ Ω, and $R_2 = 5$ Ω.

Figure 8a shows that for L_2 up to 10 μH, the values of f_{m_r} predicted from Equation (11) are within 3 ppm with respect to the numerical solutions from Equation (9). Additionally, for the same range of variation of L_2, a remarkable agreement is obtained between f_{m_el} predicted from Equation (13) and the numerical solution.

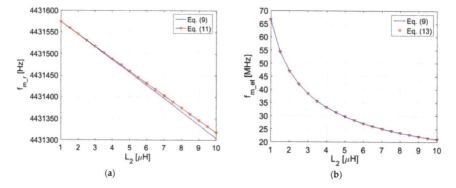

(a)

(b)

Figure 8. (a) Comparison of f_{m_r} derived from the maximum of Re{Z_1} for frequencies around f_r, in Equation (9), and the approximate value from Equation (11) as a function of L_2; (b) comparison of f_{m_el} derived from the maximum of Re{Z_1} for $f \gg f_r$, in Equation (9), and the approximate value from Equation (13) as a function of L_2.

The possibility to interrogate coil-coupled electromechanical piezoelectric resonators with the time-gated technique independently from the coupling has been previously demonstrated [21].

The RSU configuration of Figure 9 has been studied in [21], showing that the open circuit voltage $v_1(t)$ at CL$_1$ during the detection phase, after the RSU has been energized in the excitation phase, is the sum of two damped sinusoids: one at frequency f_{d_r} with exponential decaying time τ_r, and one at frequency f_{d_el} with exponential decaying time τ_{el}.

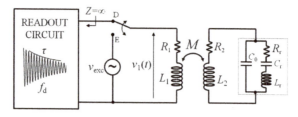

Figure 9. Block diagram of the time-gated technique applied to a coil-coupled electromechanical piezoelectric resonator.

The damped sinusoid at f_{d_r} is due to the mechanical response of the resonator, while the one at f_{d_el} is due to the electrical response of L_2 that interacts with the electrical capacitance C_0. In addition, for suitable values of L_2 and R_2, and considering the typical values of the equivalent parameters of the BVD model of a QCR, the decaying time τ_r is orders of magnitude larger than τ_{el}. Thus, the damped sinusoid at frequency f_{d_el} decays to zero much faster than the damped sinusoid at frequency f_{d_r}. Hence, the former can be neglected in the expression of $v_1(t)$, which results in

$$v_1(t) \cong k\sqrt{L_1 L_2} A_r e^{-\frac{t}{\tau_r}} \cos(2\pi f_{d\_r} t + \theta_r) - \delta(t) L_1 i_{L1}(0), \tag{14}$$

where the amplitude and phase coefficients A_r and θ_r are functions of both the initial conditions at the beginning of the detection phase ($t = 0$), and the electrical and mechanical parameters of the system. The last term represents the contribution of the initial current $i_{L1}(0)$ in the primary inductor. From Equation (14), it can be seen that k acts only as a scaling factor for the amplitude of v_1, without affecting the sensor response parameters f_{d_r} and τ_r. From a simplified analysis that considers the undamped system with $R_2 = 0$ and $R_r = 0$, under the hypothesis that $(\omega C_0)^{-1} \gg \omega L_2$ at the frequency f_r and that Q_r is large, it has been obtained that the frequency f_{d_r} can be approximated with the following relation:

$$f_{d\_r} \approx f_r \left(1 - \frac{1}{2}\frac{L_2}{L_r}\right). \tag{15}$$

It can be observed in Equation (15) that f_{d_r} depends on the ratio between L_2 and L_r. Nevertheless, if $L_2 \ll L_r$ the frequency f_{d_r} tends to the resonant frequency f_r of the electromechanical resonator. A numerical analysis that allows the calculation of the parameters f_{d_r} and τ_r of the complete system, is also reported in [21]. The results can be directly compared with Figure 8, the values of the parameters of the BVD model used in the numerical analysis being the same. Also in that case, good agreement between the values of f_{d_r} predicted from Equation (15) and the numerical results have been obtained, with a maximum deviation within 3 ppm for L_2 up to 10 μH.

3.4. Effect of Parasitic Capacitance at the Primary Coil on Coil-Coupled Capacitance Sensors

When the proposed techniques are transferred into real electronic circuits, unavoidable nonidealities result in a lumped parasitic capacitance C_P that appears in parallel to L_1. The parasitic capacitance C_P is mainly composed of the parasitic capacitance of the inductor L_1, the capacitance of the connections, and the input capacitance of the electronic interface.

The effect of C_P is now evaluated, firstly, considering the case of the RSU with the capacitance sensor, extending the treatment of Section 3.2.

With reference to Figure 10a, the real part of the impedance at the primary coil becomes

$$\text{Re}\{Z_{1P}\} = \text{Re}\left\{\frac{\left(R_1 + j\omega L_1 + \frac{\omega^2 k^2 L_1 L_2}{R_2 + j\omega L_2 + \frac{1}{j\omega C_S}}\right)\frac{1}{j\omega C_P}}{R_1 + j\omega L_1 + \frac{\omega^2 k^2 L_1 L_2}{R_2 + j\omega L_2 + \frac{1}{j\omega C_S}} + \frac{1}{j\omega C_P}}\right\}. \tag{16}$$

As discussed in [23], with $C_P \neq 0$, Equation (16) no longer allows extraction of f_S and Q_S independently from the coupling factor k, which now is in the expression of Z_{1P} and affects $\text{Re}\{Z_{1P}\}$, not only as a scaling factor. In particular, it has been shown by a numerical analysis of Equation (16) that $\text{Re}\{Z_{1P}\}$ has two maxima, corresponding, respectively, to a primary resonance near f_S and a secondary resonance near $f_P = 1/\left(2\pi\sqrt{L_1 C_P}\right)$. Both the frequencies of the maxima and the trend of $\text{Re}\{Z_{1P}\}$ are influenced by the coupling factor k [23].

Considering now the time-gated technique, the voltage $v_{1P}(t)$ at the primary coil in the detection phase can be obtained from the circuit of Figure 10b. Adopting the same approach as for the case of $C_P = 0$, it will be assumed that all the reactive elements, except the capacitor C_S, have zero initial conditions at $t = 0$. Consequently, the voltage $V_{1P}(s)$ can be expressed in the Laplace domain as

$$V_{1P}(s) = \frac{N(s)}{D(s)} =$$
$$k\sqrt{\frac{L_1}{L_2}} \frac{sV_{CS0}C_SL_2}{s^4C_SC_PL_1L_2(1-k^2)+s^3C_SC_P(L_1R_2+L_2R_1)+s^2(C_SL_2+C_PL_1+C_SC_PR_1R_2)+s(C_SR_2+C_PR_1)+1} \quad (17)$$

where V_{CS0} is the voltage across C_S at $t = 0$. From Equation (17), it can be seen that k, besides acting as a scaling factor, also features in the coefficient of fourth degree in the polynomial $D(s)$. Consequently, it is expected that the complex frequencies are dependent on k. Taking the inverse Laplace transform of Equation (17), it results that the expression of $v_{1P}(t)$ is composed of the sum of two damped sinusoids as

$$v_{1P}(t) = A_1 e^{-\frac{t}{\tau_{d1}}}\cos(2\pi f_{d1}t - \theta_1) + A_2 e^{-\frac{t}{\tau_{d2}}}\cos(2\pi f_{d2}t - \theta_2), \quad (18)$$

where A_1 and A_2 are amplitude coefficients and θ_1 and θ_2 are phase angles that depend on the parameters of the circuit and the initial conditions. The frequencies f_{d1} and f_{d2} and the decay times, τ_{d1} and τ_{d2} are obtained by the complex conjugate solutions $p_{1,2} = 1/\tau_{d1} \pm j2\pi f_{d1}$ and $p_{3,4} = 1/\tau_{d2} \pm j2\pi f_{d2}$ of $D(s) = 0$.

From the values of $p_{1,2}$ and $p_{3,4}$, it can be demonstrated that f_{d1} is close to f_P, while f_{d2} is close to f_S, but both f_{d1} and f_{d2} are dependent on k. For R_2 sufficiently smaller than R_1, a decay time τ_{d2} larger than τ_{d1} can be obtained. In this condition, in $v_{1P}(t)$ the damped sinusoid at f_{d1} falls off more rapidly than that at f_{d2}, and it becomes negligible as time elapses. Importantly, since f_{d2} depends on k, the distance-independent operation of the case $C_P = 0$ is now lost.

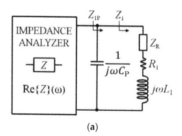

(a)

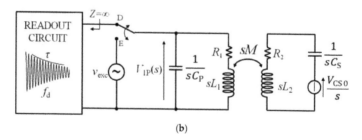

(b)

Figure 10. (a) Block diagram of the interrogation system with equivalent circuit of the impedance Z_{1P} for the technique based on impedance measurements applied to a coil-coupled capacitance sensor; **(b)** block diagram of the interrogation system with equivalent circuit in the Laplace domain to derive $V_{P1}(s)$ during the detection phase of the time-gated technique applied to a coil-coupled capacitance sensor.

The dependence of the readout frequency on the coupling factor k, introduced by the parasitic capacitance C_P, on both the proposed techniques, is investigated by numerical analysis. For the RSU and CL_1, the following sample values, which represent real conditions well, have been considered: L_2

$= 8\ \mu H$, $C_S = 100$ pF, $R_2 = 3\ \Omega$, $L_1 = L_2$, and $R_1 = 10\ \Omega$. For the impedance technique, the frequency f_{SP} has been calculated from the expression of $\mathrm{Re}\{Z_{1P}\}$, adopting the definitions in Equation (5). For the time-gated technique, f_{SP} has been calculated from f_{d2} and τ_{d2}, derived from the numerical solution of $D(s) = 0$, adopting the definitions in Equation (8).

Figure 11 compares the obtained relative deviation $(f_{SP} - f_S)/f_S$ as a function of the coupling factor k for three different values of C_P/C_S. For the considered values of the parameters, C_P ranges from 1 pF to 10 pF. As it can be observed, $(f_{SP} - f_S)/f_S$ deviates from zero, corresponding to $C_P = 0$. The deviation increases for increasing k of an amount that augments with C_P/C_S. Noticeably, both the techniques are equally affected by the inaccuracies introduced by C_P, in terms of the dependence of the readout frequency on k. These results demonstrate that C_P prevents accurate distance-independent measurements from being obtained.

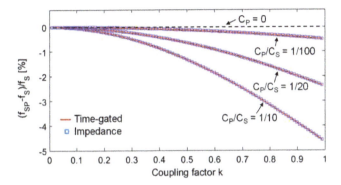

Figure 11. Comparison of the $(f_{SP} - f_S)/f_S$ obtained from the two techniques as a function of k for three different values of the ratio C_P/C_S. The exact value of f_S without the parasitic capacitance, i.e., $C_P = 0$, is $f_S = 5.626977$ MHz.

3.5. Effect of Parasitic Capacitance at the Primary Coil on Coil-Coupled Electromechanical Piezoelectric Resonators

Considering, now, the case with coil-coupled electromechanical piezoelectric resonators, the dependence on k due to C_P can be evaluated by using the same numerical approach as discussed in Section 3.3. The resonant frequency f_{rP} can be obtained from numerical analysis of the equivalent circuit in Figure 12a for the frequency-domain technique based on impedance Z_{1P}, while the equivalent circuit of Figure 12b must be considered for the time-gated technique to determine $V_{1P}(s)$.

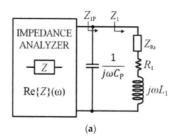

(a)

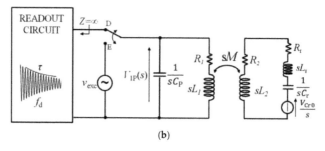

(b)

Figure 12. (**a**) Block diagram of the interrogation system with equivalent circuit of the impedance Z_{1P} for the technique based on impedance measurements applied to an electromechanical piezoelectric resonator; Z_{Rr} represents the reflected impedance of the RSU with electromechanical piezoelectric resonator. (**b**) Block diagram of the interrogation system with equivalent circuit in the Laplace domain to derive $V_{1P}(s)$ during the detection phase of the time-gated technique applied to an electromechanical piezoelectric resonator.

In both the equivalent circuits, the impedance of the static capacitance C_0 has been considered high enough to be neglected. For the time-gated technique, C_P is expected to give rise to an additional damped sinusoid in $v_{1P}(t)$, with a damped frequency related to C_P resonating with L_1. However, the numerical simulations have demonstrated that this sinusoid fades out more quickly than the damped sinusoid, due to the QCR response.

Considering the same parameter values for the QCR as adopted for the analysis of Figure 8, the obtained relative deviation $(f_{rP} - f_r)/f_r$ as a function of k for three different increasing values of the ratio C_P/C_r, is reported in Figure 13. For the considered values of the parameters, C_P ranges from 1.65 pF to 99.2 pF. The baseline, i.e., the dotted curve corresponding to $C_P = 0$, is at -54.5 ppm because of L_2, that slightly affects f_{r2} and, hence, f_{rP}, according to Equation (11). As it can be observed, f_{rP} has a maximum variation of less than 4 ppm with respect to the baseline. Remarkably, also in this case, the same behaviour with respect to C_P and k is predicted for the two techniques.

The quantitatively negligible dependence of f_{rP} on k can be ascribed to the fact that the inductive component in the RSU is dominated by L_r. In fact, L_r is three orders of magnitude larger than L_2, and it is not involved in the coupling between the primary coil and the RSU. This result shows that with coil-coupled electromechanical resonators, such as QCRs, the proposed techniques remain practically independent from the coupling factor k, despite a not-negligible C_P.

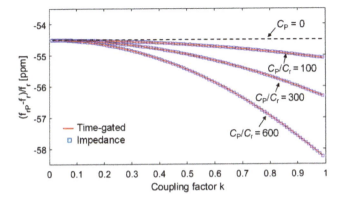

Figure 13. Comparison of the relative deviation $(f_{rP} - f_r)/f_r$ obtained from the time-gated technique and the impedance technique as a function of k for three different values of the ratio C_P/C_r.

4. Interrogation Techniques and Interface Circuits

4.1. Interrogation System Based on the Impedance-Measurement Technique with Parasitic Capacitance Compensation

The block diagram of the interrogation system, based on impedance-measurement technique, is reported in Figure 14. The primary coil CL_1 is connected to the impedance analyzer. The total parasitic capacitance C_P accounts for the contributions given by the parasitic capacitances of CL_1, the connections and the equivalent capacitance of the input of the impedance analyzer, represented in Figure 14 with C_1, C_L, and C_I, respectively.

The key idea is that connecting a proper capacitance compensation circuit to the primary coil CL_1, it is possible to cancel the effects of C_P. The proposed compensation circuit, described in Section 4.3, behaves as an equivalent negative capacitance $-C_C$. The ideal condition, where C_P is not present, i.e., $Z_{1P} = Z_1$, can be thus obtained when $C_C = C_P$. In the compensated condition, Equation (5) again applies, and k-independent measurements of the resonant frequency and quality factor can be obtained by considering the maximum of the real part of the measured impedance.

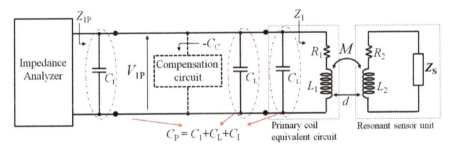

Figure 14. Block diagram of the interrogation system based on impedance measurement technique with parasitic capacitance compensation circuit.

4.2. Interrogation System Based on the Time-gated Technique with Parasitic Capacitance Compensation

The block diagram of the proposed interrogation system based on the time-gated technique is shown in Figure 15. The analog switch SW, controlled by the square-wave gate signal $v_g(t)$, alternatively connects the primary coil to the excitation signal $v_{exc}(t)$ and to the high-input impedance readout amplifier A_G during the excitation and detection phases, respectively. The noninverting amplifier A_G, with gain G, is based on a high-bandwidth operational amplifier. A frequency meter connected to the output of A_G allows measurement of the frequency of the damped sinusoidal signal $v_O(t)$.

The total parasitic capacitance C_P accounts for the contributions of the parasitic capacitances of the primary coil, the connections, the analog switch SW, and the equivalent input capacitance of the amplifier A_G, represented in Figure 15 with C_1, C_L, C_{SW}, and C_I, respectively.

Similarly to what was described in Section 4.1, a proper compensation circuit that behaves as an equivalent negative capacitance $-C_C$ can be introduced to cancel C_P. In the compensated condition, the frequency and decay time of the damped sinusoidal voltage $v_O(t)$ return to be unaffected from the coupling factor k. In this condition, Equation (8) can be used to extract the resonant frequency and quality factor of the RSU from the measured resonant frequency and decay time of $v_O(t)$.

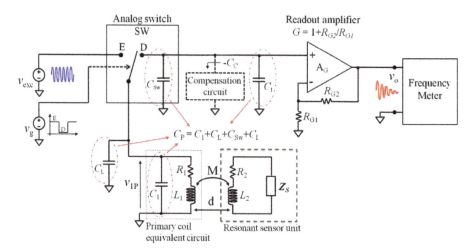

Figure 15. Block diagram of the interrogation system based on of time-gated technique with parasitic capacitance compensation circuit.

4.3. Parasitic Capacitance Compensation Circuit

Figure 16 shows the proposed capacitance compensation circuit. It is based on a high-bandwidth operational amplifier A_C operating as a negative impedance converter (NIC) to produce an effective negative capacitance $-C_C$. The voltage V_1 across CL_1 is applied across the reference capacitor C_A, thanks to the virtual short circuit at the input of A_C. The current I_{CA} through C_A is then amplified with gain $-R_{C2}/R_{C1}$, resulting in the current $I_1 = -j\omega C_A V_1(R_{C2}/R_{C1})$. The equivalent input impedance $Z_{Eq} = V_1/I_1$ is, therefore,

$$Z_{Eq} = \frac{V_1}{I_1} = \frac{V_1}{-\frac{j\omega C_A V_1 R_{C2}}{R_{C1}}} = -\frac{R_{C1}}{j\omega C_A R_{C2}} = \frac{1}{j\omega(-C_C)}. \tag{19}$$

Then, by taking C_A and R_{C1} as fixed, and making R_{C2} variable, the compensation circuit acts as an adjustable negative capacitance, given by

$$-C_C = -C_A \frac{R_{C2}}{R_{C1}}, \tag{20}$$

which can be tuned to compensate and possibly cancel C_P.

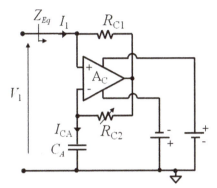

Figure 16. Schematic diagram of the parasitic capacitance compensation circuit.

5. Experimental Results and Discussion

5.1. Impedance Measurements with Coil-Coupled Capacitance Sensor and QCR

The experimental setup to test the system, according to the frequency-domain technique based on the block diagram of Figure 14, including the compensation circuit of Figure 16, is shown in Figure 17. The AD8045 (Analog Devices, Norwood, MA, USA) is used for the high-bandwidth operational amplifier A_C.

For the tests on the capacitance sensor configuration, the RSU is composed of a square planar spiral coil on Printed Circuit Board (PCB) with $L_2 = 8.51\ \mu H$, $R_2 = 3.2\ \Omega$, and a reference capacitor $C_S = 100$ pF. According to Equation (1), the resulting resonant frequency and quality factor are $f_S = 5.45$ MHz and $Q_S = 91$, respectively. A PCB square planar spiral coil has also been used for the primary coil, with $L_1 = 8.5\ \mu H$ and $R_1 = 5\ \Omega$. A fixed capacitor $C_F = 22$ pF is connected in parallel to the primary coil, in order to set the parasitic capacitance and test the effectiveness of the compensation circuit.

The real part of the impedance Z_{1P} versus frequency has been measured at varying interrogation distance d, and hence the coupling factor k, for different values of the compensation capacitance C_C. The results are shown in Figure 18.

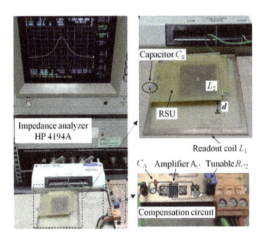

Figure 17. Experimental setup and interrogation system based on impedance-measurement technique with parasitic capacitance compensation.

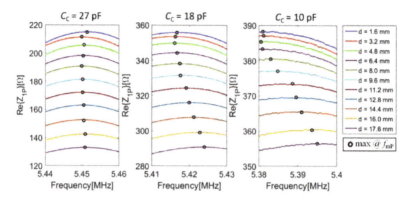

Figure 18. Measured maxima in Re{Z_{1P}} around f_S for different values of the compensation C_C, varying the distance d between CL_1 and the RSU. The frequency of the maxima at f_{mP} is highlighted with a black circle.

Figure 19 shows the measured frequency f_{mP} where the maximum of Re{Z_{1P}} near f_S occurs as a function of d, for different values of the compensation capacitance C_C. A monotonic decrease of k is expected by increasing d [29]. It can be observed that by increasing Cc, the expected undesired effect of the parasitic capacitances described in Section 3.3 decreases. With $C_C = 27$ pF, the value of f_{mP} becomes independent of d over the considered interrogation range of 16 mm, with a residual deviation of f_{mP} within 1 kHz, i.e., less than 200 ppm. The obtained value of Cc = 27 pF, slightly higher than the capacitor $C_F = 22$ pF, is ascribed to the presence of an extra capacitance of about 5 pF that concurs to form C_P. The results clearly demonstrate the effectiveness of the compensation technique and circuit.

Under ideal complete compensation condition, the measured f_{mP} approaches the unaffected value of f_m, discussed in Section 3.2, over the considered interrogation distance range. Then, for the considered RSU with a $Q_S = 91$, a relative deviation |$f_{mP} - f_S$| /f_S as low as 30 ppm is obtained from Equation (5).

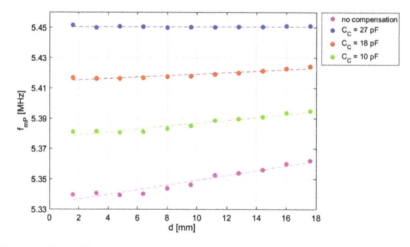

Figure 19. Measured frequency f_{mP} as a function of d for different values of C_C. The no compensation data are extrapolated from experimental values.

The same setup has been used for tests on coil-coupled electromechanical piezoelectric resonators. An AT-cut QCR with f_r = 4.432 MHz has been connected to CL$_2$. The parameters of the BVD equivalent circuit around fr of the adopted QCR are C_0 = 5.72 pF, R_r = 10.09 Ω, L_r = 77.98 mH, and Cr = 16.54 fF. The numerical analysis, discussed in Section 3.4, proves that parasitic capacitances in the order of tens of picofarads introduce negligible dependence of the measured resonant frequency on k. For this reason, the compensation circuit is not connected to the primary coil. Figure 20a shows the real part of the impedance Z_{1P}, measured in the frequency range around f_r for different values of the interrogation distance d. As it can be observed, while the magnitude of the maximum of Re$\{Z_{1P}\}$ decreases by increasing d, the frequency f_{rP}, where the maximum occurs, shows residual variations as low as 1 Hz, i.e., less than 0.3 ppm, in the explored range of d, as shown in Figure 20b. This confirms the predicted independence of f_{rP} from d, and thus from k.

5.2. Time-Gated Measurements with Coil-Coupled Capacitance Sensor and QCR

Figure 21 shows the experimental setup used to test the interrogation system based on the time-gated technique shown in Figure 15. The excitation and gate signals $v_{exc}(t)$ and $v_g(t)$ are generated by two Agilent 3320A waveform generators (Agilent Technologies, Santa Clara, CA, USA). A tailored circuit comprising the analog switch SW (MAX393, Maxim Integrated, San Jose, CA, USA), the parasitic capacitance compensation circuit, and the readout amplifier A$_G$ (OPA656, Texas Instruments, Dallas, TX, USA), has been developed. The readout output signal $v_O(t)$ has been connected to a high-resolution frequency meter Philips PM6680 (Philips International, Eindhoven, The Netherlands). The frequency meter is configured to perform measurements in a time window of duration T_M, starting after a delay time T_D from the beginning of the detection phase. The delay time T_D is used to skip the initial ringing in $v_O(t)$ [18,21]. The voltage $v_O(t)$ measured during detection phase, and the times T_D and T_M, are shown in Figure 22.

Firstly, tests have been done on the RSU with coil-coupled capacitance sensor, described in Section 5.1. The RSU has a PCB spiral coil with L_2 = 8.51 μH, R_2 = 3.2 Ω, and a capacitive sensor with C_S = 100 pF, resulting in a resonant frequency f_S = 5.45 MHz. The same PCB spiral coil described in Section 5.1, with L_1 = 8.5 μH and R_1 = 5 Ω, has been used as CL$_1$. The frequency of the excitation signal $v_{exc}(t)$ is set close to f_S to improve the transferred signal level.

Figure 23 reports the frequency f_{dP} of the damped sinusoid $v_O(t)$ during the detection phase, measured at varying d for different values of the compensation capacitance C_C. A delay time T_D = 2 μs and a measurement time T_M = 6 μs have been chosen for all the measurements. As it can be observed, for the case of compensation of C_P, the dependence of f_{dP} on d is much reduced with respect to the cases with no or partial compensation. With $C_C \approx$ 48 pF, f_{dP} has residual variations within 1.5 kHz, i.e., less than 300 ppm, across the explored interrogation range of about 17.6 mm.

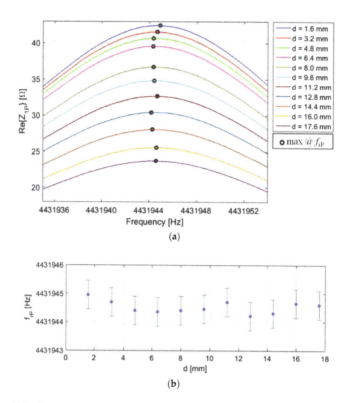

Figure 20. (**a**) Real part of Z_{1P} measured around the mechanical resonant frequency f_r of the quartz crystal resonator (QCR) connected to the primary coil CL_1 for different distances d. The frequency of the maxima at f_{rP} is highlighted with a black circle. (**b**) Frequency f_{rP} as a function of d. The error bars report the standard deviations calculated over 5 repeated measurements.

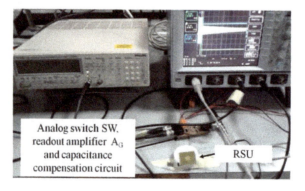

Figure 21. Picture of the experimental setup developed to implement the time-gated technique.

Under ideal complete compensation, the measured f_{dP} approaches the unaffected value of f_d discussed in Section 3.2. Then, for the considered RSU with $Q_S = 91$, a relative deviation $|f_{dP} - f_S|/f_S$ as low as 15 ppm is obtained from Equation (8).

Then, tests have been run on an RSU made by a coil-coupled 4.432-MHz AT-cut QCR. The capacitance compensation circuit has been kept inactive, due to the predicted independence of f_{rP} from k for coil-coupled QCR. The frequency f_{rP} of the damped sinusoid $v_O(t)$ has been measured with varying the interrogation distance d.

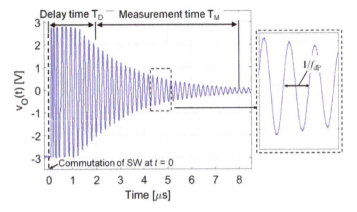

Figure 22. Measured output signal $v_O(t)$ during the detection phase. Indications of the adopted delay time T_D and measurement time T_M are reported.

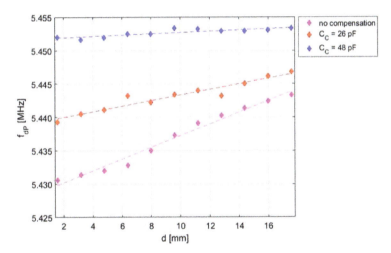

Figure 23. Frequency f_{dP} of the damped sinusoid $v_{1P}(t)$ measured as a function of the interrogation distance d for different values of the compensation capacitance C_C. A delay time $T_D = 2$ μs and a measurement time $T_M = 6$ μs have been set in the measurements.

Figure 24a shows the voltage $v_O(t)$ at the beginning of the detection phase for three different interrogation distances d. As it can be observed, the magnitude of $v_O(t)$ decreases with the increasing d, i.e., with decreasing k, while, as expected, the frequency f_{rP} is unaffected, as shown in Figure 24b. A residual variation of about 1.8 Hz, i.e., less than 0.5 ppm, has been obtained over the explored interrogation distance range of about 17.8 mm. In summary, the experimental results with coil-coupled QCRs show that the total parasitic capacitance C_P estimated in about 48 pF, causes a negligible variation of the measured frequency f_{rP} over the explored interrogation range.

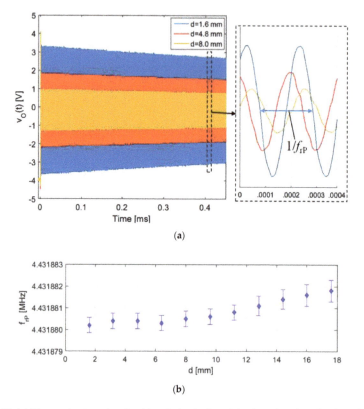

Figure 24. (**a**) Measured output signal $v_O(t)$ at the beginning of the detection phase for three different interrogation distances d. (**b**) Frequency f_{rP} as a function of d measured with a delay time $T_D = 5$ μs and a measurement time $T_M = 10$ ms. The error bars report the standard deviations calculated over 30 repeated measurements.

6. Conclusions

This work has investigated contactless interrogation techniques and readout circuits for passive sensors, exploiting the electromagnetic coupling between a primary and a secondary coil.

The sensor can be either a capacitive sensor or an electromechanical piezoelectric resonator. With both kinds of sensors, resonance can occur in the secondary circuit that can, therefore, be named resonant sensor unit (RSU). The interrogation of the RSU can be accomplished by techniques operating either in the frequency domain or in the time domain, which are ideally independent of the distance between the primary and secondary coils.

On the other hand, when unavoidable parasitic effects are considered, that combine in a lumped capacitance in parallel to the readout coil, an unwanted dependence of the readout frequency and quality factor on the interrogation distance is introduced, affecting similarly both the frequency- and time-domain techniques. Numerical analysis and experimental tests demonstrate that this dependence is detrimental on the accuracy of the readout frequency of the RSU. The inaccuracies are more relevant for the capacitive sensors, while for electromechanical piezoelectric resonators, the effect is negligible in most cases.

As a solution, an innovative approach has been proposed in which such parasitic capacitance is compensated by a purposely designed electronic circuit that has been prototyped and experimentally verified.

Micromachines **2018**, *9*, 449

In tests carried out on a capacitive RSU with the proposed compensation circuit applied, a maximum deviation as low as 300 ppm on a resonant frequency of 5.45 MHz has been obtained over an interrogation range of almost 2 cm. This successfully demonstrates the validity of the proposed approach and circuit.

In addition, the experimental results have confirmed that the effect of the input parasitic capacitance is negligible when a coil-coupled piezoelectric quartz crystal resonator is used as the RSU.

Author Contributions: M.D. worked on the theory and modeling, and numerical analyses, contributed in the experimental activity, analysis of experimental data, and in writing the paper. M.B. contributed in the theory and modeling, experimental activity, analysis of experimental data, and in writing and revising the paper. M.F. contributed in the experimental activity, analysis of experimental data, and in revising the paper. V.F. coordinated the research and contributed in the theory and modeling, and in revising the paper.

Funding: This research received no external funding.

Conflicts of Interest: The authors declare no conflict of interest.

References

1. Ferrari, M.; Ferrari, V.; Guizzetti, M.; Marioli, D. An autonomous battery-less sensor module powered by piezoelectric energy harvesting with RF transmission of multiple measurement signals. *Smart Mater. Struct.* **2009**, *18*, 085023. [CrossRef]
2. Ferrari, M.; Ferrari, V.; Guizzetti, M.; Marioli, D.; Taroni, A. Piezoelectric multifrequency energy converter for power harvesting in autonomous microsystems. *Sensor Actuator A Phys.* **2008**, *142*, 329–335. [CrossRef]
3. Tan, Y.; Dong, Y.; Wang, X. Review of MEMS electromagnetic vibration energy harvester. *J. Microelectromech. Syst.* **2017**, *26*, 1–16. [CrossRef]
4. Dalola, S.; Ferrari, M.; Ferrari, V.; Guizzetti, M.; Marioli, D.; Taroni, A. Characterization of thermoelectric modules for powering autonomous sensors. *IEEE Trans. Instrum. Meas.* **2009**, *58*, 99–107. [CrossRef]
5. Cuadras, A.; Gasulla, M.; Ferrari, V. Thermal energy harvesting through pyroelectricity. *Sensor Actuator A Phys.* **2010**, *158*, 132–139. [CrossRef]
6. Dalola, S.; Faglia, G.; Comini, E.; Ferroni, M.; Soldano, C.; Zappa, D.; Ferrari, V.; Sberveglieri, G. Planar thermoelectric generator based on metal-oxide nanowires for powering autonomous microsystem. *Procedia Eng.* **2012**, *47*, 346–349. [CrossRef]
7. Demori, M.; Ferrari, M.; Bonzanini, A.; Poesio, P.; Ferrari, V. Autonomous sensors powered by energy harvesting by von karman vortices in airflow. *Sensors* **2017**, *17*, 2100. [CrossRef] [PubMed]
8. Sample, A.P.; Yeager, D.J.; Powledge, P.S.; Mamishev, A.V.; Smith, J.R. Design of an RFID-based battery-free programmable sensing platform. *IEEE Trans. Instrum. Meas.* **2008**, *57*, 2608–2615. [CrossRef]
9. Siddiqui, A.; Mahboob, M.R.; Islam, T. A passive wireless tag with digital readout unit for wide range humidity measurement. *IEEE Trans. Instrum. Meas.* **2017**, *66*, 1013–1020. [CrossRef]
10. Demori, M.; Baù, M.; Dalola, S.; Ferrari, M.; Ferrari, V. RFID powered system for contactless measurement of a resistive sensor array. In Proceedings of the 2018 IEEE International Instrumentation and Measurement Technology Conference (I2MTC), Houston, TX, USA, 14–17 May 2018.
11. Chatzandroulis, S.; Tsoukalas, D.; Neukomm, P.A. A miniature pressure system with a capacitive sensor and a passive telemetry link for use in implantable applications. *J. Microelectromech. Syst.* **2000**, *9*, 18–23. [CrossRef]
12. Rodriguez, S.; Ollmar, S.; Waqar, M.; Rusu, A. A batteryless sensor ASIC for implantable bio-impedance applications. *IEEE Trans. Biomed. Circuit Syst.* **2016**, *10*, 533–544. [CrossRef] [PubMed]
13. Bhamra, H.; Tsai, J.W.; Huang, Y.W.; Yuan, Q.; Shah, J.V.; Irazoqui, P. A subcubic millimeter wireless implantable intraocular pressure monitor microsystem. *IEEE Trans. Biomed. Circuit Syst.* **2017**, *11*, 1204–1215. [CrossRef] [PubMed]
14. Nopper, R.; Has, R.; Reindl, L. A wireless sensor readout system—Circuit concept, simulation, and accuracy. *IEEE Trans. Instrum. Meas.* **2011**, *60*, 2976–2983. [CrossRef]
15. Huang, Q.A.; Dong, L.; Wang, L.F. LC passive wireless sensors toward a wireless sensing platform: Status, prospects, and challenges. *J Microelectromech. Syst.* **2016**, *25*, 822–840. [CrossRef]

16. Babu, A.; George, B. A linear and high sensitive interfacing scheme for wireless passive LC sensors. *IEEE Sens. J.* **2016**, *16*, 8608–8616. [CrossRef]
17. Zhang, C.; Wang, L.F.; Huang, J.Q.; Huang, Q.A. An LC-type passive wireless humidity sensor system with portable telemetry unit. *J Microelectromech. Syst.* **2015**, *24*, 575–581. [CrossRef]
18. Demori, M.; Masud, M.; Baù, M.; Ferrari, M.; Ferrari, V. Passive LC sensor label with distance-independent contactless interrogation. In Proceedings of the 2017 IEEE Sensors Conference, Glasgow, UK, 30 October–1 November 2017.
19. Wang, X.; Larsson, O.; Platt, D.; Nordlinder, S.; Engquist, I.; Berggren, M.; Crispin, X. An all-printed wireless humidity sensor label. *Sensor Actuators B Chem.* **2012**, *166*, 556–561. [CrossRef]
20. Nopper, R.; Niekrawietz, R.; Reindl, L. Wireless readout of passive LC sensors. *IEEE Trans. Instrum. Meas.* **2010**, *59*, 2450–2457. [CrossRef]
21. Baù, M.; Ferrari, M.; Ferrari, V. Analysis and validation of contactless time-gated interrogation technique for quartz resonator sensors. *Sensors* **2017**, *17*, 1264. [CrossRef] [PubMed]
22. Ferrari, M.; Baù, M.; Tonoli, E.; Ferrari, V. Piezoelectric resonant sensors with contactless interrogation for mass sensitive and acoustic-load detection. *Sensors Actuators A Phys.* **2013**, *202*, 100–105. [CrossRef]
23. Demori, M.; Baù, M.; Ferrari, M.; Ferrari, V. Electronic technique and circuit topology for accurate distance-independent contactless readout of passive LC sensors. *AEU Int. J. Electron. Commun.* **2018**, *92*, 82–85. [CrossRef]
24. Morshed, B.I. Dual coil for remote probing of signals using resistive wireless analog passive sensors (rWAPS). In Proceedings of the 2016 United States National Committee of URSI National Radio Science Meeting, Boulder, CO, USA, 21 March 2016.
25. Yang, B.; Meng, F.; Dong, Y. A coil-coupled sensor for electrolyte solution conductivity measurement. In Proceedings of the 2013 2nd International Conference on Measurement, Information and Control, Harbin, China, 6 March 2014.
26. Arnau, A.; Ferrari, V.; Soares, D.; Perrot, H. Interface electronic systems for AT-Cut QCM sensors: A comprehensive review. In *Piezoelectric Transducers and Applications*, 2nd ed.; Springer-Verlag Berlin: Heidelberg, Germay, 2008; pp. 187–203.
27. DeHennis, A.; Wise, K.D. A double-sided single-chip wireless pressure sensor. In Proceedings of the MEMS 2002 IEEE International Conference, Las Vegas, NV, USA, 21–24 January 2002.
28. Harpster, T.J.; Hauvespre, S.; Dokmeci, M.R.; Najafi, K. A passive humidity monitoring system for in situ remote wireless testing of micropackages. *J Microelectromech. Syst.* **2002**, *11*, 61–67. [CrossRef]
29. Jacquemod, G.; Nowak, M.; Colinet, E.; Delorme, N.; Conseil, F. Novel architecture and algorithm for remote interrogation of battery-free sensors. *Sensor Actuators A Phys.* **2010**, *160*, 125–131. [CrossRef]

Article

Reconfigurable Sensor Analog Front-End Using Low-Noise Chopper-Stabilized Delta-Sigma Capacitance-to-Digital Converter

Hyungseup Kim [1], Byeoncheol Lee [1], Yeongjin Mun [1], Jaesung Kim [1], Kwonsang Han [1], Youngtaek Roh [2], Dongkyu Song [2], Seounghoon Huh [2] and Hyoungho Ko [1,*

[1]   Department of Electronics Engineering, Chungnam National University, Daejeon 34134, Korea;
      hyungseup@cnu.ac.kr (H.K.); dada5891@cnu.ac.kr (B.L.); ansdud159@cnu.ac.kr (Y.M.);
      jskim1@cnu.ac.kr (J.K.); kshan1@cnu.ac.kr (K.H.)
[2]   LeoLSI Co., Ltd., Seoul 06728, Korea; ytroh@leolsi.com (Y.R.); dksong@leolsi.com (D.S.);
      iamtoto@leolsi.com (S.H.)
*   Correspondence: hhko@cnu.ac.kr; Tel.: +82-42-821-5664

Received: 15 May 2018; Accepted: 9 July 2018; Published: 10 July 2018

Abstract: This paper proposes a reconfigurable sensor analog front-end using low-noise chopper-stabilized delta-sigma capacitance-to-digital converter (CDC) for capacitive microsensors. The proposed reconfigurable sensor analog front-end can drive both capacitive microsensors and voltage signals by direct conversion without a front-end amplifier. The reconfigurable scheme of the front-end can be implemented in various multi-mode applications, where it is equipped with a fully integrated temperature sensor. A chopper stabilization technique is implemented here to achieve a low-noise characteristic by reducing unexpected low-frequency noises such as offsets and flicker noise. The prototype chip of the proposed sensor analog front-end is fabricated by a standard 0.18-μm 1-poly-6-metal (1P6M) complementary metal-oxide-semiconductor (CMOS) process. It occupies a total active area of 5.37 mm^2 and achieves an effective resolution of 16.3-bit. The total power consumption is 0.843 mW with a 1.8 V power supply.

Keywords: capacitive microsensor; analog front-end (AFE); capacitive sensor interface circuit; reconfigurable sensor readout circuit; delta-sigma modulation; capacitance-to-digital converter (CDC); temperature sensor; low-noise technique; chopper stabilization

---

1. Introduction

The emergence of the Internet of Things (IoT) in recent years has greatly influenced the field of electronics, and the demand for the development of IoT based applications has increased. In particular, as the demand for various IoT applications grows, the performances of the sensor and the sensor interface integrated circuits have become increasingly important. Low-noise characteristics and low power consumption of the sensor interface circuits have become essential requirements. Capacitive microsensors are widely adopted in various applications such as humidity sensors, accelerometers, gyroscopes, biological sensors, pressure sensors, touch screen sensors, and proximity sensors [1–9]. With the wide use of capacitive microsensors, many research works on capacitive microsensor interface circuit techniques have been reported [10–22]. A multi-stage amplification capacitive sensor readout circuit with parasitic capacitance cancellation technique has been presented [10,11]. However, the multi-stage amplification scheme requires high power consumption and a large active area, which are not suitable for IoT applications that demand low power consumption and small size. A successive approximation register (SAR) capacitance-to-digital converter (CDC) scheme for low-power applications has been presented [12–16]. The SAR CDC scheme can achieve low power consumption and small size; however, it severely suffers from the effect of parasitic capacitance due to the direct connection of the capacitive sensor to the input of the comparator without the pre-amplifier. The implementation of the pre-amplifier in the SAR CDC scheme can relieve the effect of the parasitic capacitance, but the circuit complexity and power consumption increase. A delta-sigma modulation is widely used for high resolution capacitance-to-digital conversion. A capacitive sensor readout circuit with charge sensing amplifier (CSA) for pre-amplification of the sensor signal and a delta-sigma modulator can achieve high resolution because of its low-noise characteristic [17], however, the chip size and power consumption increase due to the additional CSA. To reduce the area and power consumption, the direct conversion delta-sigma CDC can be a good solution. The direct conversion first-order delta-sigma CDC scheme can relieve the problems by directly converting the capacitance change of the capacitive sensor to digital codes [18–21]. However, the first-order delta-sigma modulation scheme suffers from the dead zone problem, which increases the nonlinearity error and leads to performance degradation [22–25].

This paper presents a reconfigurable sensor analog front-end using low-noise chopper-stabilized delta-sigma CDC. The main strength of the proposed sensor analog front-end is the reconfigurable scheme, which can drive capacitive sensors and voltage signals without a front-end amplifier by direct conversion in the second-order incremental delta-sigma converter scheme. It also employs a chopper stabilization technique to achieve a low-noise characteristic. The second-order delta-sigma scheme can relieve the dead zone problem of the first-order delta-sigma modulation scheme, which causes nonlinearity error and performance degradation. The proposed sensor analog front-end with fully integrated temperature sensor can be flexibly adopted in various IoT sensor system applications due to its reconfigurable scheme.

This paper is organized as follows: Section 2 discusses the circuit implementation of the proposed reconfigurable sensor analog front-end. Section 3 describes the measurement results of the proposed reconfigurable sensor analog front-end. Finally, Section 4 presents the discussion of the proposed reconfigurable sensor analog front-end by comparison of performance with previously reported works and presents the conclusions of this work.

2. Circuit Implementation

2.1. Top Level Architecture

The block diagram of the proposed reconfigurable sensor analog front-end is shown in Figure 1. The analog front-end circuit includes: a second-order incremental delta-sigma CDC; a current/voltage reference block with the bandgap reference and bias block with a resister string; a clock generator with an on-chip oscillator and timing generator; a fully integrated temperature sensor; a digital offset/gain correction block; and a serial peripheral interface (SPI) for interface with the host microcontroller unit (MCU). The basic scheme of the reconfigurable sensor analog front-end comprises a second-order delta-sigma modulation scheme, which relieves the nonlinearity error and performance degradation caused by the dead zone that appears when the first-order delta-sigma modulation scheme is adopted. The reconfigurable sensor analog front-end can drive capacitive microsensors and voltage signals without a front-end amplifier by direct conversion. The proposed scheme can drive the capacitive microsensors in single drive mode or differential drive mode depending on the application. The bias generation block contains a bandgap reference, current reference and a bias block. The bandgap reference generates a reference voltage and the current reference generates the reference current with the bandgap voltage. The bias voltages generated in the bias block with the reference current supplies bias voltages for each sub-block. The bandgap reference also generates the complementary to the absolute temperature (CTAT) characteristic voltage for the operation of the fully integrated temperature sensor, which can be incorporated in specific applications to measure temperature when needed. The driving mode of the capacitive microsensors, the voltage signal driving mode, and the on-chip temperature sensor as the voltage signal driving mode, can be selected by register selection.

The timing generator generates the clock signals needed by the on-chip oscillator, which can generate 1 MHz, 2 MHz, and 4 MHz master clocks by register selection or by the external input clock signal. The digital offset/gain correction block is integrated for offset/gain calibration. The SPI is used for register control and digital offset/gain correction block control with a laptop computer.

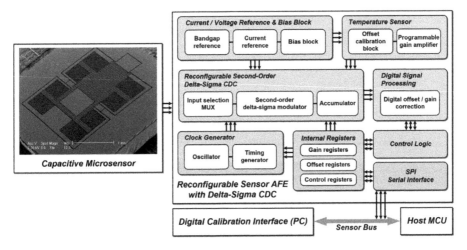

Figure 1. Block diagram of the proposed reconfigurable sensor analog front-end.

2.2. Reconfigurable Sensor Analog Front-End

The schematic of the proposed reconfigurable second-order delta-sigma CDC is shown in Figure 2. The proposed reconfigurable sensor analog front-end is based on the second-order delta-sigma CDC scheme, which operates on the same concept as the conventional delta-sigma modulator based CDC. The switch-capacitor scheme serves to balance the signal charge of the input sensor capacitor (C_{OP} or C_{ON}) with the programmable reference capacitor (C_{REF}) using the feedback capacitor of the integrator (C_{F1} and C_{F2}), which balances the average charge to zero. The programmable offset capacitor (C_{OFF}) is used for offset cancellation. The output signal through the two-stage integrator and comparator output is a digital signal, which is converted to 16-bit digital codes by the low-power digital low-pass filter (LPF) based on the accumulator. The digital data of the proposed scheme can also be acquired as bit-stream data (COMP_DOUT) depending on the application preference. The programmable feedback capacitor of the first stage integrator (C_{F1}) and second stage integrator (C_{F2}) can be controlled from 0.177 pF to 22.671 pF by using a 7-bit control register, and from 0.177 pF to 11.336 pF by using a 6-bit control register. The timing diagram of the proposed reconfigurable sensor analog front-end is shown in Figure 3. The on-chip oscillator can generate 1 MHz, 2 MHz, or 4 MHz master clocks by register selection. Moreover, the external input clock can be operated manually. The default master clock (MCLK) operates at 1 MHz. P_CMFB1 and P_CMFB2 are non-overlapping clock signals used in the switch capacitor common mode feedback (SC-CMFB) for the fully differential amplifier, which operates at 500 kHz. P1, P1d, P2, and P2d are non-overlapping clocks operating at 250 kHz. The edges of P_CMFB1, P_CMFB2, P1, P1d, P2, and P2d do not overlap. The feedback capacitor swapping non-overlapping clocks of P_SWP1 and P_SWP2 operate at 125 kHz. The chopper non-overlapping clocks operate at 32 kHz. The reset clock (RST) operates at 1 kHz when implemented with the 1 MHz master clock. The proposed sensor analog front-end adopts a low-noise technique for ensuring a low-noise characteristic.

The detailed operation timing of the integrator in the delta-sigma CDC is shown in Figure 4 (i.e., the first stage integrator with differential capacitive sensor inputs C_{OP} and C_{ON}). The operation is explained with a single-ended circuit scheme for simplicity. The RST is controlled by the accumulator in the back-end. The RST resets both of the first stage and second stage integrators after counting a number of 65,536 comparator output codes in the accumulator. The comparator output signal D and inverted signal Db are added to $P2d$ with an AND gate controlling a $VN1$ switch and a $VN2$ switch connected to C_{REF}. After the reset phase, the CDC operates with two clock phases: An initialization phase and an amplification phase. The initialization phase is shown in Figure 4a. The non-overlapping clocks $P1$ and $P1d$ enable the input sensors C_{OP}, C_{ON} and C_{OFF} to be charged while C_{REF} is initialized to be reset by the reference voltage (VCM). The total charge can be expressed as Equation (1):

$$Q_{P1\&P1d} = C_{OP} \cdot (VCM - VP1) + C_{ON} \cdot (VCM - VP2) + C_{OFF} \cdot (VCM - VN1) \tag{1}$$

The amplification phase is shown in Figure 4b. The non-overlapping clocks $P2$ and $P2d$ enable the charges stored in the input sensors C_{OP}, C_{ON} and C_{OFF} to be transferred to the first stage integrator and to be amplified. The total charge in the amplification phase can be expressed as Equation (2):

$$Q_{P2\&P2d} = C_{OP} \cdot (VCM - VP2) + C_{ON} \cdot (VCM - VP1) + C_{OFF} \cdot (VCM - VN2)$$
$$+ D \cdot C_{REF} \cdot (VCM - VN2) + Db \cdot C_{REF} \cdot (VCM - VN1) + C_F \cdot (VCM - VOUT) \tag{2}$$

The total charge during the initialization phase and the amplification phase should be equal. The total charge transferred should satisfy Equation (3):

$$Q_{P1\&P1d} = Q_{P2\&P2d} \tag{3}$$

The voltages $VP1$, $VP2$, $VN1$ and $VN2$ are set according to Equation (4):

$$VP1 = VCM + 0.5 \cdot REFP$$
$$VP2 = VCM - 0.5 \cdot REFP$$
$$VN1 = VCM - 0.5 \cdot REFN$$
$$VN2 = VCM + 0.5 \cdot REFN \tag{4}$$

By Equations (3) and (4), the simplified output of the integrator can be expressed as Equation (5):

$$VOUT = (\tfrac{1}{C_F}) \cdot (C_{OP} \cdot REFP - C_{ON} \cdot REFP - C_{OFF} \cdot REFN$$
$$- 0.5 \cdot D \cdot C_{REF} \cdot REFN + 0.5 \cdot Db \cdot C_{REF} \cdot REFN) + VCM \tag{5}$$

The output of the first stage integrator is then amplified by the second stage integrator by the same procedure. After the amplification of the second stage integrator, the comparator compares the second stage integrator and outputs bit-stream data.

The chopper stabilization technique is implemented to reduce low-frequency noises such as offsets and flicker noise [26]. The fully differential chopper amplifier is implemented as the amplifier of the integrator to obtain a low-noise characteristic. Similar fully differential chopper amplifiers are implemented for each stage. The schematic of the proposed fully differential chopper amplifier is shown in Figure 5a. The switched-capacitor common mode feedback (CMFB) circuit is implemented for low power consumption which generates the CMFB voltage for the fully differential chopper amplifier. The amplifier is designed with a DC gain of 78.68 dB and a 1.949 MHz unit gain bandwidth (UGBW). A feedback capacitor swapping scheme is adopted to enhance the common mode rejection ratio (CMRR) and thereby reduce the common mode noise of the sensor analog front-end. Figure 5b shows the resolution selectable accumulator. The accumulator consists of up-counters and resolution selection logic. The output digital code resolution can be selected by the accumulator by SEL_RESOULTION<1:0> controlling the resolution selection logic. The resolution of the output digital code can be selected as 8-bit, 12-bit and 16-bit for specific application needs.

The proposed sensor analog front-end can drive both capacitive microsensors and input voltage signals by register selection. The mode selection can be performed by controlling the registers

SEL_MODE1<1:0> to SEL_MODE4<1:0> of the analog selection multiplexers, COP_EN and CON_EN. The driving mode of the single capacitive microsensors can be selected by enabling either COP_EN or CON_EN. The driving mode of the differential capacitive microsensors can be selected by enabling both COP_EN and CON_EN. When the driving mode of the capacitive microsensors is enabled, the internal programmable capacitors C_{OP_INT} and C_{ON_INT} should be switched off for correct conversion. The capacitive sensing mode operation can be expressed as Equation (6). The computations shown in Equation (6) can be denoted as *REFP* and *REFN*.

$$VP1 - VP2 = REFP \\ VN2 - VN1 = REFN \tag{6}$$

As shown in Equation (5), the differential output voltage of the second-order delta-sigma integrator of the proposed reconfigurable sensor analog front-end can be defined as Equation (7). The term C_F is the feedback capacitor of the second-order delta-sigma integrator.

$$\Delta V_O = \left(\tfrac{1}{C_F}\right) \cdot (C_{OP} \cdot REFP - C_{ON} \cdot REFP - C_{OFF} \cdot REFN - 0.5 \cdot D \cdot C_{REF} \cdot REFN \\ + 0.5 \cdot Db \cdot C_{REF} \cdot REFN) \tag{7}$$

The input capacitance range can be defined by each conditions. When the differential output voltage of the second-order delta-sigma integrator is higher than 0 V and the bit-stream data $D[n]$ is Low (0), it is saturated and the minimum input range can be expressed as Equation (8):

$$\Delta V_O > 0 \ \& \ D[n] = 0 \quad (\text{Minimum input capacitance range}) \\ (C_{OFF} - 0.5 \cdot C_{REF}) \cdot REFN < (C_{OP} - C_{ON}) \cdot REFP \tag{8}$$

When the differential output voltage of the second-order delta-sigma integrator is lower than 0 V and the bit-stream data $D[n]$ is High (1), it is saturated and the maximum input range can be expressed as Equation (9):

$$\Delta V_O < 0 \ \& \ D[n] = 1 \quad (\text{Maximum input capacitance range}) \\ (C_{OP} - C_{ON}) \cdot REFP < (C_{OFF} + 0.5 \cdot C_{REF}) \cdot REFN \tag{9}$$

The capacitive input range of the driving mode of the capacitive microsensors can be defined as Equation (10):

$$(C_{OFF} - 0.5 \cdot C_{REF}) \cdot \frac{REFN}{REFP} < (C_{OP} - C_{ON}) < (C_{OFF} + 0.5 \cdot C_{REF}) \cdot \frac{REFN}{REFP} \tag{10}$$

The programmable capacitors C_{REF} and C_{OFF} can each be controlled from 0.177 pF to 11.158 pF by a 6-bit control register; their on and off states can also be controlled. The maximum capacitive input range of the proposed reconfigurable sensor analog front-end is 16.738 pF.

The voltage signal driving mode can be enabled by disabling COP_EN and CON_EN for the driving mode of the capacitive microsensors. When the voltage signal driving mode is enabled, the internal programmable capacitor C_{OP_INT} or C_{ON_INT} of the sampling capacitor should be switched on. A single-ended voltage mode can be selected by switching on one of the internal programmable capacitors C_{OP_INT} and C_{ON_INT}. When the internal programmable capacitor C_{OP_INT} is selected as the single-input sampling capacitor, the input signal VP_EXT should be selected by controlling SEL_MODE1<1:0>. Further, when the internal programmable capacitor C_{ON_INT} is selected as the single-input sampling capacitor, the input signal VN_EXT should be selected by controlling SEL_MODE4<1:0>. A differential voltage mode can be selected by switching on both the internal programmable capacitors C_{OP_INT} and C_{ON_INT}. When the differential input mode is selected, the internal programmable capacitors C_{OP_INT} and C_{ON_INT} should be switched on as differential sampling capacitors for both inputs. In addition, both the input signals VP_EXT and VN_EXT should be selected by controlling the SEL_MODE1<1:0> and SEL_MODE4<1:0> registers. The switching voltage can be controlled by SEL_MODE2<1:0> and SEL_MODE3<1:0>. The voltage signal driving mode with the single-ended voltage mode with VP_EXT input can be expressed as Equation (11) when the condition is as specified in the equation:

$$VP1 - VP2 = REFP, \; VP1 = V_{IN} \tag{11}$$

From Equations (10) and (11), the input range of the single-ended voltage mode can be deduced as Equation (12):

$$\left(\frac{C_{OFF} - 0.5 \cdot C_{REF}}{C_{OP\_INT}}\right) \cdot REFN + VP2 < V_{IN} < \left(\frac{C_{OFF} + 0.5 \cdot C_{REF}}{C_{OP\_INT}}\right) \cdot REFN + VP2$$
$$VP1 = VP\_EXT \tag{12}$$

The single-ended voltage mode with VN_EXT input can be expressed as for Equation (12) by changing the parameters C_{OP_INT} to C_{ON_INT}, and VP_EXT to VN_EXT. Each of the programmable capacitors C_{REF}, C_{OFF}, C_{OP_INT}, and C_{ON_INT} can be controlled from 0.177 pF to 11.158 pF by a 6-bit control register, and their on and off states can also be controlled. The maximum voltage mode input range of the proposed reconfigurable sensor analog front-end is 0 V to 1.8 V.

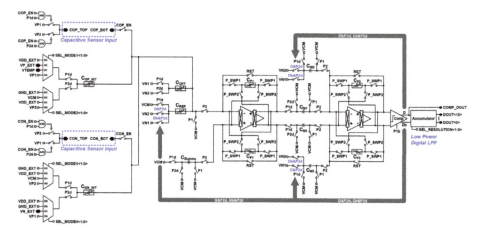

Figure 2. Schematic of the second-order delta-sigma CDC.

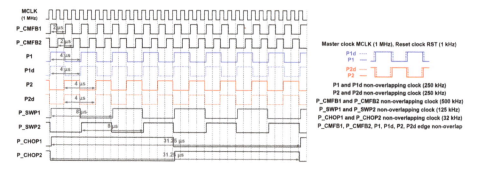

Figure 3. Timing diagram of the second-order delta-sigma CDC.

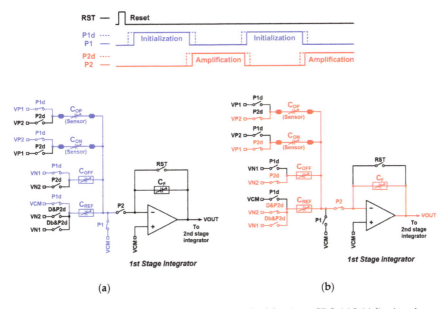

Figure 4. Detailed operation timing of the integrator in the delta-sigma CDC. (**a**) Initialization phase; (**b**) Amplification phase.

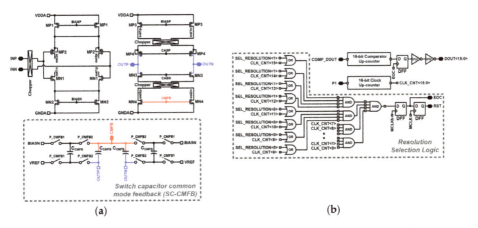

Figure 5. Schematic of fully differential chopper amplifier and accumulator. (**a**) Fully differential chopper amplifier; (**b**) Resolution selectable accumulator.

2.3. Fully Integrated Temperature Sensor

The schematic of the fully integrated temperature sensor of the proposed reconfigurable sensor analog front-end is shown in Figure 6. The temperature sensor operates and senses the temperature with the CTAT voltage generated by the bandgap reference. The output analog voltage of the temperature sensor is converted to digital codes by the voltage input mode of the proposed scheme. The scheme of the temperature sensor has been presented in [27]. The temperature sensor consists of an offset calibration block and the programmable gain amplifier (PGA). The programmable resistor (R_c) of the offset calibration block can be controlled from 52.267 kΩ to 784.016 kΩ. The value of resistor

R_a is 250.885 kΩ and that of R_b is 385.875 kΩ. The offset voltage of the temperature sensor can be expressed as Equation (13):

$$VOFFSET = (\frac{R_b + R_c}{R_a + R_b + R_c}) \cdot VCM \tag{13}$$

The PGA is implemented using a differential difference amplifier (DDA). The gain of the PGA is controlled by the 4-bit programmable resistor R_F from 522.678 kΩ to 7.840 MΩ. The gain of the PGA can be expressed as Equation (14):

$$VOUT = (1 + \frac{R_F}{R_{REF}}) \cdot (VINP - VINN) + VCM \tag{14}$$

Therefore, the output voltage of the temperature sensor can be expressed as Equation (15).

$$VTEMP\_OUT = (1 + \frac{R_F}{R_{REF}}) \cdot (VOFFSET - VTEMP\_IN) + VCM \tag{15}$$

The gain for temperature signal amplification and the offset level can be controlled by the proposed scheme depending on the application status in the temperature range of -10 °C to 120 °C.

The schematic of the bandgap reference of the fully integrated temperature sensor is shown in Figure 7. The implemented low voltage bandgap reference in the temperature sensor is a modified version of the previous bandgap scheme [28]. The bandgap reference operates with the input enable signal (EN) to be High (1) (input disable signal (ENB) to be Low (0)) which operates the start-up circuit. The output bandgap reference voltage (VBGR) is generated by ratios of the resistors R_1, R_2, R_3 and R_4, following Equation (16) (when the ratio between the two bipolar junction transistors (BJT) is Q1:Q2 = 1:24):

$$VBGR = (\frac{R_4}{R_1}) \cdot V_T \cdot ln(n) + (\frac{R_4}{R_3}) \cdot VEB_{Q2}$$
$$ln(24) = 3.178 \tag{16}$$

The bandgap resistor R4 is implemented with a 3-bit programmable resistor for voltage trimming with a range of 90.986 kΩ to 126.280 kΩ. Figure 8 shows the simulation results of the bandgap reference. The simulation result of the temperature sweep in the range of -40 °C to 120 °C is shown in Figure 8a. The simulated temperature coefficient is 3.677 ppm/°C. The generated temperature sensor voltage (VTEMP) with CTAT voltage characteristic is shown in Figure 8b. The simulation result shows that the VTEMP has CTAT characteristic with -1.750 mV/°C, which is used in the proposed on-chip temperature sensor shown as in Equation (15).

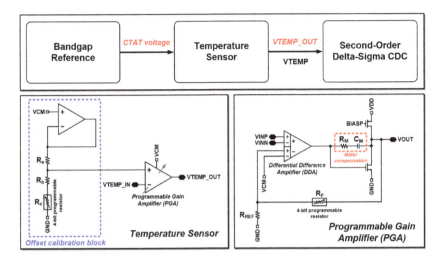

Figure 6. Schematic of fully integrated temperature sensor.

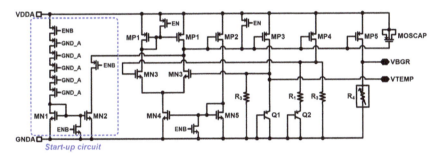

Figure 7. Schematic of bandgap reference of the fully integrated temperature sensor.

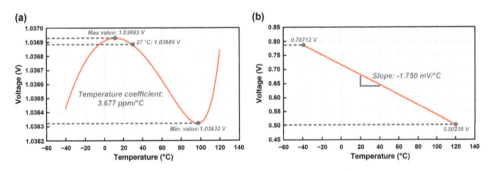

Figure 8. Simulation results of the bandgap reference. (**a**) Temperature sweep of output bandgap reference voltage (VBGR); (**b**) Generated temperature sensor voltage (VTEMP).

3. Measurement Results

3.1. Prototype Chip Implementation

The reconfigurable sensor analog front-end integrated circuit (IC) was fabricated using a standard 0.18-μm complementary metal-oxide-semiconductor (CMOS) process with an active area of 5.37 mm^2.

The die photograph is shown in Figure 9. The chip is fully integrated without other external elements. The total power consumption is 0.843 mW with 1.8 V power supply.

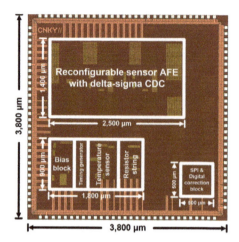

Figure 9. Die photograph of the proposed reconfigurable sensor analog front-end IC.

3.2. Measurement Environment

The measurement environment of the reconfigurable sensor analog front-end IC is shown in Figure 10. A digital oscilloscope was used for signal acquisition and data analysis. The output digital codes of the prototype IC are acquired by the logic analyzer through the laptop computer. The Fast Fourier Transform (FFT) measurement with output bit-stream data was performed by using the Audio Precision APx525. The inductance, capacitance and resistance (LCR) meter was used to measure the chip capacitor to compare with the measurement results by the proposed prototype IC for measurement evaluation. The temperature chamber was used to evaluate the performance of the on-chip temperature sensor.

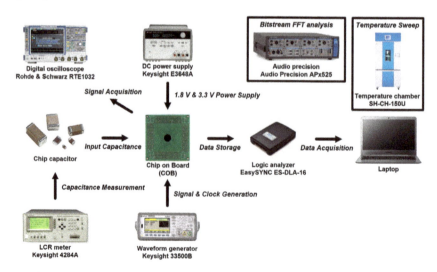

Figure 10. Measurement environment of the proposed reconfigurable sensor analog front-end IC.

3.3. Measurement Results

The FFT measurement results of the driving mode of the capacitive microsensors in the proposed reconfigurable sensor analog front-end IC are shown in Figure 11. The FFT was achieved by the bit-stream data FFT length of 65,536 points with a Blackman–Harris 3-term window. The gray line shows the measurement results without the application of the chopper stabilization technique and the black line shows the measurement results with the application of the chopper stabilization technique. The FFT result shows enhanced reduction of noise by the chopper stabilization technique implemented in the proposed scheme.

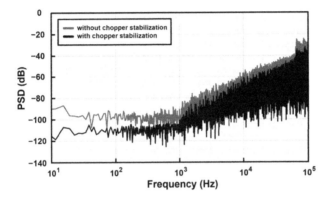

Figure 11. FFT measurement results of the proposed reconfigurable sensor analog front-end IC.

The simulation result of the capacitance linearity is shown in Figure 12. The output capacitance is indicated by the black line and the gray line indicates the trend line of the simulated output capacitance. The simulated nonlinearity is 0.028% FSO. The simulation was proceeded by Cadence Virtuoso for comparison with the measurement result. The capacitance linearity measurement result of the driving mode of the capacitive microsensors in the proposed scheme is shown in Figure 13. The capacitance linearity was measured by changing the input capacitance and acquiring the output digital codes. The output capacitance is indicated by the blue line and the red line indicates the trend line of the measured output capacitance. The measured nonlinearity is 0.711% FSO. The input capacitance was connected and measured using the LCR meter, and then connected to the analog front-end circuit; thus, the measurement results include the relatively large non-linearity because of the parasitic capacitance from the measurement environment.

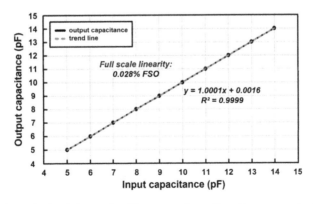

Figure 12. Linearity simulation results of the proposed reconfigurable sensor analog front-end.

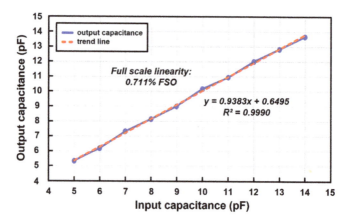

Figure 13. Linearity measurement results of the proposed reconfigurable sensor analog front-end.

The measured output codes of the capacitive microsensors of the proposed scheme are shown in Figure 14a–d. The output code error without chopper stabilization is shown in Figure 14a and its histogram is shown in Figure 14b. The output code error with the application of the chopper stabilization is shown in Figure 14c and its histogram is shown in Figure 14d. Five thousand sets of data values with fixed input capacitance of 6 pF were acquired. Figure 14a shows the peak-to-peak (P-P) noise of ±6 code variation without the application of the chopper stabilization. Figure 14c shows the measurement results of the code variation with the application of the chopper stabilization, which improved the code variation to ±2. The root mean square (*RMS*) noise is improved from 2.081 to 0.803, as shown in Figures 14b and 14d. The measured input referred capacitance *RMS* noise is 0.180 fF without the application of the chopper stabilization and 0.069 fF with the application of the chopper stabilization. The *RMS* noise and P-P noise can be acquired by the standard deviation and difference of the maximum and minimum results of the data. The effective resolution and *P-P resolution* can be acquired for performance evaluation. The effective resolution can be calculated as Equation (17) and the *P-P resolution* can be calculated as Equation (18) from the histogram results [29]:

$$Effective\ resolution = \log_2\left(\frac{P - P\ Range\ (LSBs)}{RMS\ Noise\ (LSBs)}\right) \tag{17}$$

$$P - P\ resolution = \log_2\left(\frac{P - P\ Range\ (LSBs)}{P - P\ Noise\ (LSBs)}\right) \tag{18}$$

The measured effective resolution and *P-P resolution* of the proposed scheme without the application of the chopper stabilization are 14.9-bit and 12.4-bit, respectively. The measured effective resolution and *P-P resolution* with the application of the chopper stabilization are 16.3-bit and 14-bit, respectively.

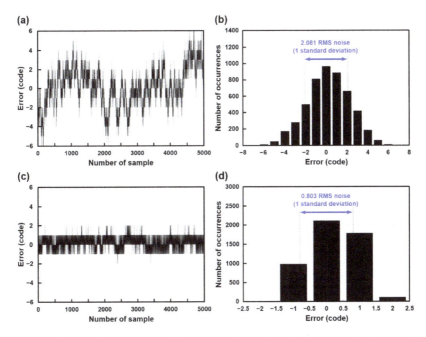

Figure 14. Measured output codes of the proposed reconfigurable sensor analog front-end IC.
(**a**) Output code error without chopper stabilization; (**b**) Histogram of output code error without
chopper stabilization; (**c**) Output code error with chopper stabilization; (**d**) Histogram of output code
error with chopper stabilization.

The measured output data of the temperature sensor with the proposed reconfigurable sensor
analog front-end IC are shown in Figures 15a and 15b. The measured temperature range is −10 °C
to 120 °C. Figure 15a shows the measured output temperature data. The blue line represents the
output temperature with two-point nonlinearity fitting. The red line is the trend line of the measured
output temperature and the black line represents the error of the two-point nonlinearity fitted output
temperature, which is shown in detail in Figure 15b. The measured nonlinearity is 0.024% FSO and the
output temperature error is −1.710/+1.693 °C.

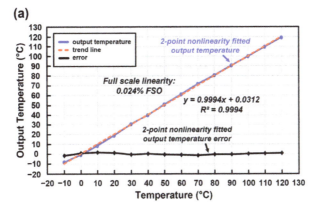

Figure 15. *Cont.*

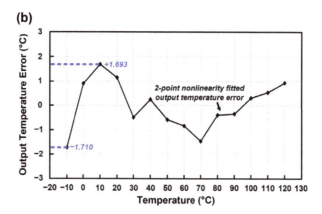

Figure 15. Measured output data of the temperature sensor of the proposed sensor analog front-end. (a) Measured output temperature data; (b) Error of the two-point nonlinearity fitted output temperature.

4. Discussion and Conclusions

The performance summary and comparison of previous works with the proposed reconfigurable sensor analog front-end scheme is shown in Table 1. The figure-of-merit (*FoM*) for the performance comparison can be calculated as given in Equation (19) [30]:

$$FoM = \frac{P_{total} \cdot T_{measurement}}{2^{resolution}} \tag{19}$$

The performance summary and comparisons show that the proposed work achieves high effective resolution, low power consumption, and low *FoM*. The power consumption of 0.843 mW and *FoM* of 13.06 pJ/step show improvements compared with previous works with similar architecture of discrete time delta-sigma CDC. The wide range of input capacitance with 16.7 pF of the proposed CDC is also an advantage compared to previous works, which makes it suitable for various capacitive microsensor applications.

This paper presented a reconfigurable sensor analog front-end using low-noise chopper-stabilized delta-sigma CDC. The proposed scheme can drive both capacitive microsensors and voltage signals by direct conversion. A fully integrated temperature sensor is implemented in the proposed reconfigurable sensor analog front-end for various applications. A low-noise technique with chopper stabilization was implemented to achieve a low-noise characteristic. The prototype IC was fabricated as per the standard 0.18-µm 1P6M CMOS process. The proposed scheme occupies a total active area of 5.37 mm^2 and the total power consumption is 0.843 mW with a 1.8 V power supply. It achieves an effective resolution of 16.3-bit and measured input referred capacitance RMS noise of 0.069 fF. The measured capacitance nonlinearity and the measured temperature nonlinearity are 0.711 % FSO and 0.024% FSO, respectively. The proposed sensor analog front-end can be flexibly adopted in various IoT sensor system applications with reasonable performance due to its reconfigurable scheme.

Table 1. Performance summary and comparisons.

Specification	This Work	[20]	[31]	[32]	[33]	[34]
Modulator order	DT 2nd	DT 1st	DT 2nd	DT 2nd	DT 4th	DT 2nd
Process (μm)	0.18	0.35	0.35	-	0.25	0.18
Re-configurability	Y	N	N	N	N	N
Supply voltage (V)	1.8 (core)/ 3.3 (pads)	3.3	3.0	5.0	2.5	2.6
Power consumption (mW)	0.843	1.44	60	3.75	6	2.34
Measurement time (ms)	1.25	0.128	1000	20	500	3.07
Effective Resolution (bit)	16.3	11.0	20.0	19.4	20.3	17.4
Capacitance range (pF)	16.7	1	1	8	5.3	10
FoM (pJ/step)	13.06	90	57220	108	2300	37
Active area (mm^2)	5.37	0.05	0.65	-	2	0.67

Author Contributions: H.K. conceived the study; H.K., B.L., Y.R., D.S., and S.H. designed the experiment; all authors participated in the testing and evaluations; H.K. wrote the paper.

Funding: This research received no external funding.

Acknowledgments: This work was supported by LeoLSI Co., Ltd., and IC Design Education Center (IDEC).

Conflicts of Interest: The authors declare no conflict of interest.

References

1. Rittersma, Z.M. Recent achievements in miniaturised humidity sensors—A review of transduction techniques. *Sens. Actuators A Phys.* **2002**, *96*, 196–210. [CrossRef]
2. Sun, H.; Fang, D.; Jia, K.; Maarouf, F.; Qu, H.; Xie, H. A low-power low-noise dual-chopper amplifier for capacitive CMOS-MEMS accelerometers. *IEEE Sens. J.* **2011**, *11*, 925–933. [CrossRef]
3. Tez, S.; Akin, T. Fabrication of a sandwich type three axis capacitive MEMS accelerometer. In Proceedings of the IEEE Sensors, Baltimore, MD, USA, 3–6 November 2013; pp. 1–4.
4. Cho, D.; Ko, H.; Kim, J.; Park, S.; Kwak, D.; Song, T.; Carr, W.; Buss, J. A novel z-axis accelerometer with perfectly-aligned, fully-offset vertical combs fabricated using the extended sacrificial bulk micromachining process. *Int. J. Comput. Eng. Sci.* **2003**, *4*, 493–496. [CrossRef]
5. Tsouti, V.; Boutopoulos, C.; Zergioti, I.; Chatzandroulis, S. Capacitive microsystems for biological sensing. *Biosens. Bioelectron.* **2011**, *27*, 1–11. [CrossRef] [PubMed]
6. Yu, H.Y.; Qin, M.; Huang, J.Q.; Huang, Q.A. A MEMS capacitive pressure sensor compatible with CMOS process. In Proceedings of the IEEE Sensors, Taipei, Taiwan, 28–31 October 2012; pp. 1–4.
7. Pedersen, T.; Fragiacomo, G.; Hansen, O.; Thomsen, E.V. Highly sensitive micro-machined capacitive pressure sensor with reduced hysteresis and low parasitic capacitance. *Sens. Actuators A Phys.* **2009**, *154*, 35–41. [CrossRef]
8. Tan, Z.; Shalmany, S.H.; Meijer, G.C.; Pertijs, M.A. An energy-efficient 15-bit capacitive-sensor interface based on period modulation. *IEEE J. Solid State Circuits* **2012**, *47*, 1703–1711. [CrossRef]
9. Dobrzynska, J.A.; Gijs, M.A.M. Polymer-based flexible capacitive sensor for three-axial force measurements. *J. Micromech. Microeng.* **2013**, *23*, 1–11. [CrossRef]
10. Song, H.; Park, Y.; Kim, H.; Cho, D.D.; Ko, H. Fully integrated low-noise readout circuit with automatic offset cancellation loop for capacitive microsensors. *Sensors* **2015**, *15*, 26009–26017. [CrossRef] [PubMed]
11. Mun, Y.; Kim, H.; Ko, Y.; Park, Y.; Koo, K.; Cho, D.D.; Ko, H. Capacitive analog front-end circuit with dual-mode automatic parasitic cancellation loop. *Microsyst. Technol.* **2017**, *23*, 515–523. [CrossRef]
12. Tanaka, K.; Kuramochi, Y.; Kurashina, T.; Okada, K.; Matsuzawa, A. A 0.026 mm^2 capacitance-to-digital converter for biotelemetry applications using a charge redistribution technique. In Proceedings of the IEEE Asian Solid-State Circuits Conference, Jeju, Korea, 12–14 November 2007; pp. 244–247.
13. Omran, H.; Arsalan, M.; Salama, K.N. An integrated energy-efficient capacitive sensor digital interface circuit. *Sens. Actuators A Phys.* **2014**, *216*, 43–51. [CrossRef]

14. Alhoshany, A.; Omran, H.; Salama, K.N. A 45.8 fJ/Step, energy-efficient, differential SAR capacitance-to-digital converter for capacitive pressure sensing. *Sens. Actuators A Phys.* **2016**, *245*, 10–18. [CrossRef]

15. Omran, H.; Alhoshany, A.; Alahmadi, H.; Salama, K.N. A 33fJ/Step SAR capacitance-to-digital converter using a chain of inverter-based amplifiers. *IEEE Trans. Circuits Syst. I Regul. Pap.* **2017**, *64*, 310–321. [CrossRef]

16. Alhoshany, A.; Sivashankar, S.; Mashraei, Y.; Omran, H.; Salama, K.N. A biosensor-CMOS platform and integrated readout circuit in 0.18-μm CMOS technology for cancer biomarker detection. *Sensors* **2017**, *17*, 1942. [CrossRef] [PubMed]

17. Xu, H.; Liu, X.; Yin, L. A closed-loop ΣΔ interface for a high-Q micromechanical capacitive accelerometer with 200 ng/ Hz input noise density. *IEEE J. Solid State Circuits* **2015**, *50*, 2101–2112. [CrossRef]

18. Liu, B.; Hoseini, Z.; Lee, K.S.; Lee, Y.M. On-chip touch sensor readout circuit using passive sigma-delta modulator capacitance-to-digital converter. *IEEE Sens. J.* **2015**, *15*, 3893–3902. [CrossRef]

19. Chiou, J.C.; Hsu, S.H.; Huang, Y.C.; Yeh, G.T.; Liou, W.T.; Kuei, C.K. A wirelessly powered smart contact lens with reconfigurable wide range and tunable sensitivity sensor readout circuitry. *Sensors* **2017**, *17*, 108. [CrossRef] [PubMed]

20. Shin, D.Y.; Lee, H.; Kim, S. A delta–sigma interface circuit for capacitive sensors with an automatically calibrated zero point. *IEEE Trans. Circuits Syst. II Exp. Briefs* **2011**, *58*, 90–94. [CrossRef]

21. Oh, S.; Jung, W.; Yang, K.; Blaauw, D.; Sylvester, D. 15.4b incremental sigma-delta capacitance-to-digital converter with zoom-in 9b asynchronous SAR. In Proceedings of the Symposium on VLSI Circuits Digest of Technical Papers, Honolulu, HI, USA, 10–13 June 2014; pp. 1–2.

22. Robert, J.; Deval, P. A second-order high-resolution incremental A/D converter with offset and charge injection compensation. *IEEE J. Solid State Circuits* **1988**, *23*, 736–741. [CrossRef]

23. Boser, B.E.; Howe, R.T. Surface micromachined accelerometers. *IEEE J. Solid State Circuits* **1996**, *31*, 366–375. [CrossRef]

24. Markus, J.; Silva, J.; Temes, G.C. Theory and applications of incremental ΔΣ converters. *IEEE Trans. Circuits Syst. I Regul. Pap.* **2004**, *51*, 678–690. [CrossRef]

25. Dong, Y.; Kraft, M.; Gollasch, C.; Redman-White, W. A high-performance accelerometer with a fifth-order sigma–delta modulator. *J. Micromech. Microeng.* **2005**, *15*, S22–S29. [CrossRef]

26. Enz, C.; Temes, G.C. Circuit techniques for reducing the effects of op-amp imperfections: Autozeroing, correlated double sampling, and chopper stabilization. *Proc. IEEE* **1996**, *84*, 1584–1614. [CrossRef]

27. Park, Y.; Kim, H.; Ko, Y.; Mun, Y.; Lee, S.; Kim, J.H.; Ko, H. Low noise CMOS temperature sensor with on-chip digital calibration. *Sensor Mater.* **2017**, *29*, 1025–1030.

28. Banba, H.; Shiga, H.; Umezawa, A.; Miyaba, T.; Tanzawa, T.; Atsumi, S.; Sakui, K. A CMOS bandgap reference circuit with sub-1-V operation. *IEEE J. Solid State Circuits* **1999**, *34*, 670–674. [CrossRef]

29. Understanding Noise, ENOB, and Effective Resolution in Analog-to-Digital Converters, Maxim Integrated, Appl. Note. AN5384. Available online: http://www.maximintegrated.com (accessed on 10 July 2018).

30. Li, B.; Sun, L.; Ko, C.T.; Wong, A.K.Y.; Pun, K.P. A high-linearity capacitance-to-digital converter suppressing charge errors from bottom-plate switches. *IEEE Trans. Circuits Syst. I Regul. Pap.* **2014**, *61*, 1928–1941. [CrossRef]

31. Gozzini, F.; Ferrari, G.; Sampietro, M. An instrument-on-chip for impedance measurements on nanobiosensors with attoFarad resoution. In Proceedings of the IEEE International Solid-State Circuits Conference—Digest of Technical Papers, San Francisco, CA, USA, 8–12 February 2009; pp. 346–348.

32. 24-Bit Capacitance-to-Digital Converter with Temperature Sensor, Analog Devices, Data Sheet AD7745/AD7746. Available online: http://www.analog.com (accessed on 10 July 2018).

33. Amini, B.V.; Ayazi, F. A 2.5-V 14-bit ΣΔ CMOS SOI capacitive accelerometer. *IEEE J. Solid State Circuits* **2004**, *39*, 2467–2476. [CrossRef]

34. Jung, Y.; Duan, Q.; Roh, J. A 17.4-b delta-sigma capacitance-to-digital converter for one-terminal capacitive sensors. *IEEE Trans. Circuits Syst. II Exp. Briefs* **2017**, *64*, 1122–1126. [CrossRef]

Article

Resonant Directly Coupled Inductors–Capacitors Ladder Network Shows a New, Interesting Property Useful for Application in the Sensor Field, Down to Micrometric Dimensions

Arnaldo D'Amico [1,2], Marco Santonico [3], Giorgio Pennazza [3,*], Alessandro Zompanti [3], Emma Scipioni [3], Giuseppe Ferri [4], Vincenzo Stornelli [4], Marcello Salmeri [1] and Roberto Lojacono [1]

[1] Department of Electronic Engineering, University of Rome Tor Vergata, Via del Politecnico, 1, 00133 Roma, Italy; damico@eln.uniroma2.it (A.D.); salmeri@eln.uniroma2.it (M.S.); lojacono@eln.uniroma2.it (R.L.)
[2] Centro Studi e Documentazione sulla Sensoristica, University of Rome Tor Vergata, Via del Politecnico, 1, 00133 Roma, Italy
[3] Unit of Electronics for Sensor Systems, Department of Engineering, Campus Bio-Medico University of Rome, Via Álvaro del Portillo, 21, 00128 Roma, Italy; m.santonico@unicampus.it (M.S.); a.zompanti@unicampus.it (A.Z.); emma.scipioni@gmail.com (E.S.)
[4] Department of Industrial and Information Engineering and Economics, University of L'Aquila, Via Giovanni Gronchi 18 - Zona industriale di Pile, 67100 L'Aquila, Italy; giuseppe.ferri@univaq.it (G.F.); vincenzo.stornelli@univaq.it (V.S.)
*   Correspondence: g.pennazza@unicampus.it

Received: 1 June 2018; Accepted: 5 July 2018; Published: 7 July 2018

Abstract: The study of ladder networks made by sequences of directly coupled inductor–capacitor single cells has led us to discover a new property, which may be of certain interest in the sensor field. In the case of n cells, the n-frequencies vector characterizing each node may allow for the identification of that capacitor (sensor), which has experienced a variation of its nominal value. This localization is possible independently from the observable node of the ladder network as proven by the application of the following multivariate data analysis techniques: principal component analysis and partial least square discriminant analysis. This property can be applied on a large scale down to micrometric dimensions in agreement with the technologic ability to shrink the capacitive sensor dimensions.

Keywords: ladder networks; capacitive sensor; sensor network; fingerprint; data analysis

---

1. Introduction

Passive ladder networks (L.N.s) made by a number of single cells showing both longitudinal and transversal impedances have been studied for a long time [1–6] due to their versatility in representing a good model for mechanical, chemical, thermal, and electronic systems and also because they have been frequently employed in passive filters [7,8]. In fact, the representation of complex dynamic systems by using the analogy of electrical networks has proven to be very useful in the realization of interfaces for monitoring integrated sensors, sensor systems, and microstructures, especially when the sensors work at the micro-dimensional level. In this analogy, the role of sensor activity is played by those electronic components, which present measurable time variability, such as inductors or capacitors. These kinds of electrical networks are called inductor–capacitor (L–C) networks and are often used in modeling a particular kind of information transmission. When the inductor (L) and capacitor (C) elements represent sensors operating in a real scenario, the content of each variation is a part of global information conveyed by the whole network of electro-mechanical sensors. The interest in L.N.s today is still alive due to new applications, for example, in analog neural networks. Furthermore, we cannot exclude in the near future their possible implications in the study of the electric behavior of both DNA and RNA structures [9] and related aspects of epigenomics.

This paper, on the other hand, also considers these kinds of networks from another viewpoint: the search of the presence of links with Fibonacci numbers. In many cases these famous numbers are present as expression of impedances, voltages, and currents and may facilitate the rapid calculation of their amplitudes [4].

The particular structure of the directly coupled L–C single cell L.N. shows very strong peculiarities, which are shown in Figure 1, reported below, and taken from D'Amico et al. [5].

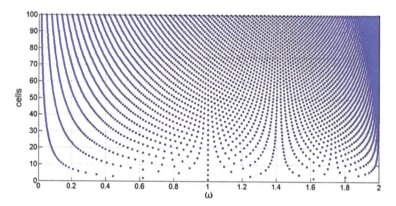

Figure 1. Normalized ω solutions in the case of an inductor–capacitor (L–C) ladder network (L.N.) formed by a number of single cells from 1 to 100.

In the vertical axes we have, for example, the number of L–C cells from 1 to 100. In the horizontal axes, we have the normalized frequencies, which means that in the case of only one cell $\omega_1 = 1/\sqrt{LC}$ is taken equal to 1. In the case of two L–C cells, the normalized ω becomes $\omega_1 = 0.618\ldots$ and $\omega_2 = 1.618$ ... (which do represent the golden section and the golden ratio, respectively) and so on. Another interesting property is represented by the fact that these two frequencies are also present in the case of 7, 12, 17, 22 ... and so on cells (i.e., starting from two cells the two solutions are present according to a period of five cells). Furthermore, the transfer function of this kind of L–C L.N. has the property to show all the ω-solutions only in the normalized interval defined by 0 and 2 (as shown in Figure 1). Another property of this L–C L.N. can be seen by looking at this figure while partly shutting one's eyes. It is possible to see many channels (finite number) that become narrower and narrower by increasing the number of cells. These are the forbidden bands similar to those that we have in a 1-dimensional (1D) array of atoms. This means that whatever the number of cells, the solutions ω_i will never enter these bands.

The novelty in this paper concerns the identification of a new property related to the L–C L.N. that can be of a certain utility in the field of sensor network. In this case we have imagined dealing with capacitive sensors for either mechanical of chemical quantities. In fact, measuring the frequencies vector in only one of the randomly selected nodes of a given L–C L.N., we have found that it is possible to determine the capacitor that has changed its value due to a given sensing action. Of course, the same property is evident if we consider the inductors as sensors. The result is the same due to the fact that the transfer function of this network is related to the ratio (K) between the longitudinal $Z_1 = j\omega L$ and transversal impedance $Z_2 = 1/j\omega C$.

In fact, being that $K = \omega^2 LC$, the same changes of either C or L (not simultaneous changes) will produce the same result.

In this paper, we have investigated, as an example, the transfer function of seven L–C cells directly coupled forming a discrete L.N. and found a new interesting property useful for applications in the field of sensors. In fact, surprisingly, each node brings the information of each cell, and when one capacitor of a cell is changed, then the voltages in the seven nodes change also. Of course, each one changes in a different way, but the identification of the modified cell can be performed whatever the testing node. This new property is found to be of interest for the control of sensorial multi-points: this attitude is strategic when applied to the monitoring of networks developed at the micrometric level, when the 'interrogation' and the localization of the 'sensor-points' could be not so easy. We have estimated the resolution of this system as a final contribution to the knowledge of this peculiar discrete network. Definitively, the purpose of this work is the study of useful electrical properties of directly coupled L–C cells forming a discrete ladder network (L–C L.N.) to be applied to the sensor field.

2. Materials and Methods

A typical L–C L.N. is shown in Figure 2.

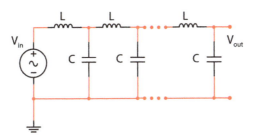

Figure 2. Ladder network formed by n-L–C elementary cells.

As shown in the literature [6], the transfer function of this L–C L.N., whatever the number of cell, can be easily determined by the use of the DFF triangle [4], which gives the modules of the coefficients of the polynomial at the denominator of the transfer function.

In the same paper, it is shown the following expression, which gives the voltage V_b in each node β of a n-length L.N. where $k(s)$ is the ratio of Z_1/Z_2 in the Laplace domain.

$$V_b = \frac{\sum_{j=0}^{n-\beta} b(n-\beta,j)k^j(s)}{\sum_{j=0}^{n} b(n,j)k^j(s)} V_{in} \tag{1}$$

This triangle is here reported in Table 1 and is framed to give the coefficients for a seven-cell L.N. (Figure 3), which is the number taken into account in this paper for the demonstration of the new property of this L.N.

Table 1. DFF triangle for a seven-cell L.N.

	Power of Monomials at the Denominator							
Cell #	X^0	X^2	X^4	X^6	X^8	X^{10}	X^{12}	X^{14}
0	1	-	-	-	-	-	-	-
1	1	−1	-	-	-	-	-	-
2	1	−3	1	-	-	-	-	-
3	1	−6	5	−1	-	-	-	-
4	1	−10	15	−7	1	-	-	-
5	1	−15	35	−28	9	−1	-	-
6	1	−21	65	−84	45	−11	1	-
7	1	−28	121	−205	165	−66	13	−1

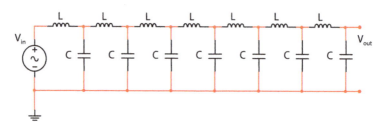

Figure 3. Ladder network of seven L–C cells.

In order to obtain a general model to be used for any kind of L–C network with n-cell, a bottom-up strategy has been used, starting from the analysis of a single L–C cell. The starting condition (assumed as a reference) for this cell is given by the following values: L = 68 uH and C = 47 nF (see Figure 4).

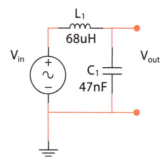

Figure 4. Single L–C cell used as a 'standard' for the reference condition of the L.N. in this work.

Studying the transfer function of this cell and simulating the relative electronic circuit in MultiSim (National Instruments, Austin, TX, USA), we obtain the magnitude curve (Figure 5), which confirms the following theoretical resonance frequency:

$$f = \frac{1}{2\pi\sqrt{LC}} = \frac{1}{2\pi\sqrt{68 \times 10^{-6} \times 47 \times 10^{-9}}} = 89.02\text{KHz} \tag{2}$$

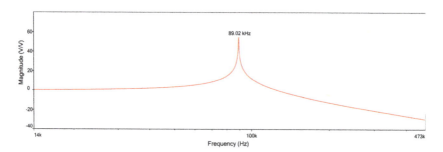

Figure 5. Magnitude vs frequency plot of the single-cell L.N. reported in Figure 3 showing the behavior of a low pass filter.

This frequency is characteristic of the elementary cell (Figure 5), and the calculus is here implemented for a n-cell ladder network.

The pattern of frequencies relative to the n poles and to the m zeros, related to the voltages at internal nodes, is typical of the ladder network. The n cells of the ladder network and the $n + m$ frequencies registered form a multidimensional $n(n + m)$ array: this array provides a dynamic picture of the network, and its elaboration via multivariate data analysis techniques gives important information on the network condition. The study of this array has been here performed with both a qualitative and a quantitative approach. Principal component analysis (PCA) has been used to explore the array variation with the aim of dynamically identifying whether a specific pattern is able to identify the point of observation on the network or the element (C or L) whose value has changed or both. Partial least square discriminant analysis (cross-validated via the leave-one-out criterion) has been used here in order to quantify the occurring variation of capacitance and/or inductance. Let us consider the seven-cell L–C ladder network with L = 68 uH and C = 47 nF as reported in Figure 6. This is the electronic circuit analyzed in the following of the work.

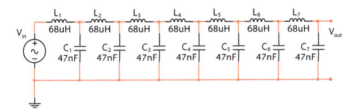

Figure 6. The seven-cell L.N. used as the reference L.N. in the work elaborations.

3. Results

3.1. Fibonacci Relations in the L–C L.N.

In the case of seven L–C L.N. cells, we have the following denominator for the transfer function:

$$-\omega^{14}L^7 C^7 + 13\omega^{12}L^6C^6 - 66\omega^{10}L^5C^5 + 165\omega^8L^4C^4 - 205\omega^6L^3C^3 + 121\omega^4L^2C^2 - 28\omega^2LC + 1 \quad (3)$$

which must be set equal to zero in order to determine the seven solutions. The seven solutions are represented by the seven resonant frequencies obtained by the following relationship [6]:

$$\omega^{(n)} = 2 \sin \{[(2i - 1)\pi]/[(2n + 1)2]\} \quad (4)$$

where n represents the number of L–C cells, and $i = 1, 2, \ldots, n$

As a consequence, according to Equation (4), the normalized solutions are the following:

$\omega_1 = 0.20906$; $\omega_2 = 0.61903$; $\omega_3 = 1$; $\omega_4 = 1.33832$; $\omega_5 = 1.61803$; $\omega_6 = 1.82713$; $\omega_7 = 1.9659$.

In this kind of L–C L.N. we have noticed that starting from the case of two or more cells (5, 7, 12, 17, 22, ...) we always get, among the others, the following two solutions: the golden ratio, $\phi = 1.618$ and the gold section, $1/\phi = 0.618$. So, even in the case under test, we have these two particular frequencies, which are related to the Fibonacci numbers, as expressed by the following relationships:

$$\phi = \log_{n-\infty} F_n / F_{(n-1)} \quad (5)$$

$$1/\phi = \log_{n-\infty} F_{(n-1)} / F_n \quad (6)$$

3.2. Sensor Localization Based on Frequency Patterns

When one of the capacitors (representing a sensor for instance) is for some reason changed (e.g., the third in the L.N. of Figure 7), all the frequency patterns of the L–C L.N. will change as a consequence of the variation of its transfer function. Depending on the node where the output is read, we will have a different set of frequencies.

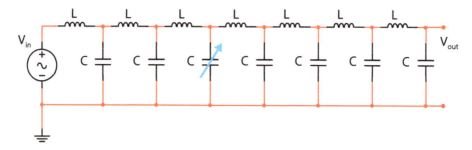

Figure 7. The L–C seven-cell L.N. with a variation of C in the third cell.

We now prove that it is possible, whatever the observed node, to localize the transversal impedance, which has changed.

This unexpected property can be of a high utility in the sensor field where a sensor network made by capacitive sensors has to be kept under control independently from the observation point.

This property has been studied by principal component analysis (PCA) in order to have a sound description of it.

Table 2 shows the first step of the analysis: the array of the characteristic frequencies of the L–C L.N. in the standard condition taken as reference (without any variation of the values of L and C). The characteristic frequencies given by the seven poles (first 7 columns of the array reported in Table 2) and given by the six zeros (the last 6 columns reported in Table 2) have been calculated for each cell (the seven rows of the array reported in Table 2).

Table 2. Array of the poles and zeros (in KHz) of the transfer function of the circuit in Figure 6. The colors used for some of the 'zero' values reported in the cells are here used to put in evidence the cancellation action of zeros and poles coincidence; thus, each couple of identical color (orange. red. yellow) corresponds to a couple of coincident pole–zero.

	Poles						
Cell #	P1	P2	P3	P4	P5	P6	P7
1	18.61	55.01	89.02	119.15	144.04	162.66	174.18
2	18.61	55.01	89.02	119.15	144.04	162.66	174.18
3	18.61	55.01	0	119.15	144.04	162.66	174.18
4	18.61	55.01	89.02	119.15	144.04	162.66	174.18
5	18.61	0	89.02	119.15	0	162.66	174.18
6	18.61	55.01	0	119.15	144.04	162.66	174.18
7	18.61	55.01	89.02	119.15	144.04	162.66	174.18

	Zeros					
Cell #	Z1	Z2	Z3	Z4	Z5	Z6
1	21.46	63.13	101.13	133.26	157.65	172.86
2	25.33	73.96	116.6	0	149.79	170.84
3	30.91	0	0	136.39	0	167.3
4	39.61	0	111.01	0	160.43	0
5	0	0	0	0	0	0
6	0	0	0	0	0	0
7	0	0	0	0	0	0

Each row of the array in Table 2 is a pattern of frequencies, which is characteristic of the adopted configuration. These seven patterns show seven different magnitude plots (reported in Figure 8) with seven different colors. Each plot represents the behavior of the magnitude of the transfer function of the whole network when read by the *i*th cell ($i = 1, \ldots, 7$).

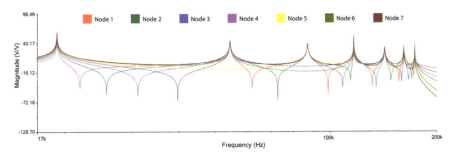

Figure 8. Magnitude plots vs frequency of the seven patterns readable by the seven nodes of the seven cells of the L–C L.N.

Thus, when C and L values are 'static' (meaning: fixed values), the 7×13 array representing the system is a static picture (Table 3). But, when the system is 'dynamic' because some elements are modified, how is the array modified? Is it possible to monitor and localize this variation by automatically checking the array variability with respect to the reference 'picture'?

Table 3. Array of the poles and zeros of the transfer function of the circuit in Figure 5 when the capacitance at node 7th has been changed from 47 nF to 44 nF.

				Poles			
Cell #	P1	P2	P3	P4	P5	P6	P7
1	18.77	55.44	89.61	119.72	144.51	162.92	174.22
2	18.77	55.44	89.61	119.72	144.51	162.92	174.22
3	18.77	55.44	89.61	119.72	144.51	162.92	174.22
4	18.77	55.44	89.61	119.72	144.51	162.92	174.22
5	18.77	55.44	89.61	119.72	144.51	162.92	174.22
6	18.77	55.44	89.61	119.72	144.51	162.92	174.22
7	18.77	55.44	89.61	119.72	144.51	162.92	174.22

			Zeros			
Cell #	Z1	Z2	Z3	Z4	Z5	Z6
1	21.67	63.69	101.85	133.87	158.01	172.98
2	25.63	74.69	117.4	0	150.34	171
3	31.35	0	90.01	137.24	0	167.61
4	40.31	0	112.3	0	161.02	0
5	0	56.33	0	0	145.41	0
6	0	0	92	0	0	0
7	0	0	0	0	0	0

To test this condition, the value of the capacitor of the third cell has been decreased, as an example, from 47 nF to 44 nF. Figure 9 shows the shift of the magnitude pattern given by this variation.

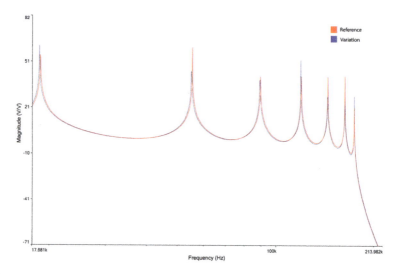

Figure 9. Comparison of the magnitude plots vs frequency of the patterns readable at the seventh node of the L–C L.N. when the capacitance at the 7th cell shifts from 47 nF to 44 nF.

Now it is possible to obtain the array of the resonance frequencies for each node of the L.N. by varying each capacitor of the L.N. Table 4 reports an example: the array given by the variation of the capacitor in the 7th cell. This array is given by reading each node of the L.N.

Table 4. Root-mean-square error in cross validation (RMSECV) in the identification of the capacitance shifts (from C1 to C7), as obtained from the partial least square discriminant analysis (PLS-DA) model by using the leave-one-out cross-validation criterion. Each row of the table reports the node (the point of observation for monitoring the 'sensor' variation) in the first column and the minimum detectable variation in that node, in the second column.

Node	RMSECV [nF]
1	0.36
2	0.19
3	0.17
4	0.31
5	2.08×10^{-6}
6	0.16
7	0.20

In Figure 10, three examples of the magnitude plot shifting for three different conditions: (a) C shift in cell 1 read by node 1; (b) C shift in cell 2 read by node 2; and (c) C shift in cell 5 read by node 5.

Using multivariate data analysis techniques, it is possible to face the complexity of the information content of the 7×13 arrays. This approach allows the reduction of the problem dimension and the representation of a multidimensional issue on a 2- or 3-dimensional plane, which can effectively map the L.N. conditions. Principal component analysis is the simplest explorative (unsupervised) method to obtain this 'map'. The PCA elaboration of the seven-cell L–C L.N. of Figure 5 has given the scores plot reported in Figure 11.

The scores plot in Figure 11 appears to be like a map of the L.N.: the central 'corridor' is the reference condition of the L.N. corresponding to the starting value of 47 nF for the capacitor. Along the PC2, the shift of the C value is mapped, either increasing (towards the upper portion of the plot) or decreasing (towards the lower portion of the plot) the value of C. Along the PC1, it is possible to localize the cell. This 'mapping' action is better represented in Figure 12, where the same plot of Figure 11 is repeated with a figurative representation of the localization action, which can be performed using the PCA model of Figure 11 in finding out the variation that occurred.

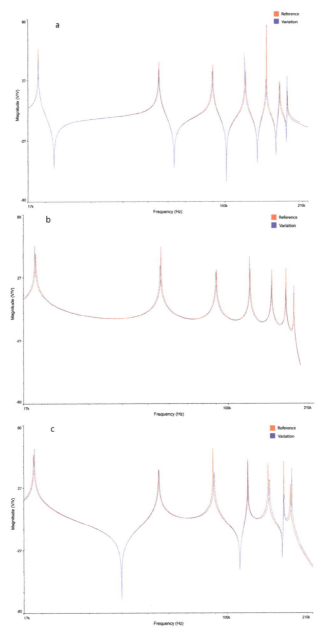

Figure 10. Magnitude plot shifting for three different conditions: (**a**) C shift in cell 1 read by node 1; (**b**) C shift in cell 2 read by node 2; and (**c**) C shift in cell 5 read by node 5.

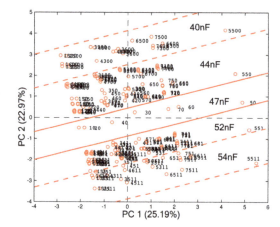

Figure 11. Score plot of the first two PCs of the principal component analysis (PCA) model built in the 7 × 13 data array of resonance frequency of the seven-cell L–C L.N. of Figure 5.

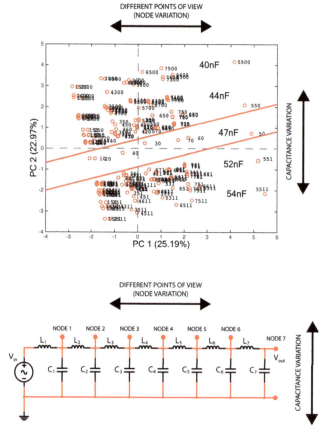

Figure 12. Representation of the localization action, which can be performed using the PCA model of Figure 11 in finding out the variation that occurred.

Micromachines **2018**, *9*, 343

Considering the capability of the multivariate model to follow also the increasing/decreasing of the C value supposed to be modified, a supervised technique could be applied in order to test the performance of the model in the quantification of this change. A partial least square model has been calculated on the L.N., and the root-mean-square error in cross validation (RMSECV) has been estimated by applying the leave-one-out criterion. The rather interesting results are reported in Table 4. The RMSECV confirms the capability of the system to detect variations of capacitance down to 10^{-6} nF; thus, it could be used in the management of sensors with optimal resolution power, which is crucial when monitoring very small deviations of micrometric sensors' responses.

4. Conclusions

Ladder networks have been employed in many applications in the engineering context, and in this paper, we have shown that another important property can be attributed to them in the special case when the L.N. is formed by longitudinal inductors and transversal capacitors.

The results obtained in this work demonstrate that one of the transversal elements, capacitors in this example, can be univocally identified by using the arrays of the resonance frequencies, which can be easily determined by the transfer function of the L.N. itself. Moreover, by analyzing these arrays with multivariate data analysis technique, it is possible to localize the element where in the L.N. the variation is occurring and to quantify this variation independently from the observation node. The model here presented has a general validity and can be used for any kind of network as far as the number of cells is concerned.

This method could be of particular utility in cases of complex network configurations, when the identification of the variation of single sensorial element is not easy, such as in the case of sensor networks operating at the micrometric dimensional level. Of course, there is an important aspect to be considered when dimensions of sensors are reduced, which deals with the possibility of keeping the overall performance analysis when operating frequencies become higher and higher. The identification of limits in this direction is a challenge for near-future technological work. Moreover, whenever the L.N. represents a sensor network, an automated localization system based on such model could be useful to speed up the identification process and the potential warning activation, especially in case of hazardous or extended areas.

Author Contributions: A.D. and R.L. conceived and designed the experiments; M.San., G.P., A.Z. and E.S. performed the experiments; M.San., M.Sal., V.S. and G.F. analyzed the data; M.San., G.P. and A.D. wrote the paper.

Funding: This research received no external funding.

Conflicts of Interest: The authors declare no conflict of interest.

References

1. Morgan-Voyce, A. Ladder network analysis using Fibonacci numbers. *IRE Trans. Circuit Theory.* **1959**, *6*, 321–322. [CrossRef]
2. Ferris, G.; Faccio, M.; D'Amico, A. A new numerical triangle showing links with Fibonacci numbers. *Fibonacci Q.* **1991**, *29*, 316–321.
3. Faccio, M.; Ferri, G.; D'Amico, A. Fibonacci numbers and ladder network impedances. *Fibonacci Q.* **1992**, *30*, 62–67.
4. Faccio, M.; Ferri, G.; D'Amico, A. A new fast method for ladder networks characterization. *IEEE Trans. Circuit Syst.* **1991**, *38*, 1377–1382. [CrossRef]
5. D'Amico, A.; Falconi, C.; Bertsch, M.; Ferri, G.; Lojacono, R.; Mazzotta, M.; Santonico, M.; Pennazza, G. The presence of Fibonacci numbers in passive ladder networks: The case of forbidden bands. *IEEE Antennas Propag. Mag.* **2014**, *56*, 275–287. [CrossRef]
6. Faccio, M.; Ferri, G.; D'Amico, A. The DFF and DFFz triangles and their mathematical properties. In Proceedings of the Fifth International Conference on Fibonacci Numbers and Their Applications, St. Andrews, UK, 20–24 July 1992.

7. Fialkov, A.A. A theorem on general LC-R ladder filters. *IEEE Trans. Circuit Syst.* **1983**, *3*, 293–296. [CrossRef]
8. Johns, D.A.; Snelgrove, W.M.; Sedra, A.S. Ortonormal ladder filters. *IEEE Trans. Circuit Syst.* **1989**, *36*, 337–343. [CrossRef]
9. Marshall, R. Modeling DNA/RNA strings using resistor-capacitor (RC) ladder networks. *Comput. J.* **2010**, *53*, 644–660. [CrossRef]

Article

The Evolution of Integrated Interfaces for MEMS Microphones

Piero Malcovati [1,*,†] and Andrea Baschirotto [2,†]

1   Department of Electrical, Computer, and Biomedical Engineering, University of Pavia, 27100 Pavia, Italy
2   Department of Physics "G. Occhialini", University of Milano-Bicocca, 20126 Milano, Italy; andrea.baschirotto@unimib.it
*   Correspondence: piero.malcovati@unipv.it; Tel.: +39-0382-985256
†   These authors contributed equally to this work.

Received: 23 May 2018; Accepted: 22 June 2018; Published: 26 June 2018

Abstract: Over the last decade, MEMS microphones have become the leading solution for implementing the audio module in most portable devices. One of the main drivers for the success of the MEMS microphone has been the continuous improvement of the corresponding integrated interface circuit performance in terms of both dynamic range and power consumption, which enabled the introduction in mobile devices of additional functionalities, such as Hi-Fi audio recording or voice commands. As a result, MEMS microphone interface circuits evolved from just simple amplification stages to complex mixed-signal circuits, including A/D converters, with ever improving performance. This paper provides an overview of such evolution based on actual design examples, focusing, finally, on the latest cutting-edge solutions.

Keywords: MEMS microphones; microsensor interface circuits; data converters

1. Introduction

After the invention of the first microphone in 1876, carbon microphones were introduced in 1878 as key components of early telephone systems. In 1942, ribbon microphones were developed for radio broadcasting. The invention of the self-biased condenser or electret microphones (ECM) in 1962 represented the first significant breakthrough in this field. Indeed, ECMs, ensuring high-sensitivity and wide bandwidth at low cost, have dominated the market for high-volume applications until the last decade, when MEMS microphones started to gain popularity [1].

The first microphone based on silicon micro-machining (MEMS microphone) was introduced in 1983. Thanks to the use of advanced fabrication technologies, MEMS microphones offer several advantages with respect to ECMs: better performance, smaller size, compatibility with high-temperature automated printed circuit board (PCB) mounting processes, and lower sensitivity to mechanical shocks. Moreover, MEMS microphones can be integrated together with the CMOS electronics on the same chip or, more commonly, within the same package [2], thus reducing area, complexity, and costs, while increasing efficiency, reliability, and performance. As a result, around 2014 MEMS microphones overcame ECMs in terms of sold units, with an annual market size increase of more than 11%, as shown in Figure 1.

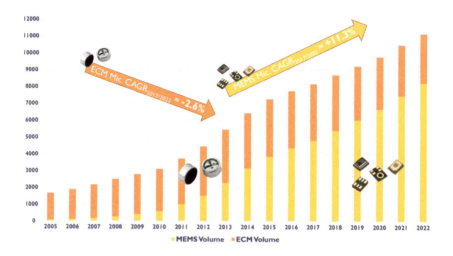

Figure 1. The microphone market in million units since 2005 [3].

MEMS microphones can be realized exploiting different transduction principles, such as piezoresistive, and optical detection. However, more than 80% of the produced MEMS microphones are based on capacitive transduction, since it achieves higher sensitivity, consumes lower power, and is more compatible with batch production. Piezoelectric MEMS microphones are also gaining popularity as an alternative to capacitive devices, since they do not require a biasing voltage, but so far they have not reached the same level of performance and cost effectiveness.

The interface circuit is of paramount importance for MEMS microphones, since it represents one of the most significant competitive advantages with respect to ECMs. Therefore, the development of high-performance interface circuits has been proceeding in parallel with the evolution of MEMS microphones since the very beginning [4–12]. The main target in the optimization of these interface circuits is the constant improvement of the audio performances, such as signal-to-noise ratio (SNR), dynamic range (DR), and total harmonic distortion (THD), while maintaining or even reducing the power consumption. This trend is mainly driven by portable applications, in which the audio-related functionalities have been expanding significantly. For example, voice interfaces are becoming pervasive. A growing number of people now talk to their mobile devices, asking them to send e-mails and text messages, to search for directions, or to find information on the internet. These functions require continuous listening, thus introducing severe constraints on the power consumption of the microphone modules. On the other hand, mobile devices nowadays are also used to perform high-fidelity (Hi-Fi) audio/video recording, which require high performance in terms of DR and THD. Such different scenarios are clearly characterized by different performance and power consumption requirements in the microphone module. Different operating modes are required when the same device is re-used in different systems (with different specifications) or when, in the same system, the specifications change depending on the performed function.

In the first case, applications with different DR requirements lead to different component choices, like, for instance, different microphones and/or audio processors. In this situation, the microphone interface circuit has to achieve different performance levels depending on the hardware to which it is connected. In the second case, portable devices supporting voice commands require the audio module to be always active, featuring low DR with low power consumption in stand-by mode (to extend battery life) [13]. However, as soon as an audio input signal is detected, the DR and, hence, the power consumption of the audio module have to be increased to effectively perform the required functions. Then, as soon as the input signal vanishes, the system has to return in stand-by mode. For instance, in always running applications, the bandwidth and *DR* requirements are typically relaxed (e.g., 4-kHz bandwidth and *DR* > 70 dB), but power consumption has to be extremely low [14–16], whereas, in Hi-Fi applications, the required bandwidth is 20 kHz and the *DR* has to be larger than 90–100 dB, but a relatively high (e.g., around 1 mW) power consumption can be tolerated [17–24].

As a consequence, in the last decade, MEMS microphone interface circuits evolved from just simple amplification stages to complex mixed-signal circuits, including A/D converters, with ever increasing performance.

This paper is organized as follows. Section 2 provides a short overview of MEMS microphones, briefly describing their operating principle. Then, Section 3 discusses the basic principles of the interface circuits for MEMS microphones, illustrating the most important design options and trade-offs, as well as the evolution of both the architecture and the performance over the last decade. This evolution is then analyzed in detail with four actual design examples, which are described in Sections 4–7, respectively. Finally, in Section 8, we draw some conclusions and discuss future trends.

2. Capacitive MEMS Microphones

A microphone is a transducer, which translates a perturbation of the atmospheric pressure, i.e., sound, into an electrical quantity. In a capacitive MEMS microphone, the pressure variation leads to the vibration of a mechanical mass, which, in turn, is transformed into a capacitance variation.

Sound pressure is typically expressed in dB_{SPL} (sound-pressure-level). A sound pressure of 20 µPa, corresponding to 0 dB_{SPL}, is the auditory threshold (the lowest amplitude of a 1-kHz signal that a human ear can detect). The sound pressure level of a face-to-face conversation ranges between 60 dB_{SPL} and 70 dB_{SPL}. The sound pressure rises to 94 dB_{SPL} if the speaker is at a distance of one inch from the listener (or the microphone), which is the case, for example, in mobile phones. Therefore, a sound pressure level of 94 dB_{SPL}, which corresponds to 1 Pa, is used as a reference for acoustic applications. The performance parameters for acoustic systems, such as *SNR*, are typically specified at 1-Pa and 1-kHz.

A MEMS microphone, whose simplified structure is shown in Figure 2, consists of two conductive plates at a distance x. The top plate, in this case, is fixed and cannot move, while the bottom plate is able to vibrate with the sound pressure, producing a variation of x (Δx) with respect to its steady-state value (x_0), proportional to the instantaneous pressure level (P_S). Different arrangements of the electrodes and fabrication solutions are possible [25–31], but the basic principle does not change.

The capacitance of a MEMS microphone can then be written as

$$C(P_S) = \frac{\epsilon_0 A}{x(P_S)} = \frac{\epsilon_0 A}{x_0 + \Delta x(P_S)},\tag{1}$$

where A is the area of the smallest capacitor plate and ϵ_0 is the vacuum dielectric permittivity.

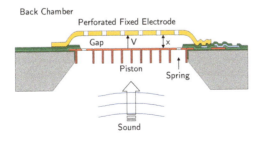

Figure 2. Basic structure and working principle of a MEMS microphone.

Denoting with C_0 the MEMS capacitance in the absence of sound, i.e., when $x = x_0$, and assuming linear the relationship between the sound pressure P_S and the deformation x ($\Delta x = -\kappa \Delta P_S$), which is actually true for $\Delta x \ll x_0$, we can calculate the output signal (ΔV) as a function of ΔP_S. If the MEMS capacitor is initially charged to a fixed voltage V_B, the charge $Q = C_0 V_B$ remains constant, independently of P_S. As a consequence, the capacitance variation due to a sound pressure variation ΔP_S leads to a voltage signal (ΔV) given by

$$\Delta V = \frac{Q}{C(P_S)} - \frac{Q}{C_0} = \frac{Q \Delta x}{\epsilon_0 A} = -\frac{\kappa C_0 V_B \Delta P_S}{\epsilon_0 A} = -\kappa_V \Delta P_S, \tag{2}$$

where κ_V denotes the voltage sensitivity of the microphone.

According to (2), κ_V depends on the bias voltage V_B. Therefore, in order to increase the microphone sensitivity and, hence, the *SNR*, the value of V_B has to be pretty high, typically ranging from 5 V to about 15 V. As a consequence, a charge pump is usually required to generate the desired value of V_B, starting from the standard CMOS power supply voltage (1.8 V, 2.5 V, or 3.3 V).

In practical implementations, a MEMS microphone is not just a capacitor, but some additional parasitic components have to be taken into account. The equivalent circuit of an actual MEMS microphone is shown in Figure 3.

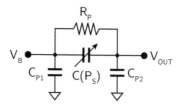

Figure 3. Equivalent circuit of a MEMS microphone.

Besides the variable capacitance $C(P_S)$, the equivalent circuit includes two parasitic capacitances C_{P1} and C_{P2}, connected between each plate of the MEMS microphone and the substrate, as well as a parasitic resistance R_P, connected in parallel to $C(P_S)$. The value of these parasitic components depends on the specific implementation of the microphone, but typically C_{P1} and C_{P2} are of the order of few pF, while R_P is in the GΩ range.

3. MEMS Microphone Interface Circuits

The interface circuit for a MEMS microphone has to read-out the electrical signal, ΔV, and convert it in the digital domain. Digital output is, indeed, a must for MEMS microphones, in order to gain a competitive advantage over ECMs, in terms of area and cost at system level. Therefore, the interface circuit for a MEMS microphone, whose block diagram is shown in Figure 4, typically consists of a preamplifier followed by an A/D converter (ADC). Moreover, for capacitive MEMS microphones, a charge pump is usually required for generating the microphone bias voltage V_B. For piezoelectric MEMS microphones, the bias voltage is not required, but, besides this, the interface circuits are basically the same as for capacitive devices.

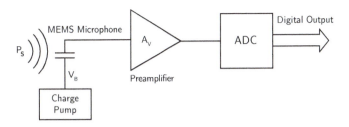

Figure 4. Typical block diagram of the interface circuit for a MEMS microphone.

3.1. Preamplifier

The topology and the functionality of the preamplifier in a MEMS microphone interface circuit has to buffer the microphone output voltage, eventually introducing some gain, providing a suitable signal, with low output impedance, to the subsequent ADC, as shown in Figure 5a. In this case, the input impedance of the preamplifier has to be extremely high (larger than 10 GΩ), in order to guarantee that the charge stored on the microphone capacitance is maintained, while providing, at the same time, a suitable DC bias voltage at the preamplifier input node. The biasing network at the preamplifier input is, therefore, very critical and represents typically the most challenging part of the preamplifier design. The solutions usually adopted to implement R_B are based on inversely biased diodes or switched networks [32]. Resistor R_B introduces a high-pass filter with cut-off frequency $f_{HP} \approx 1/\left(2\pi R_B C_0\right)$, which has to be lower than 20 Hz to avoid loss of signal.

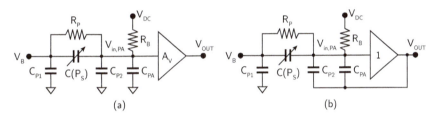

Figure 5. Block diagram of the preamplifier without (**a**) and with (**b**) parasitic capacitance bootstrapping.

The parasitic capacitance at the preamplifier input (C_{PA}) is also particularly important, considering that the output voltage of the microphone ΔV, given by (2), in the presence of parasitic capacitances (both C_{P2} and C_{PA}), is actually attenuated, leading to

$$V_{in,PA} = \Delta V \frac{C_0}{C_0 + C_{P2} + C_{PA}} = -\Delta P_S \frac{\kappa_V C_0}{C_0 + C_{P2} + C_{PA}} \qquad (3)$$

This attenuation can often be quite substantial, thus leading to a degradation of the actual microphone sensitivity and, hence, of the *SNR*. This problem can be mitigated by bootstrapping C_{P2} and, eventually, also C_{PA}, as shown in Figure 5b. In this case, the voltage across the parasitic capacitances is kept constant, independently of the signal, and, therefore, $V_{in,PA} \approx \Delta V$. In order to achieve proper bootstrapping, the gain of the preamplifier (or, at least, of the preamplifier first stage) has to be unitary and, hence,

$$V_{OUT} = -\kappa_V \Delta P_S \qquad (4)$$

Quite often, the overall preamplifier gain is programmable, in order to adapt the microphone output signal range, which can change depending on the used microphone and/or the fabrication tolerances, to the ADC input signal range.

3.2. A/D Converter

The large majority of the ADCs for audio applications are realized with sigma-delta ($\Sigma\Delta$) modulators, in view of their inherent linearity and low power consumption. The main reason that makes $\Sigma\Delta$ modulators particularly suited for audio applications is the relatively small bandwidth of audio signals ($B = 20$ Hz, $\cdots$, 20 kHz), which allows fairly large oversampling ratios, $M = f_S / (2B)$, to be achieved, while maintaining the sampling frequency (f_S) at acceptable values (few MHz). By trading accuracy with speed, $\Sigma\Delta$ modulators achieve *SNR* values larger than 60 dB with simple hardware and small area, considering that the *SNR* of a $\Sigma\Delta$ modulator of order L with N-bit quantizer and oversampling ratio M, is ideally given by [33–35]

$$SNR = \frac{2^{2N} 3 \, (2L+1) \, M^{2L+1}}{2\pi^{2L}} \tag{5}$$

Following this trend, $\Sigma\Delta$ modulators represent the dominant solution for implementing the ADC also in the interface circuits for MEMS microphones [5,7,9–12,36–38].

Audio $\Sigma\Delta$ modulators can be implemented using either continuous-time (CT) or discrete-time (DT) architectures [33,34]. CT $\Sigma\Delta$ modulators represent the most promising solution for minimizing power consumption, since they require operational amplifiers with lower bandwidth with respect to their DT counterparts for the same *SNR*. However, they are more sensitive to clock jitter and process variations. The Schreier figure-of-merit [39], defined as

$$FoM_S = DR + 10 \log \frac{B}{P} \tag{6}$$

B being the bandwidth and P the power consumption, is a useful indicator to compare different ADC solutions. Figure 6 shows the values of FoM_S of ADCs published in the last 20 years as a function of the Nyquist frequency $F_N = 2B$.

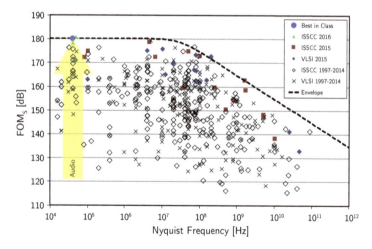

Figure 6. ADC state-of-the-art based on FoM_S from [40].

As expected, the top of class performance in the audio field is achieved with a CT $\Sigma\Delta$ modulator. Moreover, it is possible to verify the trend in the direction of increasing the *DR* while maintaining or reducing the power consumption, as discussed in Section 1.

To understand this evolution of both the architecture and the performance of the ADCs for MEMS microphones, it is useful to consider four actual design examples, which span from the very first experiments, targeting a *DR* of the order of 60–70 dB with a power consumption in the mW range, to the latest top-of-class achievements (*DR* > 100 dB with power consumption lower than 1 mW).

4. Example 1: Third-Order DT ΣΔ Modulator

As a first design example, we consider a DT ΣΔ modulator used in one of the very first MEMS microphone interface circuits [7,41]. In this interface circuit, considering the sampling frequency $f_S = 2.52$ MHz and, hence, the oversampling ratio $M = 63$, according to Equation (5), a third-order ($L = 3$), single-bit ($N = 1$) ΣΔ modulator is sufficient to achieve the required $SNR \geq 60$ dB. The block diagram of the third-order DT ΣΔ modulator is shown in Figure 7.

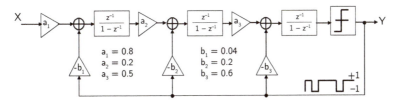

Figure 7. Block diagram of the third-order DT ΣΔ modulator (example 1).

The signal transfer function (*STF*) and the noise transfer function (*NTF*) are given by

$$STF = \frac{0.06z}{(z - 0.92)(z^2 - 1.47z + 0.55)},\tag{7}$$

$$NTF = \frac{(z - 1)^3}{(z - 0.92)(z^2 - 1.47z + 0.55)}\tag{8}$$

respectively.

Figure 8 shows the switched-capacitor (SC) implementation of the ΣΔ modulator.

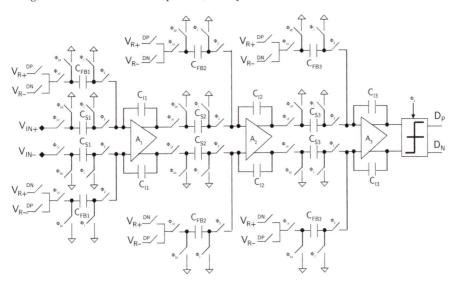

Figure 8. Schematic of the SC implementation of the third-order DT ΣΔ modulator (example 1).

The feedforward and feedback paths are implemented using separate capacitors, thus relaxing the settling requirements of the operational amplifiers. The feedback path contains an extra switch, to select between positive and negative reference voltage (V_{R+} or V_{R-}). The first integrator has reduced output swing, but the capacitors are large to keep the kT/C noise low, while the second and third integrator use smaller capacitors, but the output swing is large. Therefore, all the integrators have almost the same settling requirements for the operational amplifiers. Bottom-plate sampling is used in the whole $\Sigma\Delta$ modulator to minimize the distortion due to charge-injection from switches.

The operational amplifiers used for the integrators are based on a telescopic-cascode topology. The common-mode feedback is realized with an SC network. The comparator used consists of a differential stage with regenerative load, followed by a set–reset flip-flop.

Experimental Results

The interface circuit has been fabricated using a 0.35-μm CMOS technology with four metal and two polysilicon layers. The circuit consumes 210 μA for the analog section and 90 μA for the logic, respectively, leading to an overall power consumption of 1.0 mW with a sampling frequency of 2.52 MHz and a power supply voltage of 3.3 V. The chip area is 3.15 mm^2 (1930 μm × 1630 μm), including pads.

Figure 9 shows the achieved *SNDR* as a function of the input signal amplitude with an input signal frequency of 1 kHz. The peak *SNDR* equal to 61 dB is achieved with an input signal amplitude of −13 dB$_{FS}$, corresponding to a sound pressure of 104 dB$_{SPL}$ for the considered MEMS microphone. By considering both noise and distortion contributions, the achieved *ENOB* is equal to 9.8. The achieved *DR* is 76 dB.

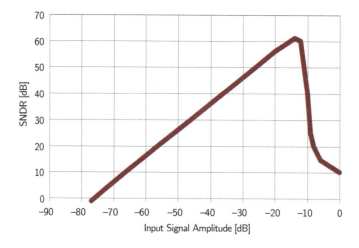

Figure 9. Measured *SNDR* as a function of the input signal amplitude (example 1)

Finally, Table 1 summarizes the most important measured performances.

Table 1. Measured performance summary (example 1).

Parameter	Value
Technology	0.35-μm CMOS
Bandwidth (B)	20 kHz
Dynamic range (DR)	76 dB
Signal-to-noise and distortion ratio ($SNDR$)	61 dB
Effective number of bits ($ENOB$)	9.8
Power supply voltage	3.3 V
ADC power consumption	360 μW
ADC figure of merit (FoM_S)	153 dB
Total power consumption	1 mW

5. Example 2: Second-Order Multi-Bit DT ΣΔ Modulator

The second design example is a MEMS microphone interface circuit again based on DT ΣΔ modulator [12]. Considering a sampling frequency f_S = 2.048 MHz, with a signal bandwidth B = 20 kHz, and hence an oversampling ratio M = 51, according to (5), the required $SNR \geq 80$ dB and a single-bit output stream can be achieved, for example, with a single-bit quantizer (N = 1) and a fourth-order noise shaping (L = 4). However, this solution suffers from instability for large input signals, thus requiring watch-dog circuits in order to guarantee saturation recovery. Moreover, at least four operational amplifiers have to be used to design the loop filter.

Another possible solution is to use a 2-2 multi-stage noise shaping (MASH) ΣΔ modulator [33,34] to achieve the required SNR, while overcoming instability issues. However, this solution does not provide a single-bit output stream because of the additional digital filter required to combine the outputs of the cascaded modulators, and suffers from quantization noise leakage problems, due to mismatches between the analog integrators and the digital filter. Moreover, it still requires four operational amplifiers.

According to (5), the required SNR is also obtained with L = 2 and $3 < N < 4$ (e.g., 12-level quantizer). This solution can be easily designed to be stable even for a large input signal and requires only two operational amplifiers to implement the loop filter. Moreover, multi-bit feedback alleviates the slew-rate requirements of the operational amplifiers. However, this solution does not provide fourth-order noise shaping nor single-bit output stream. These drawbacks can be solved by connecting at the output of the multi-bit, second-order, analog ΣΔ modulator a single-bit, fourth-order, digital ΣΔ modulator, operated at the same sampling frequency f_S, which truncates the multi-bit output down to a single bit and shapes the resulting truncation error with a fourth-order transfer function. The digital, fourth-order ΣΔ modulator is less critical than its analog counterpart, since it can be easily verified under any operating conditions, and, by using sufficiently large word-length in the integrators and a suitable noise transfer function, instability can be avoided. This solution, whose block diagram is shown in Figure 10, is very promising to achieve the specifications of power consumption and resolution of the system. In order to verify the achievable performance with the used ΣΔ modulator architecture and derive the specifications for the building blocks, behavioral simulations, including most of the non-idealities (kT/C noise, jitter, operational amplifier noise, gain, bandwidth and slew rate), have been performed using a dedicated toolbox [35]. The achieved SNR is 82.4 dB, which corresponds to an effective number of bits ($ENOB$) of 13.4.

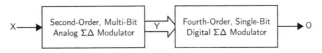

Figure 10. Block diagram of the ΣΔ modulator (example 2).

Several solutions are available in literature to obtain a DT analog second-order ΣΔ modulator [39]. Among them, the second-order ΣΔ modulator architecture, whose block diagram is shown in Figure 11 [42], is particularly suited for the considered application, since, thanks to the feedforward paths from the input of the integrators to the input of the quantizer, the output of the integrators consists of quantization noise only, thus allowing low-performance (and hence low-power) operational amplifiers to be used.

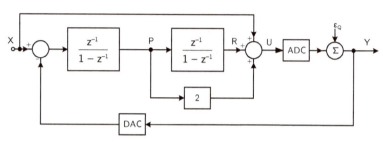

Figure 11. Block diagram of the DT analog second-order ΣΔ modulator (example 2).

The analog ΣΔ modulator consists of two integrators, one adder, a flash ADC, and a multi-bit digital-to-analog converter (DAC). The circuit features $STF = 1$, and

$$NTF = \left(1 - z^{-1}\right)^2,\tag{9}$$

with second-order noise shaping. Both the integrator outputs consist of quantization noise only, whose maximum amplitude is equal to $V_{ref} / (k + 1)$, where V_{ref} is the reference voltage (i.e., the full scale value) and $k = 2^N$ is the number of levels in the quantizer.

Figure 12 shows the SC implementation of the DT analog second-order ΣΔ modulator. The circuit is actually fully-differential, although, for simplicity, Figure 12 shows a single-ended version. An active block has been used to implement the adder before the quantizer, in order to reduce the capacitive load for the two integrators, thus reducing the power consumption. This solution requires an additional operational amplifier but, thanks to the reduced capacitive load, it consumes less power anyway than a solution based on a passive adder.

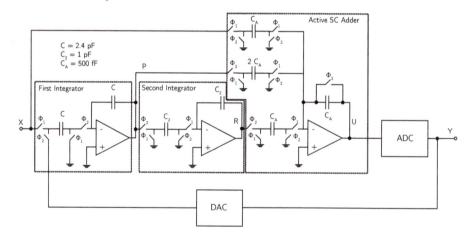

Figure 12. Schematic of the SC implementation of the DT analog second-order ΣΔ modulator (example 2).

The operational amplifiers used for the integrators and the adder are based on a folded-cascode topology. The common-mode feedback is realized with an SC network.

The quantizer (flash ADC) consists of $k = 11$ comparators, thus leading to a 12-level output code. The comparator used in the flash ADC consists of a pre-amplifier followed by a clock-driven regenerative latch. The fully-differential comparison between the input signals and the threshold voltages is performed before the pre-amplification stage by an SC network.

The DAC is realized by splitting the input capacitance C of the first integrator into 12 identical parts, which are alternately connected to $V_{ref,p}$, $V_{ref,n}$ or V_{agnd}, according to the quantizer output.

The block diagram of the DT digital fourth-order, single-bit $\Sigma\Delta$ modulator is shown in Figure 13. Denoting with Y and ϵ_Q the modulator input and the quantization noise, respectively, the modulator output signal O is given by

$$O(z) = Y(z) + \epsilon_Q(z)\frac{(z-1)^2\,(z^2 - 1.99z + 0.99)}{(z^2 - 1.079z + 0.3014)\,(z^2 - 1.794z + 0.8294)} \tag{10}$$

thus leading to a unitary *STF* in the audio band and an *NTF* with fourth-order noise shaping. The coefficients of the $\Sigma\Delta$ modulator are implemented as the sum of no more than two terms, each expressed as a power of 2, thus avoiding the use of multipliers.

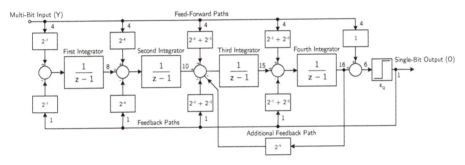

Figure 13. Block diagram of the fourth-order, digital $\Sigma\Delta$ modulator (example 2).

The word-length in the internal registers is 8 bits for the first integrator, 10 bits for the second integrator, 15 bits for the third integrator, 16 bits for the fourth integrator, and 6 bits for the final adder, in order to avoid saturation and truncation, under any operating conditions.

Experimental Results

The interface circuit has been fabricated using a 0.35-µm CMOS technology with four metal and two polysilicon layers. The circuit consumes 215 µA for the analog section and 95 µA for the digital section, respectively, leading to an overall power consumption of 1.0 mW with a clock frequency of 2.048 MHz and a power supply voltage of 3.3 V. The chip area is 3 mm^2 (1755 µm $\times$ 1705 µm), including pads. The full-scale input signal amplitude is equal to the DAC reference voltage ($V_{ref} = V_{ref,p} - V_{ref,n}$), which has been set to $\pm$400 mV, i.e., $V_{in} = 800$ mV peak-to-peak, which, for the considered MEMS microphone, corresponds to about 106 dB$_{SPL}$.

Figure 14 shows the achieved *SNDR* as a function of the input signal amplitude with an input signal frequency of 1 kHz. The peak *SNDR* is equal to 71 dB. By considering both noise and distortion contributions, the achieved *ENOB* is equal to 11.5. The achieved *DR* is 77 dB. The use of a feedforward path in the analog, second-order $\Sigma\Delta$ modulator allows the peak *SNDR* to be achieved for an input signal amplitude as large as -1.8 dB$_{FS}$.

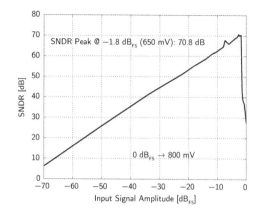

Figure 14. Measured *SNDR* as a function of the input signal amplitude (example 2).

Finally, Table 2 summarizes the most important measured performances.

Table 2. Measured performance summary (example 2).

Parameter	Value
Technology	0.35-μm CMOS
Bandwidth (*B*)	20 kHz
Dynamic range (*DR*)	77 dB
Signal-to-noise and distortion ratio (*SNDR*)	71 dB
Effective number of bits (*ENOB*)	11.5
Power supply voltage	3.3 V
ADC power consumption	760 μW
ADC figure of merit (*FoM$_S$*)	148 dB
Total power consumption	1 mW

6. Example 3: Fourth-Order MASH DT ΣΔ Modulator

The third design example belongs to the new generation of MEMS microphone interface circuits. This interface circuit is based on a reconfigurable MASH 2-2 DT ΣΔ modulator, which can efficiently target different functions and/or applications, as discussed in Section 1 [22,24]. The reconfigurable DT ΣΔ modulator can operate in different modes depending on the target function or application. In particular, it is possible to select the ΣΔ modulatror order (second or fourth), the sampling frequency (768 kHz, 2.4 MHz, or 3.6 MHz), the signal bandwidth (4 kHz or 20 kHz), and the bias current level (50%, 75%, or 100% of the nominal value). Among the several resulting operating modes, the three most common ones are:

- Low-Power (LP) mode (second order, $f_S = 768$ kHz, 4-kHz bandwidth, 50% bias current level);
- Standard (ST) mode (fourth order, $f_S = 2.4$ MHz, 20-kHz bandwidth, 75% bias current level);
- High-Resolution (HR) mode (fourth order, $f_S = 3.6$ MHz, 20-kHz bandwidth, 100% bias current level).

The block diagram of the ΣΔ modulator is shown in Figure 15. It consists of two cascaded second-order stages and a digital recombination filter. The MASH topology has been selected for several reasons. Firstly, it can be made unconditionally stable for input signals bounded within the full-scale, value independently of the operating mode. Moreover, in the presence of accidental signal overload beyond the full-scale value, it guarantees fast recovery. The inherent stability feature allows the *SNR* to be maintained close to the ideal value given by Equation (5).

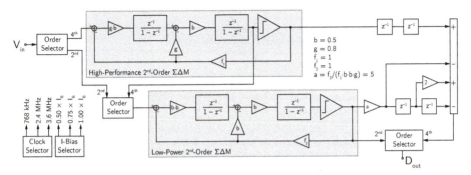

Figure 15. Block diagram of the reconfigurable DT MASH ΣΔ modulator (example 3).

With three selectors, it is possible to reconfigure the ΣΔ modulator in a fourth-order or in a second-order topology. When the fourth-order topology is selected, both stages are active, the input is applied to the first stage, the output of the second integrator of the first stage is fed into the second stage, and the multi-bit output is read after the digital recombination network, which merges the bitstreams produced by the two stages. On the other hand, when the second-order topology is selected, only the second stage is active (while the first stage is turned-off), and the input is applied directly to the second stage from which the single-bit output is read.

The first and the second stages of the DT MASH ΣΔ modulator structure are topologically identical. The fully-differential SC implementation of each second-order stage is shown in Figure 16.

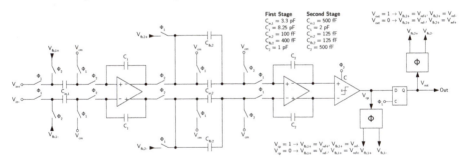

Figure 16. Schematic of the SC implementation of a single stage of the reconfigurable DT MASH ΣΔ modulator (example 3).

In each second-order ΣΔ modulator stage of the MASH structure, the coefficients are optimized to ensure that the integrator output swing remains within the allowed range under any operating conditions. The coefficients of the digital recombination filter have, then, been set accordingly, in order to properly cancel the first-stage quantization noise from the global ΣΔ modulator output in the operating modes featuring fourth-order noise shaping.

The noise requirements of the second stage are relaxed with respect to the first stage both with fourth-order noise shaping (when the second-stage requirements are reduced by the first-stage gain) and with second-order noise shaping (when lower target specification are required). The softened noise requirements for the second stage are exploited for reducing the capacitance values and the bias current with respect to the first stage. In the same way, inside each stage, the second integrator is designed with lower noise performance (i.e., lower capacitance values and lower bias current) with respect to the first integrator.

Experimental Results

The reconfigurable MASH SC ΣΔ modulator has been fabricated in a 0.18-μm CMOS process. The chip area is 0.5×0.8 mm^2, including the ΣΔ modulator, the reference buffers, and an LDO regulator to stabilize the power supply voltage. The reference voltages V_{ref+} and V_{ref-} are ±500 mV around the common mode voltage $V_{cm} = 850$ mV (i. e. the ΣΔ modulator full-scale input signal is 2 $V_{pp,diff}$). These reference voltages are constant independently of the operating mode (they are actually produced by a bandgap reference circuit shared with other blocks in the complete audio module).

Figure 17 shows the measured *SNDR* of the ΣΔ modulator as a function of the input signal amplitude at 1 kHz in the three main modes of operation (HR, ST, and LP).

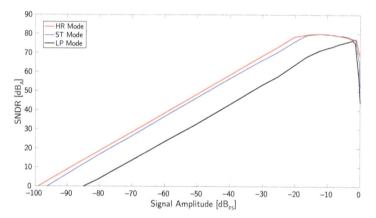

Figure 17. Measured *SNDR* as a function of the input signal amplitude in the three main operating modes (example 3).

The circuit achieves a *DR* of 99 dB in HR mode, 96 dB in ST mode, and 85 dB in LP mode. The peak *SNDR* is limited in all operating modes to about 80 dB by the harmonic distortion of the signal source available for the measurements (in the considered application, the *SNDR* for sound pressures larger than 100 dB$_{SPL}$ is anyway limited to about 75 dB by the harmonic distortion of the microphone).

The achieved *DR* and power consumption of the reconfigurable ΣΔ modulator for all the available operating modes are reported in Table 3, demonstrating the flexibility of the device.

Table 3. *DR* and power consumption in the different operating modes (example 3).

f_S [MHz]	B [kHz]	Second-Order Single-Bit Output		Fourth-Order Multi-Bit Output	
		DR [dB]	*P* [mW]	*DR* [dB]	*P* [mW]
0.768	4	85 (LP)	0.10	99	0.48
	20	59		97	
2.4	4	95	0.15	98	0.73
	20	77		96 (ST)	
3.6	4	96	0.20	102	0.97
	20	85		99 (HR)	

Finally, Table 4 summarizes the the most important measured performances.

Table 4. Measured performance summary (example 3).

Parameter	HR Mode	ST Mode	LP Mode
Bandwidth (*B*) [kHz]	20	20	4
Clock frequency (*f_S*) [MHz]	3.6	2.4	0.768
Noise-shaping order (*L*)	4th	4th	2nd
Dynamic range (*DR*) [dB]	99	96	85
ADC power consumption [mW] §	0.97	0.73	0.10
ADC figure of merit (*FoM_S*) [dB]	172	170	161
Total power consumption [mW] §	1.33	1.01	0.18
Signal-to-noise and distortion ratio (*SNDR*) [dB] *		80	
Power supply voltage [V]		1.7–3.6	
Technology		0.18-µm CMOS	

* Limited by the harmonic distortion of the available signal source; § Measured with a power supply voltage equal to 1.8 V.

7. Example 4: Third-Order CT ΣΔ Modulator

The last example, one of the top-of-class interface circuits for MEMS microphones, is based on a third-order, multi-bit CT ΣΔ modulator [23]. The block diagram of the ΣΔ modulator is illustrated in Figure 18.

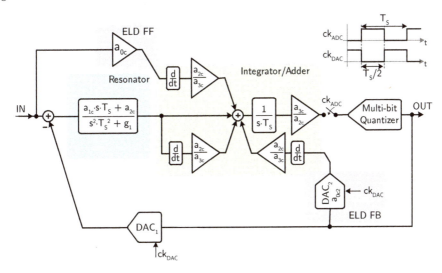

Figure 18. Block diagram of the third-order CT ΣΔ modulator (example 4).

The loop filter consists of a resonator (second-order transfer function) followed by an integrator. A local feedback DAC around the quantizer (DAC$_2$) and a dedicated feedforward path are used for compensating the excess loop delay (ELD). The feedforward paths of the loop filter and the local ELD feedback are differentiated and added at the input of the integrator, in order to avoid an active adder at the input of the quantizer. The multi-bit quantizer drives a 15-level DAC (DAC$_1$) with dynamic element matching (DEM) to close the main feedback loop of the CT ΣΔ modulator.

The schematic of the active-RC implementation of the CT ΣΔ modulator is shown in Figure 19.

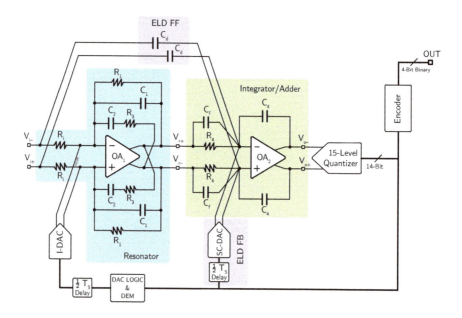

Figure 19. Schematic of the active-RC implementation of the third-order CT ΣΔ modulator (example 4).

The resonator is implemented using a single operational amplifier and no active adder is used at the input of the quantizer, thus requiring only two operational amplifiers for implementing the third-order loop-filter transfer function. The local feedback DAC for ELD compensation is implemented with an SC structure, whereas the main feedback DAC is realized with a three-level (−1, 0, +1) current-steering topology, which guarantees minimum noise for small input signals. Indeed, with the three-level topology, the unused DAC current sources are not connected to the resonator input and, hence, they do not contribute to the CT ΣΔ modulator noise. The multi-bit quantizer is realized with 14 identical differential comparators and a resistive divider from the analog power supply for generating the threshold voltages.

The values of the passive components used for implementing the CT ΣΔ modulator are summarized in Table 5. The value of R_i has been chosen as low as 47 kΩ to fulfill the thermal noise requirements, while R_1, R_3, R_4, C_1, C_2, C_f, and C_4 are obtained consequently to achieve the desired CT ΣΔ modulator coefficients. Eventually, resistors R_i can be removed if the preamplifier is realized with a transconductor which provides directly an output current. Both operational amplifiers are realized with a two-stage, Miller compensated topology in which transistor size and bias current are sized to fulfill the noise requirements (the values in the second operational amplifier are scaled with respect to the first one, since its noise contribution is negligible).

Table 5. Passive component values in the third-order ΣΔ modulator (example 4).

Resistor	Value	Capacitor	Value
R_i	47 kΩ	C_1	18.5 pF
R_1	5.7 MΩ	C_2	18.7 pF
R_3	57 kΩ	C_f	2.1 pF
R_4	1 MΩ	C_4	1 pF

Experimental Results

The third-order CT ΣΔ modulator has been fabricated using a 0.16-μm CMOS technology. The chip area is 0.21-mm².

Figure 20 shows the measured *SNDR* as a function of the input signal amplitude at 1 kHz. The full-scale input signal (0 dB$_{FS}$) corresponds to 1 V$_{rms}$ differential. The achieved *DR* is 106 dB (A-weighted), corresponding to an *ENOB* > 17 bits, whereas the peak *SNDR* is 91.3 dB. The change of slope in the *SNDR* curve for input signal amplitudes larger than −17 dB$_{FS}$ is due to the increased current-steering DAC noise when more than one three-level DAC element is used (acceptable for the microphone application, where the performance for large input signals is limited by the microphone itself).

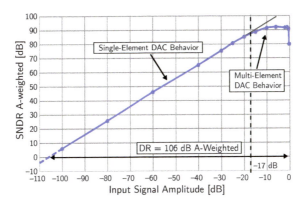

Figure 20. Measured *SNDR* as a function of the input signal amplitude (example 4).

The analog section of the third-order ΣΔ modulator consumes 350 μW, while the digital blocks (i.e., DEM and thermometer-to-binary converter) consume 40 μW, both from a 1.6-V power supply and during conversion. The achieved value of *FoM$_S$* is 180 dB, which is among the highest reported for audio ΣΔ modulators. Table 6 summarizes the achieved performance.

Table 6. Measured performance summary (example 4).

Parameter	Value
Technology	0.16-μm CMOS
Bandwidth (*B*)	20 kHz
Dynamic range (*DR*)	103.1 dB
Dynamic range A-weighted (*DR$_A$*)	106 dB
Signal-to-noise and distortion ratio (*SNDR*)	91.3 dB
Effective number of bits (*ENOB*)	17
Power supply voltage	1.6 V
ADC power consumption	390 μW
ADC figure of merit (*FoM$_S$*)	180 dB

8. Conclusions

Looking at the performance evolution in the four reported MEMS microphone interface circuit design examples, summarized in Table 7, it appears clearly that in the last decade the trend has been in the direction of increasing the *SNDR* and the *DR*, while maintaining the power consumption in the hundreds of μW range, with the goal of reaching Hi-Fi audio quality (*DR* > 100 dB) in portable devices, eventually introducing some reconfigurability to tackle scenarios, such as voice commands, where a power consumption lower than 100 µW is required. This trend, obviously is reflected in a constant increase of *FoM_S*.

Table 7. Evolution of MEMS microphone interface circuits

Parameter	Example 1	Example 2	Example 3 LP	HR	Example 4
Year	2008	2011	2015		2016
Technology	0.35 µm	0.35 µm	0.18 µm		0.16 µm
Bandwidth (*B*) [kHz]	20	20	4	20	20
Noise-shaping order (*L*)	3rd	4th	2th	4nd	3rd
Dynamic range (*DR*) [dB]	76	77	85	99	103
			Evolution →		
ADC power consumption [mW]	0.36	0.76	0.10	0.97	0.39
ADC figure of merit (*FoM_S*) [dB]	153	151	161	172	180
			Evolution →		
Power supply voltage [V]	3.3	3.3	1.7–3.6		1.6

Further improvements of the audio quality beyond 110-dB *DR* are not desirable nor necessary, since the physical limitations in the microphone itself (such as Brownian noise) would anyway prevent the exploitation of such performance at system level. Therefore, the next goal in the development of MEMS microphone interface circuits is toward the reduction of the power consumption below 100 µW, while maintaining the *DR* performance. Indeed, in this direction, there is still a lot of space for improvements, especially by exploiting the intrinsic features of the audio signals to dynamically adapt the power consumption. Voice activity detection, adaptive biasing, and tracking ADCs are some of the topics being investigated to achieve this target.

Author Contributions: The authors contributed equally to this work.

Funding: This research received no external funding.

Acknowledgments: The authors wish to acknowledge Davide Cattin, Fabrizio Conso, Marco De Blasi, Andrea Fornasari, Massimo Gottardi, Marco Grassi, Syed Arsalan Jawed, Nicola Massari, Luca Picolli, Gino Rocca, Andrea Simoni, and Lei Zou for their contributions to the design of the integrated circuits.

Conflicts of Interest: The authors declare no conflict of interest.

References

1. Hsu, Y.C.; Chen, J.Y.; Wang, C.H.; Liao, L.P.; Chou, W.C.; Wu, C.Y.; Mukherjee, T. Issues in path toward integrated acoustic sensor system on chip. In Proceedings of the IEEE International Conference on Sensors, Lecce, Italy, 26–29 October 2008; pp. 585–588.
2. Malcovati, P.; Maloberti, F. Interface circuitry and microsystems. In *MEMS: A Practical Guide to Design, Analysis and Applications*; Korvink, J., Paul, O., Eds.; Springer: Dordrecht, The Netherlands, 2005; pp. 901–942.
3. Yole Développement. Available online: http://www.yole.fr/AcousticMEMS_AudioSolutions_Overview.aspx (accessed on 15 March 2018).
4. Van der Zwan, E.J.; Dijkmans, E.C. A 0.2-mW CMOS ΣΔ modulator for speech coding with 80-dB dynamic range. *IEEE J. Solid-State Circuits* **1996**, *31*, 1873–1880. [CrossRef]
5. Bajdechi, O.; Huijsing, J.H. A 1.8-V ΔΣ modulator interface for an electret microphone with on-chip reference. *IEEE J. Solid-State Circuits* **2002**, *37*, 279–285. [CrossRef]
6. Pernici, S.; Stevenazzi, F.; Nicollini, G. Fully integrated voiceband codec in a standard digital CMOS technology. *IEEE J. Solid-State Circuits* **2004**, *39*, 1331–1334. [CrossRef]

7.   Jawed, S.A.; Cattin, D.; Gottardi, M.; Massari, N.; Baschirotto, A.; Simoni, A. A 828-μW 1.8-V 80-dB dynamic-range readout interface for a MEMS capacitive microphone. In Proceedings of the 34th European Solid-State Circuit Conference (ESSCIRC), Edinburgh, Scotland, 15–19 September 2008; pp. 442–445.

8.   Citakovic, J.; Hovesten, P.F.; Rocca, G.; van Halteren, A.; Rombach, P.; Stenberg, L.J.; Andreani, P.; Bruun, E. A compact CMOS MEMS microphone with 66-dB SNR. In Proceedings of the IEEE International Solid-State Circuit Conference Digest of Technical Papers (ISSCC), San Francisco, CA, USA, 8–12 February 2009; pp. 350–351.

9.   Chiang, C.T.; Huang, Y.C. A 14-bit oversampled ΔΣ modulator for silicon condenser microphones. In Proceedings of the IEEE Instrumentation and Measurement Technology Conference (IMTC), Singapore, 5–7 May 2009; pp. 1055–1058.

10. Le, H.B.; Lee, S.G.; Ryu, S.T. A regulator-free 84-dB DR audio-band ADC for compact digital microphones. In Proceedings of the IEEE Asian Solid-State Circuit Conference (ASSCC), Beijing, China, 8–10 November 2010; pp. 1–4.

11. Zare-Hoseini, H.; Kale, I.; Richard, C.S.M. A low-power continuous-time ΔΣ modulator for electret microphone applications. In Proceedings of the IEEE Asian Solid-State Circuit Conference (ASSCC), Beijing, China, 8–10 November 2010; pp. 1–4.

12. Picolli, L.; Grassi, M.; Fornasari, A.; Malcovati, P. A 1.0-mW, 71-dB SNDR, fourth-order ΣΔ interface circuit for MEMS microphones. *Analog Integr. Circuits Signal Process.* **2011**, *66*, 223–233. [CrossRef]

13. Badami, K.M.H.; Lauwereins, S.; Meert, W.; Verhelst, M. A 90-nm CMOS, 6-μW Power-Proportional Acoustic Sensing Frontend for Voice Activity Detection. *IEEE J. Solid-State Circuits* **2016**, *51*, 291–302.

14. Park, H.; Nam, K.Y.; Su, D.K.; Vleugels, K.; Wooley, B.A. A 0.7-V 870-μW digital-audio CMOS ΣΔ modulator. *IEEE J. Solid-State Circuits* **2009**, *44*, 1078–1088. [CrossRef]

15. Yang, Z.; Yao, L.; Lian, Y. A 0.5-V 35-μW 85-dB DR double-sampled ΔΣ modulator for audio applications. *IEEE J. Solid-State Circuits* **2012**, *47*, 722–735. [CrossRef]

16. Christen, T. A 15-bit 140-μW scalable-bandwidth inverter-based ΔΣ modulator for a MEMS microphone with digital output. *IEEE J. Solid-State Circuits* **2013**, *48*, 1605–1614. [CrossRef]

17. Yang, Y.Q.; Chokhawala, A.; Alexander, M.; Melanson, J.; Hester, D. A 114-dB 68-mW chopper-stabilized stereo multibit audio ADC in 5.62 mm². *IEEE J. Solid-State Circuits* **2003**, *38*, 2061–2068. [CrossRef]

18. Nguyen, K.; Adams, R.; Sweetland, K.; Chen, H. A 106-dB SNR hybrid oversampling analog-to-digital converter for digital audio. *IEEE J. Solid-State Circuits* **2005**, *40*, 2408–2415. [CrossRef]

19. Choi, M.Y.; Lee, S.N.; You, S.B.; Yeum, W.S.; Park, H.J.; Kim, J.W.; Lee, H.S. A 101-dB SNR hybrid ΔΣ audio ADC using post-integration time control. In Proceedings of the IEEE Custom Integrated Circuit Conference (CICC), San Jose, CA, USA, 21–24 September 2008; pp. 89–92.

20. Kim, Y.G.; Cho, M.H.; Kim, K.D.; Kwon, J.K.; Kim, J.D. A 105.5-dB, 0.49-mm² audio ΣΔ modulator using chopper stabilization and fully randomized DWA. In Proceedings of the IEEE Custom Integrated Circuit Conference (CICC), San Jose, CA, USA, 21–24 September 2008; pp. 503–506.

21. Luo, H.; Han, Y.; Cheung, R.C.C.; Liu, X.; Cao, T. A 0.8-V 230-μW 98-dB DR inverter-based ΣΔ modulator for audio applications. *IEEE J. Solid-State Circuits* **2013**, *48*, 2430–2441. [CrossRef]

22. Grassi, M.; Conso, F.; Rocca, G.; Malcovati, P.; Baschirotto, A. A multi-mode SC audio ΣΔ modulator for MEMS microphones with reconfigurable power consumption, noise-shaping order, and DR. In Proceedings of the European Solid-State Circuit Conference (ESSCIRC), Lausanne, Switzerland, 12–15 September 2016; pp. 245–248.

23. De Berti, C.; Malcovati, P.; Crespi, L.; Baschirotto, A. A 106-dB A-weighted DR low-power continuous-time ΣΔ modulator for MEMS microphones. *IEEE J. Solid-State Circuits* **2016**, *51*, 1607–1618. [CrossRef]

24. Zou, L.; Rocca, G.; De Blasi, M.; Grassi, M.; Malcovati, P.; Baschirotto, A. ΣΔ ADC based adaptive readout ASIC for digital audio sensor. *Analog Integr. Circuits Signal Process.* **2017**, *92*, 383–392. [CrossRef]

25. Je, S.S.; Kim, J.H.; Kozicki, M.N.; Chae, J.S. A directional capacitive MEMS microphone using nano-electrodeposits. In Proceedings of the IEEE International Conference on Micro-Electro-Mechanical Systems (MEMS), Sorrento, Italy, 25–29 January 2009; pp. 96–99.

26. Weigold, J.W.; Brosnihan, T.J.; Bergeron, J.; Zhang, X. A MEMS condenser microphone for consumer applications. In Proceedings of the IEEE International Conference on Micro-Electro-Mechanical Systems (MEMS), Istanbul, Turkey, 22–26 January 2006; pp. 86–89.

27. Bergqvist, J.; Gobet, J. Capacitive microphone with a surface micromachined backplate using electroplating technology. *IEEE/ASME J. Microelectromech. Syst.* **1994**, *3*, 69–75. [CrossRef]

28. Kasai, T.; Sato, S.; Conti, S.; Padovani, I.; David, F.; Uchida, Y.; Takahashi, T.; Nishio, H. Novel concept for a MEMS microphone with dual channels for an ultrawide dynamic range. In Proceedings of the IEEE International Conference on Micro-Electro-Mechanical Systems (MEMS), Cancun, Mexico, 23–27 January 2011; pp. 605–608.

29. Leinenbach, C.; van Teeffelen, K.; Laermer, F.; Seidel, H. A new capacitive type MEMS microphone. In Proceedings of the IEEE International Conference on Micro-Electro-Mechanical Systems (MEMS), Hong Kong, China, 24–28 January 2010; pp. 659–662.

30. Martin, D.T.; Liu, J.; Kadirvel, K.; Fox, R.M.; Sheplak, M.; Nishida, T. A micromachined dual-backplate capacitive microphone for aeroacoustic measurements. *IEEE/ASME J. Microelectromech. Syst.* **2007**, *16*, 1289–1302. [CrossRef]

31. Zou, Q.B.; Li, Z.J.; Liu, L.T. Design and fabrication of silicon condenser microphone using corrugated diaphragm technique. *IEEE/ASME J. Microelectromech. Syst.* **1996**, *5*, 197–204.

32. Croce, M.; De Berti, C.; Crespi, L.; Malcovati, P.; Baschirotto, A. MEMS microphone fully-integrated CMOS cap-less preamplifiers. In Proceedings of the IEEE Ph.D. Research in Microelectronics and Electronics (PRIME), Giardini Naxos, Italy, 12–15 June 2017; pp. 37–40.

33. Temes, G.C.; Schreier, R.; Norsworthy, S.R. $\Delta\Sigma$ *Data Converters*; IEEE Press: New York, NY, USA, 1996.

34. Maloberti, F. *Data Converters*; Springer: Dordrecht, The Netherlands, 2007.

35. Malcovati, P.; Brigati, S.; Francesconi, F.; Maloberti, F.; Cusinato, P.; Baschirotto, A. Behavioral modeling of switched-capacitor $\Sigma\Delta$ modulators. *IEEE Trans. Circuits Syst. Part I Fundam. Theory Appl.* **2003**, *50*, 352–364. [CrossRef]

36. Deligoz, I.; Naqvi, S.R.; Copani, T.; Kiaei, S.; Bakkaloglu, B.; Je, S.S.; Chae, J.S. A MEMS-based power-scalable hearing aid analog front-end. *IEEE Trans. Biomed. Circuits Syst.* **2011**, *5*, 201–213. [CrossRef] [PubMed]

37. Lu, C.; Lemkin, M.; Boser, B.E. A monolithic surface micromachined accelerometer with digital output. *IEEE J. Solid-State Circuits* **1995**, *30*, 1367–1373. [CrossRef]

38. Wu, J.F.; Carley, L.R. Electromechanical $\Delta\Sigma$ modulation with high-Q micromechanical accelerometers and pulse density modulated force feedback. *IEEE Trans. Circuits Syst. Part I Regul. Pap.* **2006**, *53*, 274–287.

39. Schreier, R.; Temes, G.C. *Understanding $\Delta\Sigma$ Data Converters*; Wiley-Interscience: New York, NY, USA, 2005.

40. Murman, B. ADC Performance Survey 1997–2018. Available online: http://web.stanford.edu/~murmann/adcsurvey.html (accessed on 17 February 2018).

41. Jawed, S.A.; Cattin, D.; Massari, N.; Gottardi, M.; Baschirotto, A. A MEMS microphone interface with force-balancing and charge-control. In Proceedings of the IEEE Ph.D. Research in Microelectronics and Electronics (PRIME), Istanbul, Turkey, 22–25 June 2008; pp. 97–100.

42. Kwon, S.; Maloberti, F. A 14-mW multi-bit $\Sigma\Delta$ modulator with 82-dB SNR and 86-dB DR for ADSL2+. In Proceedings of the IEEE International Solid-State Circuit Conference Digest of Technical Papers (ISSCC), San Francisco, CA, USA, 6–9 February 2006; pp. 68–69.

Article

Chopper-Stabilized Instrumentation Amplifier with Automatic Frequency Tuning Loop

Chen-Mao Wu [1], Hsiao-Chin Chen [2], Ming-Yu Yen [2,*] and San-Ching Yang [3]

[1]   Asmedia Technology Inc., New Taipei 231, Taiwan; alexwuee2b@gmail.com
[2]   Department of Electrical Engineering, National Taiwan University of Science and Technology,
       Taipei 10607, Taiwan; hcchen@mail.ntust.edu.tw
[3]   Inventec Corporation, Taipei 11107, Taiwan; m10207414@mail.ntust.edu.tw
*   Correspondence: d10207401@mail.ntust.edu.tw; Tel.: +886-2-2733-3141 (ext. 7399)

Received: 14 May 2018; Accepted: 29 May 2018; Published: 8 June 2018

Abstract: A variable-gain chopper-stabilized instrumentation amplifier (chopper IA), which employs a low pass filter (LPF) to attenuate the up-converted noise at the chopping frequency, is presented. The circuit is designed and fabricated with Taiwan Semiconductor Manufacturing Company (TSMC) (Hsinchu, Taiwan) 0.18 μm complementary metal-oxide-semiconductor (CMOS) technology. Consuming 1.1 mW from a 1.2 V supply voltage, the chopper IA achieves a variable gain of 20.7–48.5 dB, with a minimum bandwidth of 6.7 kHz and a common-mode rejection ratio (CMRR) of 95 dB below 10 kHz. By using the chopper technique, the input-referred noise of the chopper IA can be reduced to 0.28 μVrms (0~96 kHz), with a chopping frequency of 83.3 kHz. An automatic frequency tuning loop (ATL) is employed to adjust the corner frequency of the LPF dynamically so that the frequency ratio between the chopping frequency and the LPF corner frequency is 8.3, ensuring a noise reduction of 36.7 dB.

Keywords: automatic frequency tuning loop; chopper technique; instrumentation amplifier; low-pass filter

---

1. Introduction

To meet a variety of healthcare demands, physiological signal acquisition can be performed by implantable, wearable, or portable monitoring systems [1,2]. Recently, systems that can monitor physiological signals, e.g., electroencephalography (EEG), electrocardiography (ECG), blood pressure and glucose, have been proposed and demonstrated [3–5]. Chopper IAs are widely adopted in these systems for their advantageous low noise, high input impedance, and high common mode rejection ratio (CMRR).

The chopper modulation operation is describeted as follows [6]: The bandwidth of the signal is assumed to be less than half the chopping frequency. The input chopper up-converts the signal to the chopping frequency and its odd harmonics, and then delivers it to the amplifier. After amplification, the signal is then down-converted to its original band by the output chopper. Because the DC offset and noise only go through the chopper modulation once, they are up-converted to the chopping frequency and its odd harmonics. The low-pass filter (LPF) then attenuates the up-converted noise. The amount of noise reduction depends on the ratio of the LPF corner frequency to the chopping frequency. However, both the corner frequency of the LPF and the chopping frequency may change due to process variations, which can diminish the amount of noise reduction.

In this work, strong correlation is built up between the corner frequency of the LPF and the chopping frequency so that the noise reduction is not affected by process variations. The rest of the paper is organized as follows. The system architecture and the way that the chopper IA cooperates with the automatic frequency tuning loop (ATL) to achieve the above-mentioned goal is introduced in

Section 2. The design of the building blocks is addressed in Section 3. The measurement results are reported in Section 4. Finally, this work is summarized in Section 5.

2. System Architecture

A block diagram of the proposed chopper IA, which employs an ATL to control the corner frequency of the LPF for noise-reduction, is shown in Figure 1. CLK_chop is the chopping signal and CLK_ATL is the reference clock signal of the ATL. The former is generated from the configuration of an on-chip ring oscillator followed by a divide-by-12 circuit, while the latter is generated from the configuration of the same ring oscillator followed by a divide-by-25 circuit. The chopping frequency is represented by f_chop, and the frequency of the ATL reference clock, by f_ATL. Note that the corner frequency of the LPF is equal to one fourth of f_ATL. In this way, the ratio between the chopping frequency f_chop and the LPF corner frequency is always 8.3, even though the oscillating frequency of the ring oscillator changes with process variations. As a result, the LPF ensures an attenuation of 36.7 dB at the chopping frequency to provide adequate noise reduction in the chopper IA. In this work, an on-chip ring oscillator at 1 MHz is implemented. Therefore, the chopping signal of 83.33 kHz is delivered to the chopper IA, while the reference clock of 40 kHz is delivered to the ATL. During the operation, the input of the LPF is first connected to the divide-by-four circuit to form the frequency tuning loop for corner frequency calibration. After the calibration is completed, the input of the LPF is connected to the chopper IA for noise reduction.

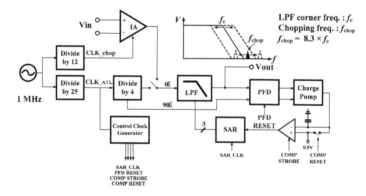

Figure 1. Block diagram of the proposed chopper IA with automatic frequency tuning loop (ATL).

In addition to the LPF, the ATL consists of a divide-by-four circuit, a phase frequency detector (PFD), a charge pump (CP), a comparator and a successive approximation register (SAR) [7,8]. The divide-by-four circuit generates a pair of quadrature signals at 10 kHz, namely, signals with 90° phase difference. In Figure 1, the one that is sent to the LPF is defined as the 0° signal and the other is defined as the 90° signal. When the 0° signal passes though the LPF, the filter introduces a frequency-dependent phase delay. Theoretically, the introduced phase delay should be 90° at the corner frequency of the LPF. Therefore, the frequency tuning/calibration can be performed by measuring the introduced phase delay. There are three key steps in each tuning cycle. First, the output signal of the LPF, the 0° signal with introduced phase delay, is compared with the 90° signal in the PFD. Secondly, the PFD output signals modulate the charge/discharge currents of CP, and the CP output is compared with a reference voltage of 0.9 V in the comparator to deliver a digital output. Then, the SAR logic sets one bit of the 3-bit control code of the LPF in accordance with this digital output signal. It takes three tuning cycles to complete the frequency tuning. Ideally, the Sallen-Key LPF would exhibit the corner frequency of 10 kHz after the frequency tuning.

3. Circuit Design

3.1. Chopper Instrumentation Amplifier: Chopper IA

The two-stage variable-gain chopper IA is developed from a difference amplifier, as depicted in Figure 2 [9]. The variable-gain function is realized by a switch-resistor array and a 3-to-8 decoder, where a unit resistor of 1.14 kΩ is adopted and the maximum resistance is 333 kΩ. The chopper stabilization technique is performed by using two chopper-stabilized operational amplifiers, OP1 and OP2, in the first stage because the noise of the first stage is most critical [9].

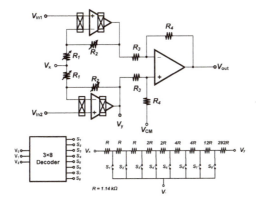

Figure 2. Tunable gain chopper IA [9].

3.1.1. Chopper Operational Amplifier

A schematic of the chopper-stabilized operational amplifier is shown in Figure 3 [9]. As previously mentioned, the noise performance of a two-stage amplifier is dominated in the first stage. If the noise origin of the operational amplifiers in the first stage can be removed, the noise performance of the IA can be significantly improved. The chopper modulator at the input, represented by chopper1, translates the input signal from its original band to the chopping frequency. The other two chopper modulators, chopper2 P-type and chopper2 N-type, then translate the desired signal back to its original band while converting the flicker noise, DC offsets, or noises well below the chopping frequency to the chopping frequency.

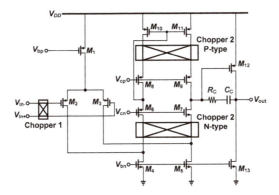

Figure 3. Chopper operational amplifier [9].

3.1.2. Chopper Modulator

The configuration of the chopper modulator and the switch implementation are shown in Figure 4a,b, respectively. To deal with imperfections such as the charge injection and clock feedthrough, dummies are added to the switches at both the sources and drains. When the switches are off, the channel charges are canceled by the dummies to prevent an electric potential error at the output. The switches are driven by non-overlapping clocks $\phi1$ and $\phi2$. During the operation, the input signals at nodes in1 and in2 are alternatively directed to either the node out1 or out2.

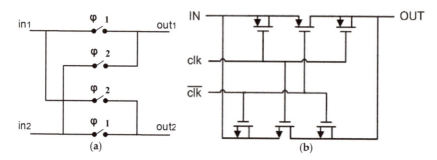

Figure 4. (a) Chopper modulation topology; (b) Switch topology.

The non-overlapping clock generator is shown in Figure 5a, and the waveform of the non-overlapping clock signals $\phi1$ and $\phi2$ is shown in Figure 5b. The non-overlapping clock generator is used to provide the required clocks $\phi1$ and $\phi2$ for the chopper modulator. The signal ϕ_{chop} is a square wave generated from the configuration of the on-chip ring oscillator followed by a divide-by-12 circuit, as previously mentioned. Notably, $\phi1$ and $\phi2$ need to be a pair of non-overlapping clock signals so that the switches driven by different clock signals are not turned on simultaneously. The inverting clock signals are also generated to control the dummy switches. The multi-inverter buffer stage is adopted to boost the driving capability of the clock signals.

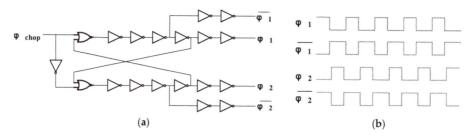

Figure 5. (a) Non-overlapping clock generator; (b) Non-overlapping clock signals.

The input-referred noise simulation results are obtained from the chopper IA before and after the chopper modulator are activated, as shown in Figure 6. The input-referred noise is greatly reduced after the chopper modulator is activated, with the chopping clock at 83.3 kHz. When the chopper modulator is activated, the input-referred noise at 100 Hz and 1 kHz are 32.2 nV/$\sqrt{Hz}$ and 27.9 nV/$\sqrt{Hz}$, respectively. The transient simulation is also performed, as shown in Figure 7. A 1 kHz differential signal, with a DC level of 600 mV and an amplitude of 0.5 mV, is applied at the input of the chopper IA. According to the simulation results, the output signals exhibit ignorable distortion, where the total harmonic distortions observed at the IA output node and LPF output node are 74.6 dB and 51.6 dB, respectively.

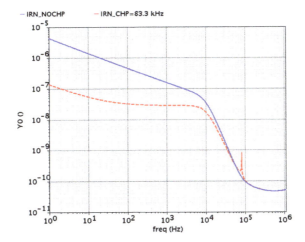

Figure 6. Input-referred noises of the chopper IA before (red dot line) and after (blue solid line) the chopper modulator is activated.

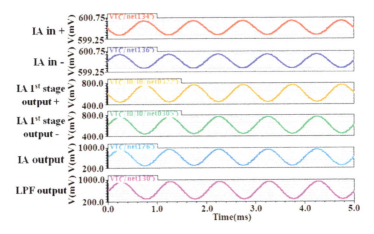

Figure 7. Transient simulation of the chopper IA.

3.2. Sallen-Key Low Pass Filter

As the last stage in the chopper IA, the LPF attenuates the up-converted noise at the chopping frequency. A schematic of the Sallen-Key LPF [10], where both variable capacitors C1 and C2 are realized by 3-bit cap-arrays and R1–2 = 1 MΩ, is shown in Figure 8a. The schematic of the cap-array is shown in Figure 8b, where the capacitance of a unit capacitor is 104.0 fF. With a 3-bit binary-to-thermometer decoder, the LPF can be operated in 8 modes, where the capacitors C1 and C2 can be varied from 14.6 pF to 29.7 pF and 7.3 pF to 14.9 pF, respectively. The frequency response simulation results of the LPF are shown in Figure 9, where 8 different corner frequencies are realized. According to the simulation results, the corner frequency of the LPF can be varied from 6.9 kHz to 13.6 kHz with a step size of 0.8~1 kHz.

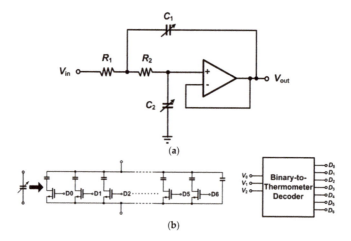

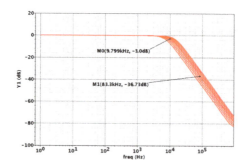

Figure 8. (**a**) Sallen-Key low-pass filter; (**b**) Cap-array schematic.

Figure 9. Frequency response simulation results of the low pass filter (LPF).

3.3. Divide-by-Four Circuit

The divide-by-four circuit is used to generate the required quadrate signals. The D flip-flop topology is shown in Figure 10a. The nodes "D" and "QN" are connected to form a divide-by-two circuit. The divide-by-four circuit is realized by two divide-by-two circuits in cascade, as shown in Figure 10b. The input clock and output signal waveforms obtained from the simulation of the divide-by-four circuit are shown in Figure 10c. The 0° signal (OUT_0) and the 180° signal (OUT_180) are differential signals that are fed to the LPF, while the 90° signal (OUT_90) is sent to the PFD.

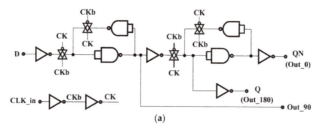

Figure 10. *Cont.*

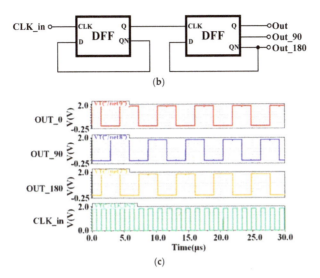

(b)

(c)

Figure 10. (**a**) D-flip-flop logic diagram; (**b**) Divide-by-four block diagram; (**c**) Divide-by-four simulation results.

3.4. Control Clock Generator

The required timing control signals are generated by a control clock generator that is designed with Verilog code and then realized through logic synthesis. The transient waveforms of the input clock and the four timing control clocks, generated from the control clock generator, are shown in Figure 11. The timing control of the ATL is performed as follows. The comparator would be activated by the "Comp strobe", which is negative-edge triggered. The result of the comparison is then sent to the SAR logic. At the same time, the PFD is deactivated by the "PFD reset", which is positive-edge triggered. Then, the SAR logic is activated by "SAR CLK" to determine one bit of the binary codes according to the comparison result. Finally, the comparator is deactivated by the "Comp reset", which is positive-edge triggered.

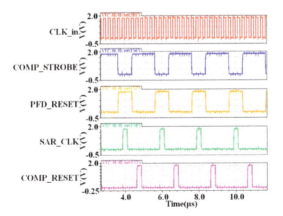

Figure 11. Simulation of the timing control.

3.5. Automatic Frequency Tuning Loop (ATL)

When the ATL is applied with different input clocks, the 3-bit digital output of the SAR logic can be observed to verify the frequency tuning function. The digital code is 111 when an input clock of 24.8 kHz is applied to the ATL, as shown in Figure 12a. The digital code is 011 when an input clock of 42.8 kHz is applied to the ATL, as shown in Figure 12b. The digital code is 000 when an input clock of 60 kHz is applied to the ATL, as shown in Figure 12c. Note that the 3-bit digital code controls the variable capacitors in the LPF and determines the corner frequency of the LPF. Therefore, according to the simulation results, the corner frequency of the LPF can be adjusted by the input clock.

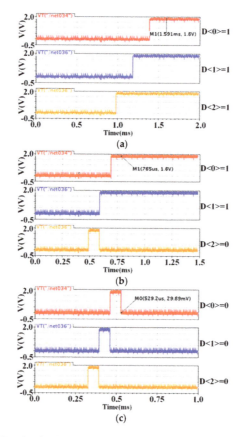

Figure 12. The 3-bit digital code observed in the ATL simulation with an input clock of (**a**) 24.8 kHz, (**b**) 42.8 kHz and (**c**) 60.0 kHz.

4. Measurement

4.1. Chopper IA

The measurement of the chopper IA is performed with the Anritsu network analyzer MS4630B. The measured frequency response of the chopper IA is shown in Figure 13, where the gain of the chopper IA can be varied from 20.7 dB to 48.5 dB and the corner frequency is 6.7~7.7 kHz. The measured CMRR of the chopper IA is shown in Figure 14. The CMRR is above 95 dB in the frequency range below 10 kHz. The noise measurement is performed using the R&S UPV audio analyzer (Rohde & Schwarz, Munich, Germany). During the measurement, the ATL is activated to perform the frequency tuning, where an input clock of 40 kHz is provided by the configuration of the 1-MHz on-chip ring oscillator followed by a divide-by-25 circuit, so that the corner frequency of the LPF is set to 10.1 kHz. Three chip samples have been tested. The average of the input-referred noises obtained from these chips, before and after the chopper modulator is activated, is shown in Figure 15. The in-band noise is lowered by 40 dB after the chopper modulator is activated. When the chopper IA operates in the highest-gain mode, the input-referred noise, integrated from 0 to 96 kHz, is 0.28 uVrms.

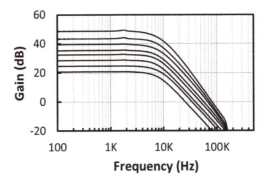

Figure 13. The measured frequency responses of the variable-gain chopper IA.

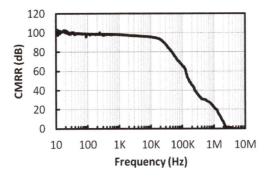

Figure 14. The measured CMRR of the chopper IA.

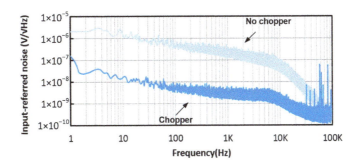

Figure 15. The measured input-referred noise of the chopper IA before and after the chopper modulator is activated.

4.2. LPF and ATL

The measurement of the LPF is performed with the Anritsu network analyzer MS4630B (Anritsu Company Inc., Kanagawa Prefecture, Japan). The measured gain and phase frequency responses of the LPF are shown in Figure 16. The corner frequency of the LPF can be varied from 6.7 kHz to 12.8 kHz with a step size of 0.9–1.0 kHz. Note that the frequency at which the phase delay reaches 90° is from 7.5 kHz to 14.4 kHz.

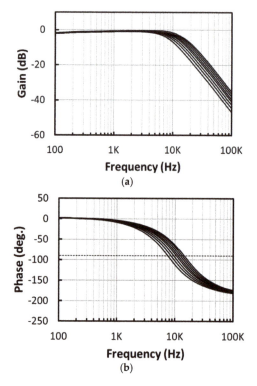

Figure 16. The measured (**a**) gain and (**b**) phase frequency responses of the LPF.

The function of the ATL was verified by observing the digital output of the ATL under different input clocks. During the measurement, the 3-bit digital output of the SAR logic was observed with a logic analyzer, where the input clock was provided by a function generator. The measurement results of digital output under input clocks from 32.8 kHz to 58.4 kHz are listed in Table 1.

Table 1. Digital Codes under Different Input Clocks.

CLK/4 (kHz)	Digital Codes
>14.6	000
13.7~14.5	001
12.5~13.6	010
11.4~12.4	011
10.4~11.3	100
9.2~10.3	101
8.3~9.1	110
<8.2	111

The digital outputs of the SAR logic, observed with the logic analyzer under three different clocks, are shown in Figure 17. When an input clock of 24.8 kHz is applied, the observed digital code is 111 after frequency tuning. When an input clock of 42.8 kHz is applied, the observed digital code is 100 after frequency tuning. When an input clock of 60.0 kHz is applied, the observed digital code is 000 after frequency tuning. According to the measurement results, the corner frequency of the LPF can be controlled by the input clock. The frequency response of the LPF for an ATL input clock of 28 kHz, 42.8 kHz and 60 kHz, where the corner frequency of the LPF is adjusted to 6.7 kHz, 10.1 kHz and 12.8 kHz, respectively, is shown in Figure 18.

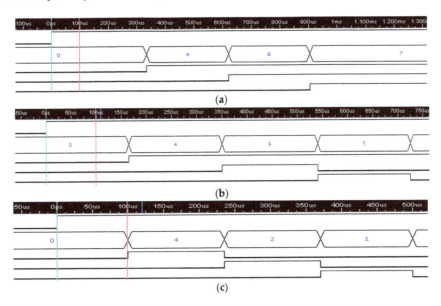

Figure 17. The measurement results of ATL: (**a**) Input clock of 24.8 kHz; ATL digital outputs = 111; (**b**) Input clock of 42.8 kHz; ATL digital outputs = 100; (**c**) Input clock of 60.0 kHz; ATL digital outputs = 000.

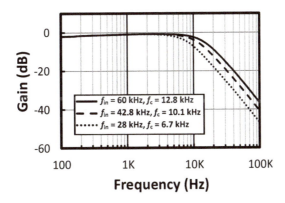

Figure 18. The measured frequency responses of LPF for an ATL input clock of 28, 42.8 and 60 kHz.

The chopper IA was fabricated with TSMC 0.18 µm CMOS technology. The chip micrograph, where the chip occupies an area of 2.13 mm^2, is shown in Figure 19. The performance of the chopper IA, along with other previous works for comparison [11–13], is summarized in Table 2.

Figure 19. Chip micrograph of the chopper IA with an ATL.

Table 2. Performance Summary of the Chopper IA.

Parameter (Unit)	This Work	[11]	[12]	[13]
Technology (nm)	180	65	180	65
Supply Voltage (V)	1.2	1.2	0.5	1
Chopping Frequency (kHz)	83.3	50	5	5
Gain (dB)	20.7~48.5	34	39.6	100
f3dB (kHz)	6.7~7.7	11	0.25	0.7
Common Mode Rejection Ratio (dB)	>95	>94	>106	134
Power Supply Rejection Ratio (dB)	>95	>100	>73	120
Input-Referred Noise (nV/$\sqrt{\text{Hz}}$)	4.2	37	112	60
Input-Referred Noise (uVrms)	0.205 (0.5–100 Hz) 0.213 (0.5–250 Hz) 0.345 (0.0–96 kHz)	N/A	2.8 (0.5–250 Hz)	6.7 (0.5–100 Hz)
Noise Efficiency Factor [14]	6.13	2.0	8.7	3.9
Power (mW)	1.1	0.0014	0.0013	0.0021
Chip Size(mm^2)	2.13	N/A	1	0.2

5. Conclusions

A low-noise IA is designed and implemented by using the chopper technique, where an LPF is employed to attenuate the up-converted noise at chopping frequency. With an ATL, the corner frequency of the LPF can be controlled with the input clock. The on-chip ring oscillator and dividers are employed to generate the input clock of the ATL and the clock of the chopper modulator, so that the noise reduction can be immune to process variations as the two clocks are correlated. During the measurement, the corner frequency of the LPF is set to 10.1 kHz, while the chopper modulator operates at a clock of 83.3 kHz. The chopper IA consumes 1.1 mW from a supply voltage of 1.2 V. The chopper IA delivers a variable gain from 20.7 dB to 48.5 dB and achieves a minimum bandwidth of 6.7 kHz. The input-referred noise of 0.28 μVrms (0~96 kHz) is achieved.

Author Contributions: H.-C.C. conceived this work; C.-M.W., M.-Y.Y., and S.-C.Y. designed the circuits and implemented the chip; C.-M.W. wrote the major draft; H.-C.C. assisted with review of the paper.

Acknowledgments: This work was supported in part by MediaTek and the Ministry of Science and Technology, Taiwan, under the contract number MOST 105-2622-8-002-002, and in part by the Ministry of Science and Technology, Taiwan, under the contract number MOST 106-2221-E-011-158. We are grateful to the National Chip Implementation Center of Taiwan for their technical support during the chip fabrication.

Conflicts of Interest: The authors declare no conflict of interest.

Micromachines **2018**, *9*, 289

References

1. Yazicioglu, R.F.; Kim, S.; Torfs, T.; Kim, H.; van Hoof, C. A 30 μW Analog signal processor ASIC for portable biopotential signal monitoring. *IEEE J. Solid-State Circuits* **2011**, *46*, 209–223. [CrossRef]
2. Gyselinckx, B. Human++: Emerging Technology for Body Area Networks. In Proceedings of the 2006 IFIP International Conference on Very Large Scale Integration, Nice, France, 16–18 October 2006; pp. 175–180.
3. Moy, T.; Huang, L.; Rieutort-Louis, W.; Wu, C.; Cuff, P.; Wagner, S.; Sturm, J.C.; Verma, N. An EEG acquisition and biomarker-extraction system using low-noise-amplifier and compressive-sensing circuits based on flexible, thin-film electronics. *IEEE J. Solid-State Circuits* **2017**, *52*, 309–321. [CrossRef]
4. Mohan, R.; Zaliasl, S.; Gielen, G.G.E.; van Hoof, C.; Yazicioglu, R.F.; van Helleputte, N. A 0.6-V, 0.015-mm^2, time-based ECG readout for ambulatory applications in 40-nm CMOS. *IEEE J. Solid-State Circuits* **2017**, *52*, 298–308. [CrossRef]
5. Song, K.; Ha, U.; Park, S.; Bae, J.; Yoo, H.J. An impedance and multi-wavelength near-infrared spectroscopy IC for non-invasive blood glucose estimation. *IEEE J. Solid-State Circuits* **2015**, *50*, 1025–1037. [CrossRef]
6. Bakker, A.; Thiele, K.; Huijsing, J.H. A CMOS nested-chopper instrumentation amplifier with 100-nV offset. *IEEE J. Solid-State Circuits* **2000**, *35*, 1877–1883. [CrossRef]
7. Rogin, J.; Kouchev, I.; Brenna, G.; Tschopp, D.; Huang, Q. A 1.5-V 45-mW direct-conversion WCDMA receiver IC in 0.13-μm CMOS. *IEEE J. Solid-State Circuits* **2003**, *38*, 2239–2248. [CrossRef]
8. Chen, H.C.; Wang, T.; Chiu, H.W.; Yang, Y.C.; Kao, T.H.; Huang, G.W.; Lu, S.S. A 5-GHz-band CMOS receiver with low LO self-mixing front end. *IEEE Trans. Circuits Syst. I Regul. Pap.* **2009**, *56*, 705–713. [CrossRef]
9. Lyu, Y.J.; Wu, Q.X.; Huang, P.S.; Chen, H.C. CMOS analog front end for ECG measurement system. In Proceedings of the 2012 International Symposium on Intelligent Signal Processing and Communications Systems, Taipei, Taiwan, 4–7 November 2012; pp. 327–332.
10. Kuo, P.Y.; Sie, L.F. Analyze the behavior model based on Verilog-A for Sallen-Key low-pass filter. In Proceedings of the 2015 IEEE International Conference on Consumer Electronics-Taiwan, Taipei, Taiwan, 6–8 June 2015; pp. 460–461.
11. Chandrakumar, H.; Marković, D. A simple area-efficient ripple-rejection technique for chopped biosignal amplifiers. *IEEE Trans. Circuits Syst. II Express Briefs* **2015**, *62*, 189–193. [CrossRef]
12. Zhu, Z.; Bai, W. A 0.5-V 1.3-μW analog front-end CMOS circuit. *IEEE Trans. Circuits Syst. II Express Br.* **2016**, *63*, 523–527. [CrossRef]
13. Fan, Q.; Sebastiano, F.; Huijsing, J.H.; Makinwa, K.A.A. A 1.8 μW 60 nV/$\sqrt{Hz}$ Capacitively-coupled chopper instrumentation amplifier in 65 nm CMOS for wireless sensor nodes. *IEEE J. Solid-State Circuits* **2011**, *46*, 1534–1543. [CrossRef]
14. Zheng, J.; Ki, W.H.; Hu, L.; Tsui, C.Y. Chopper capacitively coupled instrumentation amplifier capable of handling large electrode offset for biopotential recordings. *IEEE Trans. Circuits Syst. II Express Briefs* **2017**, *64*, 1392–1396. [CrossRef]

Article

A Low Power Energy-Efficient Precision CMOS Temperature Sensor [†]

Rongshan Wei * and Xiaotian Bao

College of Physics and Information Engineering, Fuzhou University, Fuzhou 350116, Fujian, China;
n161120014@fzu.edu.cn
* Correspondence: wrs08@fzu.edu.cn
† This work was supported by the National Natural Science Foundation of China (Grant No. 61404030) and the Natural Science Foundation of Fujian Province, China (Grant No. 2018J01803).

Received: 11 April 2018; Accepted: 17 May 2018; Published: 24 May 2018

Abstract: This paper presents a low power, energy-efficient precision CMOS temperature sensor. The front-end circuit is based on bipolar junction transistors, and employs a pre-bias circuit and bipolar core. To reduce measurement errors arising from current ratio mismatch, a new dynamic element-matching mode is proposed, which dynamically matches all current sources in the front-end circuit. The first-order fitting and third-order fitting are used to calibrate the output results. On the basis of simulation results, the sensor achieves 3σ-inaccuracies of $+0.18/-0.13$ °C from -55 °C to $+125$ °C. Measurement results demonstrate sensor 3σ-inaccuracies of ±0.2 °C from 0 °C to $+100$ °C. The circuit is implemented in 0.18 µm CMOS, and consumes 6.1 µA with a 1.8 V supply voltage.

Keywords: mode matching methods; temperature sensor; calibration

---

1. Introduction

Knowing the die temperature of transistors employed in precision sensor systems is often quite important because this information can be used to mitigate the cross sensitivity of a system to temperature [1,2]. In this manner, temperature sensors have been employed to compensate for the temperature dependence of MEMS resonators [1], to compensate for the curvature in a band-gap voltage reference [2], or in temperature measurements and over-temperature protection directly. In such systems, the inaccuracy of temperature sensors is a significant component of the total error budget, and thus often limits their ultimate performance.

Wu et al. [3] presented a thermistor-based sensor that achieved an inaccuracy of ±0.5 °C from 0 °C to 100 °C with one-point calibration. Although a thermistor-based sensor has the advantage of low power consumption, it usually requires multi-point calibration to attain high accuracy because of the non-linearity between resistance and temperature. Chen et al. [4] proposed a time-to-digital converter based temperature sensor that achieved an inaccuracy of $-0.7/+0.9$ °C from 0 °C to 100 °C. Testi et al. [5] presented a ring oscillator-based temperature sensor that achieved a maximum inaccuracy of ±3 °C from 0 °C to 120 °C after two-point calibration. While both of these latter temperature sensors have the advantage of low power consumption, they failed to achieve high accuracies.

Sensors based on bipolar junction transistors (BJTs) can achieve high accuracy because the base-emitter voltage V_{BE} offers advantageous temperature characteristics. Lee et al. [6] proposed a BJT-based temperature sensor that achieved an inaccuracy of ±1 °C from -55 °C to 125 °C. Aita et al. [7] presented a BJT-based temperature sensor that achieved an inaccuracy of ±0.25 °C from -70 °C to 130 °C using dynamic element matching (DEM).

This paper proposes a temperature sensor circuit based on BJTs for operation over the temperature range of 0 °C to 100 °C. Compared with the DEM approaches employed previously to reduce mismatch related errors [8,9], we propose a new DEM approach, denoted as all DEM (ALL-DEM), that provides greater temperature measurement precision by dynamically matching all current sources in the front-end circuit. Moreover, compared with the employment of a second-order sigma-delta analog-to-digital converter (ADC) [10] and a first-order zoom ADC [11], the sensor employs a second-order zoom ADC, which can improve the resolution and reduce the required conversion time. In addition, the temperature sensor employs voltage calibration to improve its performance.

The remainder of this paper is organized as follows. Section 2 describes the operation of the BJT-based temperature sensor front-end circuit, and discusses its main error sources. Section 3 discusses the proposed temperature sensor front-end circuit employing the ALL-DEM approach in detail. Section 4 describes the structure and operating modes of a zoom ADC. Section 5 discusses the voltage calibration and the means of conducting first-order fitting and third-order fitting. Section 6 presents the simulation and measurement results of the chip and discusses this work. Section 7 concludes the paper.

2. Sensor Operating Principles and Error Budgeting

As shown in Figure 1, the front-end circuit consists of a pre-bias circuit and a bipolar core built around several current sources, four substrate PNP transistors, and an opamp. Two branches of current with a ratio of 1:p_b bias a pair of PNPs (Q_{LB} and Q_{RB}).

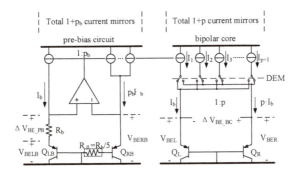

Figure 1. Conventional bipolar junction transistor (BJT) based temperature sensor front-end circuit.

The base-emitter voltages V_{BE} of the PNPs (V_{BELB} and V_{BERB}) are complementary to the absolute temperature (CTAT), whereas the difference between the two values of V_{BE}, denoted as ΔV_{BE_PB}, is proportional to the absolute temperature (PTAT). For a BJT, these voltages can be given by

$$V_{BE} = \eta \frac{kT}{q} ln\left(\frac{I_C}{I_S}\right) \qquad (1)$$

$$\Delta V_{BE\_PB} = V_{BERB} - V_{BELB} = \eta \frac{kT}{q} ln(p_b) \qquad (2)$$

respectively, where η is a process-dependent nonideality factor, k is the Boltzmann constant, q is the electron charge, T is the temperature in Kelvin, and I_C and I_S are the collector and saturation currents of the BJT. An opamp forces ΔV_{BE_PB} across a resistance of R_b to generate a PTAT bias current $I_b = \Delta V_{BE\_PB}/R_b$. The PTAT current is mirrored to the bipolar core, and two current branches with a ratio of 1:p are directed to two PNPs (Q_L and Q_R) to generate two additional V_{BE} (V_{BEL} and V_{BER}) and ΔV_{BE_BC} values.

Because the current gain β of the PNPs is finite and the biasing current is directed to a PNP via its emitter, the ratio of I_C (Q_{LB} and Q_{RB}) is not the same as a current branch. Using a β-compensating resistance of $R_\beta = R_b/5$ in the pre-bias circuit suppresses the effect of β on V_{BE} [12].

Generally, as shown in Figure 2a, temperature can be measured as $\alpha \cdot \Delta V_{BE}$ with respect to a reference voltage $V_{REF} = V_{BEL} + \alpha \cdot \Delta V_{BE\_BC}$, where α is a constant [9]. This provides the parameter $\mu_{PTAT} = \alpha \cdot \Delta V_{BE\_BC}/V_{REF}$, which varies linearly from ~0.3 to ~0.7 over the temperature range considered [12]. Alternatively, as shown in Figure 2b, a zoom ADC is employed for this purpose to reduce the power consumption, die area, and required conversion time [8,13].

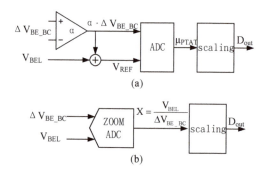

Figure 2. Operating principles of analog-to-digital converters (ADCs): (**a**) sigma-delta ADC; (**b**) zoom ADC.

The ADC provides the parameter $X = V_{BEL}/\Delta V_{BE\_BC}$, which varies nonlinearly from ~28 to ~8 over the temperature range considered [8]. In this case, the parameter μ_{PTAT} can be determined in the digital back-end according to the relationship $\mu_{PTAT} = X/(\alpha + X)$, where α is a calibration parameter. The discretized output D_{out} based on the parameter μ_{PTAT} can then be converted to units of °C by a linear fit as follows [8]:

$$D_{out} = A \cdot \mu_{PTAT} + B = A \cdot \frac{\alpha}{X+\alpha} + B = A \cdot \frac{\alpha \cdot \Delta V_{BE\_BC}}{V_{BEL} + \alpha \cdot \Delta V_{BE\_BC}} + B \qquad (3)$$

Here, A and B are calibration parameters with approximate values of 600 and −273, respectively. According to Equation (3), the sensitivity of D_{out} to error in V_{BEL} and ΔV_{BE_BC} can be respectively expressed by

$$S_{V_{BEL}}^{D_{out}}(T) = \frac{\partial D_{out}}{\partial V_{BEL}} = A \cdot \frac{\partial \mu_{PTAT}}{\partial V_{BEL}} = -\frac{T}{V_{REF}} \qquad (4)$$

$$S_{\Delta V_{BE\_BC}}^{D_{out}}(T) = \frac{\partial D_{out}}{\partial \Delta V_{BE\_BC}} = A \cdot \frac{\partial \mu_{PTAT}}{\partial \Delta V_{BE\_BC}} = \frac{A-T}{V_{REF}}\alpha \qquad (5)$$

where the approximation $\mu_{PTAT} \approx T/A$ has been employed in the final forms. For example, supposing that $V_{REF} = 1.2$ V, $A = 600$, and $\alpha = 14$, a 0.1 °C temperature error is approximately equal to a 0.3 mV error in V_{BEL} at +126.85 °C or a 0.02 mV error in ΔV_{BE_BC} at −73.15 °C. Therefore, the accuracy of the sensor is limited by the error in V_{BEL} and ΔV_{BE_BC}.

The main source of error in ΔV_{BE_BC} is a current ratio mismatch Δp between the two current branches in the bipolar core. The absolute error in ΔV_{BE_BC} can then be given as follows:

$$\Delta V_{BE\_BC} - \Delta V_{BE\_BC}|_{\Delta p=0} = \eta \frac{kT}{q}ln(p+\Delta p) - \eta \frac{kT}{q}ln(p) = \eta \frac{kT}{q}ln\left(1+\frac{\Delta p}{p}\right) \approx \eta \frac{kT}{q}\frac{\Delta p}{p} \qquad (6)$$

Here, T is in units of Kelvin. With a carefully designed layout of the current sources, $\Delta p/p = 0.1\%$ can be expected [14], and the temperature error due to mismatch is then 0.091 K according to Equation (5).

Error due to Δp can be reduced by dynamically interchanging the current sources in the bipolar core [15] using DEM [16]. This is illustrated for the case of the bipolar core in Figure 1. One of the current sources is directed to Q_L, whereas the other current sources are directed to Q_R. This averaging process cancels the first-order error in ΔV_{BE_BC} whereas the second-order error remains, which is given as follows [12]:

$$\left|\Delta V_{BE\_BC} - \Delta V_{BE\_BC}|_{\Delta p=0}\right| < \frac{1}{2}\eta\frac{kT}{q}\left(\frac{\Delta p}{p}\right)^2 \qquad (7)$$

If, for instance, $\Delta p/p = 1\%$, this corresponds to a temperature error of at most 4.6 mK, which is sufficient to obtain a temperature error well below 0.1 K.

Similarly, a current ratio mismatch exists in the pre-bias circuit, which results in PTAT errors in I_b and V_{BEL}. The absolute error in V_{BEL} can then be given as follows:

$$V_{BEL} - V_{BEL,ideal} = \eta\frac{kT}{q}ln\left(\frac{p+\Delta p}{p}\right) \approx \eta\frac{kT}{q}\cdot\frac{\Delta p}{p} \qquad (8)$$

If, for example, $\Delta p/p = 1\%$, the error in V_{BEL} corresponds to a temperature error of at most 65 mK.

To reduce temperature measurement errors, most conventional circuits match only current sources in the bipolar core dynamically [8,9,13], and the mismatch in the pre-bias circuit is regarded as a relatively minor problem.

3. Temperature Sensor Front-End Circuit

According to the discussion in the previous section, a conventional circuit reduces temperature measurement errors by averaging Δp to some extent, but cannot make full use of the circuit because current sources in the pre-bias circuit do not participate in the averaging process. Therefore, we employed the proposed ALL-DEM approach in the temperature sensor front-end circuit, which matches all current sources in both the pre-bias circuit and bipolar core dynamically. Assuming that $p_b = p = 5$, the proposed circuit is illustrated in Figure 3.

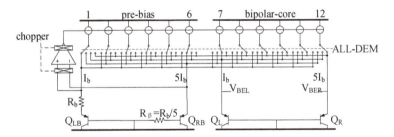

Figure 3. Front-end circuit employing the all dynamic element matching (ALL-DEM) approach.

The ALL-DEM approach employs the following steps:

Step 1: Number all current sources from 1 to 12.

Step 2: Under the control of ALL-DEM, current source 1 is directed to Q_{LB}, current sources 2–6 are directed to Q_{RB}, current source 7 is directed to Q_L, and current sources 8–12 are directed to Q_R.

Step 3: After a single integral sampling period, current sources are cyclically shifted, and Step 2 is repeated, i.e., current source 2 is directed to Q_{LB}, current sources 3–7 are directed to Q_{RB}, current source 8 is directed to Q_L, and current sources 9–12 and current source 1 are directed to Q_R.

An ALL-DEM cycle consists of 12 periods. In addition to dynamically matching the current sources in the pre-bias circuit (rather than only in the bipolar core), the ALL-DEM approach offers another advantage, in that it provides a greater number of conditions in the bipolar core compared with conventional DEM, which is increased from 6 to 12.

The ALL-DEM approach can reduce the mismatch in the pre-bias circuit, and, hence, can reduce temperature measurement errors caused by the pre-bias circuit. In addition, the proposed circuit employs chopping to suppress the offset of the opamp. The benefits of the ALL-DEM approach are demonstrated by the simulation results presented in Figure 4, which shows the maximum temperature errors obtained with different DEM schemes. As the results show, the maximum temperature error caused by the ALL-DEM approach is at least 0.82 °C less than that obtained without the DEM approach. Moreover, the average maximum temperature error caused by the ALL-DEM approach is 0.07 °C less than that of the conventional DEM approach. The ALL-DEM approach can therefore achieve a higher accuracy than the conventional DEM approach.

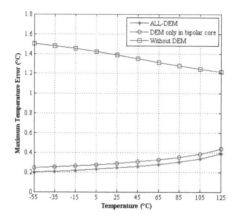

Figure 4. Maximum temperature errors simulations with different dynamic element matching (DEM) schemes.

4. Zoom Analog-to-Digital Converter

As shown in Figure 5, the zoom ADC is a two-step ADC structure that consists of a successive approximation (SAR) ADC and a sigma-delta ADC. The conversion process of the zoom ADC can be divided into two operating modes. Here, the SAR ADC first converts the input $x(t)$ to obtain the output of the most significant bit (*MSB*), which is denoted as coarse conversion. Then, the zoom ADC enters into the second operating mode, where the sigma-delta ADC converts the input $x(t)$ according to *MSB*, and generates the output of the least significant bit (*LSB*), which is denoted as fine conversion. Finally, we obtain the output $D[n]$ by combining *MSB* and *LSB*. Therefore, the zoom ADC combines the rapid conversion of an SAR ADC with the high precision of a sigma-delta ADC.

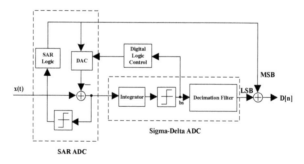

Figure 5. Structure of the zoom ADC. (Note: SAR: successive approximation; LSB: least significant bit; MSB: most significant bit; DAC: digital-to-analog converter).

5. Calibration

Figure 6 presents an overview of the temperature sensor. It consists of a front-end circuit that generates V_{BE} and ΔV_{BE}, which are fed to the zoom ADC. The output of the zoom ADC in the normal operating mode is the ratio $X_N = V_{BE}/\Delta V_{BE}$. However, the ADC can be configured to output $X_c = V_{ext}/\Delta V_{BE}$ when the temperature sensor chip is placed in the calibration mode. A PT-100 thermistor, which was calibrated to an error of less than 1 mK and placed in good thermal contact with the temperature sensor, was used to obtain the reference temperature T_{chip} [17].

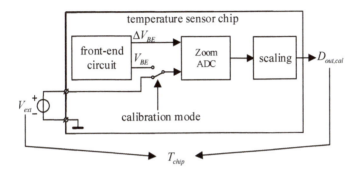

Figure 6. Overview of the temperature sensor.

We adopted voltage calibration, which employs the following steps.

Step 1: Change the operating mode of the temperature sensor chip into the calibration mode. Then, input testing voltage V_{ext}, and obtain ΔV_{BE} as follows:

$$\Delta V_{BE} = \frac{V_{ext}}{X_{ext}} \tag{9}$$

We can then calculate η using ΔV_{BE} and T_{chip} according to Equation (2).

Step 2: Change the operating mode of the temperature sensor chip into the normal operating mode. Take 20 temperature reading samples over 11 testing points in the temperature range from 0 °C to +100 °C, and obtain X and D_{out} from each testing point, respectively. The average value X_{AVG} at each testing point can be calculated from the values of X obtained at each testing point. Then, the calibration parameters A, B, and α can be calculated according to Equation (3).

Step 3: The voltage calibration temperature T_D can be calculated using η, Equations (2) and (9).

Step 4: Then, the ideal voltage calibration output X_{ideal} can be calculated using T_D, A, B, and α according to Equation (3). In addition, we can obtain the actual output X_D from the chip.

Step 5: Output D is then obtained from A, B, α, X_{ideal}, and X_D as follows:

$$D = A \cdot \frac{\alpha}{X + X_{ideal} - X_D + \alpha} + B \tag{10}$$

Here, Equation (10) represents the first-order fitting. Actually, the fitting accuracy can be improved by adopting the following fixed third-order polynomial:

$$D = A \cdot \left(\frac{\alpha}{X' + \alpha}\right)^3 + B \cdot \left(\frac{\alpha}{X' + \alpha}\right)^2 + C \cdot \left(\frac{\alpha}{X' + \alpha}\right) + E \tag{11}$$

where $X' = X + X_{ideal} - X_D$, A, B, C, and E are calibration parameters that are calculated in Step 1. In this paper, the voltage calibration employed single-point calibration, and the value T_D was set to 37 °C.

6. Experimental Results and Discussion

The circuit was implemented in 0.18 µm CMOS technology provided by Semiconductor Manufacturing International Corp. (SMIC, Shanghai, China), and all current sources employed a current of 180 nA. The chip consumed 6.1 µA with a 1.8 V supply voltage, where the current consumption of the front-end circuit was 4.6 µA and the current consumption of the zoom ADC was 1.5 µA. The core area of the chip was 860 µm × 580 µm. A micrograph of the chip is shown in Figure 7.

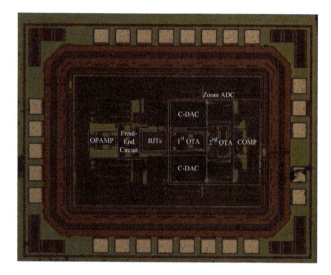

Figure 7. Chip micrograph. (Note: OTA: operational transconductance amplifier; C-DAC: capacitive digital-to-analog converter; COMP: comparator).

Figure 8 presents the simulation results of the front-end circuit obtained via 20 Monte Carlo simulations. Here, Figure 8a presents the simulation results of the first-order fitting, which exhibits 3σ-inaccuracies of +0.12/−0.06 °C from −55 °C to +125 °C. In addition, Figure 8b presents the simulation results of the third-order fitting, which exhibits 3σ-inaccuracies of ±0.08 °C from −55 °C to +125 °C.

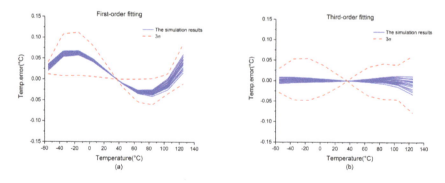

Figure 8. Simulation results of the front-end circuit: (**a**) first-order fitting; (**b**) third-order fitting.

The simulation results of the chip are presented in Figure 9. Here, Figure 9a presents the results of first-order fitting, which exhibits 3σ-inaccuracies of +0.25/−0.13 °C over the temperature range considered. In addition, Figure 9b presents the results of third-order fitting, which exhibits 3σ-inaccuracies of +0.18/−0.13 °C over the temperature range considered.

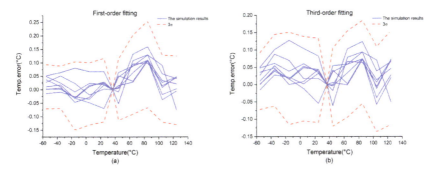

Figure 9. Simulation results for the chip: (**a**) first-order fitting; (**b**) third-order fitting.

Figure 10 presents the measurement results of the chip. During measurements, we added a shielding box to improve the accuracy of the temperature sensor. As shown in Figure 10a, the chip exhibits 3σ-inaccuracies of +0.15/−0.3 °C from 0 °C to +100 °C with first-order fitting. Figure 10b presents the measurement results of third-order fitting, which shows that the chip can achieve 3σ-inaccuracies of ±0.2 °C from 0 °C to +100 °C.

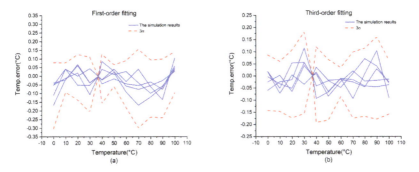

Figure 10. Measurement results of the chip: (**a**) first-order fitting; (**b**) third-order fitting.

As demonstrated by the simulation and measurement results, third-order fitting can achieve a greater measurement than first-order fitting. The measured performance of the temperature sensor is compared with the performances of previously reported state-of-the-art temperature sensor implementations in Table 1. Because of the employment of the second-order zoom ADC, the parameter figure-of-merit (FOM) of the sensor is better than those presented in References [6,15], which shows that the proposed sensor provides better resolution and a reduced conversion time. However, the measurement temperature range of this work is only from 0 °C to 100 °C because of the limitations of the measurement equipment. As a result, the *Rel.InAcc* value of the proposed circuit is 0.4%.

Table 1. Performance Comparison with Previously Reported Temperature Sensor Schemes.

Item	[8]	[9]	[17]	[18]	This Work
Year	2013	2005	2017	2014	2018
Process (μm)	0.16	0.7	0.16	0.7	0.18
Area (mm^2)	0.08	4.5	0.16	0.8	0.5
V$_{DD}$ (V)	1.5–2	2.5–5.5	1.5–2	2.9–5.5	1.8
Supply Current (μA)	3.4	75	4.6	55	6.1
Temperature Range (°C)	−55 to +125	−55 to +125	−55 to +125	−45 to +130	0 to +100
Resolution (°C) T$_{conv}$ (ms)	0.02 (5.3)	0.01 (100)	0.015 (5)	0.003 (2.2)	0.01 (3.4)
Inaccuracy (°C)	±0.15	±0.1	±0.06	±0.15	±0.2
FOM * (pJ°C^2)	11	1875	7.8	3.2	3.8
Rel.InAcc. ** (%)	0.17	0.11	0.07	0.17	0.4

* FOM = (Power·T$_{conv}$) × (Resolution)^2. ** Rel.InAcc = (2 × Inaccuracy/Range) × 100%.

The present work has taken errors into account as much as possible and employs the ALL-DEM approach and calibration to improve the accuracy of the proposed temperature sensor. Among the remaining errors, the curvature error is the largest source of error. Therefore, a curvature calibration or a curvature compensation technology can be expected to improve the accuracies of the temperature sensor. In addition, while the BJT-based temperature sensors provide higher accuracy than thermistor-based sensors, they also require greater power consumption. A higher-order zoom ADC can reduce the power consumption, although its implementation will also require a greater die area. The miniaturization of BJT-based temperature sensors is also an important consideration, and the means of reducing the die area while simultaneously reducing the power consumption of the temperature sensor will be the objective of future research.

7. Conclusions

This paper proposed a low power, energy-efficient precision CMOS temperature sensor circuit implemented in 0.18 μm CMOS technology provided by SMIC. Using the novel ALL-DEM approach, all current sources in the proposed front-end circuit are matched dynamically to reduce system errors arising from current ratio mismatch. Single-point calibration was adopted to improve the accuracy of the sensor. According to the experimental results, the proposed circuit provides a maximum temperature error of ±0.2 °C over the temperature range from 0 °C to +100 °C. The proposed circuit is applicable to a wide range of temperature sensor applications.

Author Contributions: Rongshan Wei provided the initial concepts, prototypes and wrote the paper. Xiaotian Bao conducted the measurement of the temperature sensor and analyzed the data.

Conflicts of Interest: The authors declare no conflict of interest.

References

1. Zaliasl, S.; Salvia, J.C.; Hill, G.C.; Chen, L.; Joo, K.; Palwai, R.; Arumugam, N.; Phadke, M.; Mukherjee, S.; Lee, H.C.; et al. A 3 ppm 1.5 × 0.8 mm^2 1.0 μA 32.768 kHz MEMS-based oscillator. *IEEE J. Solid-State Circuits* **2015**, *50*, 291–302. [CrossRef]
2. Maderbacher, G.; Marsili, S.; Motz, M.; Jackum, T.; Thielmann, J.; Hassander, H.; Gruber, H.; Hus, F.; Sandner, C. A digitally assisted single-point-calibration CMOS bandgap voltage reference with a 3σ inaccuracy of ±0.08% for fuel-gauge applications. In Proceedings of the 2015 International IEEE ISSCC, San Francisco, CA, USA, 22–26 February 2015; pp. 1–3.
3. Wu, C.K.; Chan, W.S.; Lin, T.H. A 80 kS/s 36 μW resistor-based temperature sensor using BGR-free SAR ADC with a unevenly-weighted resistor string in 0.18 μm CMOS. In Proceedings of the 2011 Symposium on VLSI Circuits (VLSIC), Honolulu, HI, USA, 15–17 June 2011; pp. 222–223.
4. Chen, P.; Chen, C.-C.; Tsai, C.-C.; Lu, W.-F. A time-to-digital-converter-based CMOS smart temperature sensor. *IEEE J. Solid-State Circuits* **2005**, *40*, 1642–1648. [CrossRef]
5. Testi, N.; Yang, X. A 0.2 nJ/sample 0.01 mm^2 ring oscillator based temperature sensor for on-chip thermal management. In Proceedings of the IEEE International Symposium on Quality Electronic Design, Santa Clara, CA, USA, 4–6 March 2013; pp. 696–702.

6. Lee, H.-Y.; Hsu, C.-M.; Luo, C.-H. CMOS thermal sensing system with simplified circuits and high accuracy for biomedical application. In Proceedings of the 2006 IEEE International Symposium on Circuits and Systems, Island of Kos, Greece, 21–24 May 2006; pp. 4367–4370.

7. Aita, A.L.; Pertijs, M.A.P.; Makinwa, K.A.A.; Huijsing, J.H. A CMOS smart temperature sensor with a batch-calibrated inaccuracy of ±0.25 °C (3σ) from −70°C to 130 °C. In Proceedings of the 2009 IEEE International Solid-State Circuits Conference—Digest of Technical Papers, San Francisco, CA, USA, 8–12 February 2009; pp. 342–343.

8. Souri, K.; Chae, Y.; Makinwa, K.A.A. A CMOS temperature sensor with a voltage-calibrated inaccuracy of ±0.15 °C (3σ) from −55 °C to 125 °C. *IEEE J. Solid-State Circuits* **2013**, *48*, 292–301. [CrossRef]

9. Pertijs, M.A.P.; Makinwa, K.A.A.; Huijsing, J.H. A CMOS smart temperature sensor with a 3σ inaccuracy of ±0.1 °C from −55 °C to 125 °C. *IEEE J. Solid-State Circuits* **2005**, *40*, 2805–2815. [CrossRef]

10. Pertijs, M.A.P.; Niederkorn, A.; Ma, X.; Bakker, A.; Huijsing, J.H. A CMOS smart temperature sensor with a 3σ inaccuracy of ±0.5 °C from −50 °C to 120 °C. *IEEE J. Solid-State Circuits* **2005**, *40*, 454–461. [CrossRef]

11. Souri, K.; Kashmiri, M.; Makinwa, K. A CMOS temperature sensor with an energy-efficient zoom ADC and an Inaccuracy of ±0.25 °C (3σ) from −40 °C to 125 °C. In Proceedings of the IEEE International Solid-State Circuits Conference, San Francisco, CA, USA, 7–11 February 2010; pp. 310–311.

12. Pertijs, M.A.P.; Huijsing, J. *Precision Temperature Sensors in CMOS Technology*; Springer: Dordrecht, The Netherlands, 2006.

13. Souri, K.; Makinwa, K.A.A. A 0.12 mm² 7.4 μW micropower temperature sensor with an inaccuracy of ±0.2 °C (3σ) from −30 °C to 125 °C. *IEEE J. Solid-State Circuits* **2011**, *46*, 1693–1700. [CrossRef]

14. Hastings, A. *The Art of Analog Layout*; Prentice Hall: Upper Saddle River, NJ, USA, 2006.

15. Klaassen, K.B. Digitally controlled absolute voltage division. *IEEE Trans. Instrum. Meas.* **1975**, *24*, 106–112. [CrossRef]

16. Van De Plassche, R.J. Dynamic element matching for high-accuracy monolithic D/A converters. *IEEE J. Solid-State Circuits* **1976**, *11*, 795–800. [CrossRef]

17. Yousefzadeh, B.; Shalmany, S.H.; Makinwa, K.A.A. A BJT-Based Temperature-to-Digital Converter with ±60 mK (3σ) Inaccuracy From −55 °C to +125 °C in 0.16-μm CMOS. *IEEE J. Solid-State Circuits* **2017**, *52*, 1044–1052. [CrossRef]

18. Heidary, A.; Wang, G.; Makinwa, K.; Meijer, G. 12.8 A BJT-based CMOS temperature sensor with a 3.6pJ·K2-resolution FoM. In Proceedings of the 2014 IEEE International Solid-State Circuits Conference Digest of Technical Papers (ISSCC), San Francisco, CA, USA, 9–13 February 2014; pp. 224–225.

 *micromachines*

Article

An Adaptable Interface Conditioning Circuit Based on Triboelectric Nanogenerators for Self-Powered Sensors

Yongshan Hu [1,2,3], Qiuqin Yue [4], Shan Lu [1,2,3], Dongchen Yang [1,2,3], Shuxin Shi [1,2,3], Xiaokun Zhang [1,2,3] and Hua Yu [1,2,3,*]

1   Key Laboratory for Optoelectronic Technology and Systems, Ministry of Education of China, Chongqing 400044, China; 20113211@cqu.edu.cn (Y.H.); 20103160@cqu.edu.cn (S.L.); 20113210@cqu.edu.cn (D.Y.); 20160802007t@cqu.edu.cn (S.S.); 20160813100@cqu.edu.cn (X.Z.)
2   Key Laboratory of Fundamental Science of Micro/Nano-Device and System Technology, Chongqing University, Chongqing 400044, China
3   College of Optoelectric Engineering, Chongqing University, Chongqing 400044, China
4   Department of Electro-Mechanic Engineering, Chongqing College of Electronic Engineering, Chongqing 401331, China; 200923008@cqcet.edu.cn
*   Correspondence: yuhua@cqu.edu.cn; Tel./Fax: +86-23-6511-1022

Received: 29 December 2017; Accepted: 23 February 2018; Published: 1 March 2018

Abstract: In order to solve the limited life problem of typical battery power supply, a self-powered method that is based on the environmental energy harvesting has emerged as an amazing power supply approach. The Tribo-electric-Nano-generator (TENG) has been widely studied because of its high efficiency, low fabrication cost, and high output voltage. However, low output power conversion efficiency has restricted its practical application because of its own extremely high output impedance. In order to match the high output impedance of TENG and increase the output power, this paper presents an adaptable interface conditioning circuit, which is composed of an impedance matching circuit, a synchronous rectifier bridge, a control circuit, and an energy storage device. In the impedance matching circuit, the energy loss of coupling inductance could be reduced by using the bi-directional switch to increase the frequency, and impedance matching circuit can be used to increase the output efficiency of TENG. Experimental results show that, in about 3.6 s, the storing capacitor voltage was basically stable at 5.5 V by using the proposed adapted interface conditioning circuit in this paper. The charging efficiency has increased by 50%.

Keywords: adaptable interface conditioning circuit; impedance matching; TENG; self-powered sensors

1. Introduction

The use of wireless sensors and the wearable devices has developed rapidly in recent years. In traditional way, they are usually powered by standard batteries. However, this approach has become a bottleneck restricting the development of wireless sensors and the wearable devices because batteries usually become depleted within a relatively short timeframe, and the replacement or recharge of batteries can increase the cost. The self-powered method based on the environmental energy harvesting provides a new solution for power supply of wireless sensor nodes and wearable devices [1–4]. Environmental energy harvester has been used as a battery to power-up the wireless sensor node or the wearable device. Usually, the environmental energy is weak and discontinuous, such as vibration energy, so the high efficiency, low power consumption is essential [5] The triboelectric nanogenerator (TENG), first invented by Zhong Lin Wang et al. In 2012, is able to produce electrical output based on triboelectrification and electrostatic induction in response to an external mechanical input. Its fundamental physics and output characteristics can be attributed to the Maxwell's displacement current [6,7]. Up to now, the area power density of TENGs has reached 313 W/m² and their volume energy density has reached 490 kW/m³ [8]. When compared with other energy generators, the TENG has high efficiency, low fabrication cost, and high output voltage. These advantages make TENG more suitable for self-powered wireless sensors and the wearable devices. Some studies of TENG have shown that charging efficiency decays quickly after several charging cycles, the maximum voltage of the energy storage device is much smaller than the open-circuit voltage of the TENG, regardless of the energy conversion efficiency of the TENG [9]. Also, the TENG has poor load capacity because of its high output impedance. In order to convert the output voltage of the TENG to a stable DC voltage and increase the energy-storage efficiency, an interface conditioning circuit is essential. Some studies have shown that the DC-DC circuit is effective in working as a conditioning circuit that can stabilize the output voltage successfully [10,11]. However, maximizing the power extraction from TENG is still unresolved, so impendence matching is a major consideration in circuit design and also it is the most efficient way to increase the output power. The fully-integrated self-powered wireless sensor node contains TENGs, which is an interface conditioning circuit, energy storage elements, and load circuits (wireless sensor node).

The objective of this paper is to present an adaptable interface conditioning circuit based on triboelectric nanogenerator. Firstly, we will discuss the output characteristics of TENG. Then, analysis of the interface conditioning circuit will be done in detail. Finally, the experimental results will be discussed.

2. Modeling of TENG

The fundamental working principle of TENGs is triboelectrification. Electrostatic induction is the main mechanism that converts mechanical energy to electricity. Any TENG contains two pairs of frictional electrified layers face to each other, the distance between the two layers is X. X will change when the external force applied, so the capacitance between the layers C will change. Triboelectric charges will be generated after the external force works, there will be induced charges between the two layers, as shown in Figure 1a. In order to get more charges, materials for triboelectrification is very important. According to the triboelectric series [8], polydimethylsiloxane and aluminum are selected as the materials for triboelectrification. In one contact- separation process, output voltage of TENG without any load is shown in Figure 1b, which reaches the maximum at $X = 0$ and $X = Xmax$. When we apply an external force on TENG periodically, output voltage is shown in Figure 1c. We can assume that the induced voltage between the two electrodes is V, transferred charges between the two layers is Q. The electrical potential difference V consists of two parts, one part is from the polarized triboelectric charges, and the other part is the already transferred charges Q, so V is given by the V-Q-X equation:

$$V = -\frac{1}{C(X)}Q + V_{oc}(X) \tag{1}$$

Operating characteristics of TENG have been described in Equation (1), so we can get its inherent capacitive behavior from theoretical analysis [8,12,13]. From the V-Q-X equation of triboelectric nanogenerators, equivalent SPICE (Simulation program with integrated circuit emphasis) model can be easily obtained. As seen in Equation (1), there are two terms at the right side. Two circuit components are used to represent them. First, due to the inherent capacitance between the two electrodes of TENG, a capacitor C_s is used to express its capacitance characteristics. The other term $V_{oC}(X)$ is an open circuit voltage term, which is resulting from the separation of the polarized tribo-charges and could be represented by a voltage source (V_{oc}). From these two terms, the whole equivalent SPICE model can be represented by a double-ended device that consists of an ideal voltage source a serial with a capacitor, as shown in Figure 1d. So, we can consider the TENG as a capacitive device in electrical analysis, and this is the reason why it has a poor load capacity. TENG's output voltage is provided with different loads. In Figure 1e, the load voltage decreases as the load capacitance increases. In Figure 1f, the load voltage increases as the load resistance increases. The experimental results are consistent with the theoretical analysis.

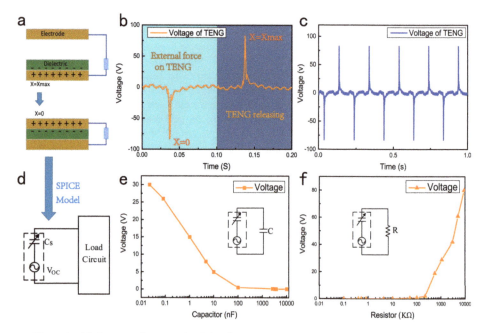

Figure 1. (**a**) Structure diagram of a Tribo-electric-Nano-generator (TENG). (**b**) Output voltage waveform of TENG in one working cycle without any load. (**c**) Open-circuit voltage of TENG. (**d**) Equivalent SPICE model of TENG. (**e**) Load voltage curve while the capacitor ranging from 22 pF to 10 μF is loaded. (**f**) Load voltage curve while the resistor ranging from 0.1 kΩ to 9.1 MΩ is loaded.

Also, when we talk about a certain TENG, a theoretical calculation is an important method to get the characteristics of TENG, such as finite element method (FEM). Using FEM simulation software, such as COMSOL and ANSYS, the finite element calculation can be easily done. Another general method to get the characteristics of TENG is utilizing SPICE software, such as OrCad, Mulitisim. From the TENG equivalent SPICE model, the TENG can be obtained in theoretical calculation using SPICE software as a basic element consisting of a voltage source in serial connection with a capacitor [14]. After the motion process and the initial condition are generated, the powerful SPICE software can easily calculate the real-time output of any TENG systems.

When the signal source is used to drive a certain load, the voltage, current, total power consumption will change with the different load parameters. The main purpose of the impedance matching in the circuit is to adjust the load impedance, so that we can get the required optimal power with a certain power supply. To achieve the impedance matching in an AC circuit, the most effective way is to use the coupling inductances, the coupling inductances can not only achieve the impedance matching, but also regulate the output voltage [14].

As shown in Figure 2a, we assume that the turns ratio of the coupling inductance is *n*, the load capacitance is C_L. So, we can get the equivalent circuit shown in Figure 2b. Figure 2bi shows the equivalent primary circuit of the coupling inductance. Figure 2bii shows the equivalent secondary circuit of the coupling inductance, the following equations are satisfied:

$$C'_L = n^2 C_L \tag{2}$$

$$C'_S = \frac{C_S}{n^2}, \quad V'_S = \frac{V_S}{n^2} \tag{3}$$

According to the above analysis, using the coupling inductance, the output voltage of TENG can be reduced to $1/n$ of the source output, the output current is increased by n times and output impedance is reduced to $1/n^2$. However, for an ideal capacitive load, it cannot extract energy from TENG because the average power of the load capacitor in one cycle is zero. When considering the load capacitance in one period is still very helpful. In Figure 2c, we assume that the load capacitance is C_L, the voltage extract from TENG is shown below:

$$V(C_L) = \frac{C_S}{C_S + C_L} V_S \tag{4}$$

$$E(C_L) = \frac{1}{2} C_L V_L^2 = \frac{1}{2} C_s V_s^2 \left(\frac{1}{2 + \beta + 1/\beta} \right) \tag{5}$$

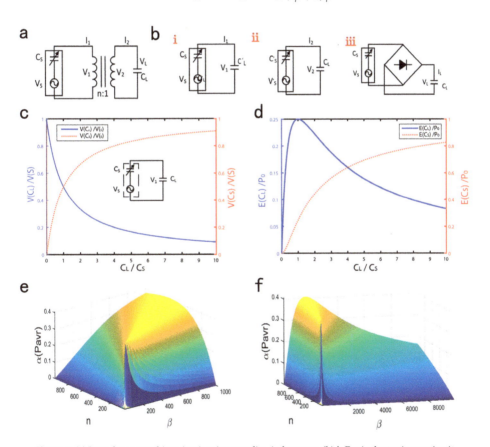

Figure 2. (a) Impedance matching circuit using coupling inductance. (b) i: Equivalent primary circuit of the coupling inductance; ii: The equivalent secondary circuit of the coupling inductance; iii: Charge a capacitor via a rectifier bridge. (c) Voltage curves of the C_L and C_s when C_L/C_s changes from 1 to 10. (d) Power curves of the C_L and C_s when C_L/C_s changes from 1 to 10. (e) Average charge efficiency diagram (β ranges from 0 to 1000). (f) Average charge efficiency diagram (β ranges from 1000 to 8000).

Among them, $\beta = C_L/C_s$, define $P_o = \frac{1}{2}C_s V_{SMAX}^2$, so in half period, when V_s gets the maximum value V_{smax}, the $V(C_L)$, $E(C_L)$, also get the maximum value, the curve of $V(C_L)$ and $E(C_L)$ are shown in Figure 2c,d. To prevent current reflow, we consider using a rectifier bridge, as shown in Figure 2biii. Assume that the voltage loss of the rectifier bridge is V_D. So, in the first period:

Initial value:

$$V(C_L)_0 = V(C_S)_0 = 0 \; V_{S0} = V_D \tag{6}$$

During the charging process, the circuit KCL (Kirchhoff's current law) equation is:

$$V_S = V(C_S) + V(C_L) + V_D \tag{7}$$

So, we can get the voltage $V(C_L)$, $V(C_S)$, shown below:

$$V(C_L)_1 = V(C_L)_0 + \Delta V(C_L)_1 = \frac{1}{1+\beta}(V_{SMAX} - V_D) \tag{8}$$

$$V(C_S)_1 = V(C_S)_0 + \Delta V(C_S)_1 = \frac{\beta}{1+\beta}(V_{SMAX} - V_D) \tag{9}$$

After n periods, we get $V(C_L)_n$, $P(C_L)_n$, shown below:

$$V(C_L)_n = [1 - \frac{\beta(\beta-1)^{n-1}}{(1+\beta)^n}](V_{SMAX} - V_D) \tag{10}$$

$$P(C_L)_n = \frac{1}{2}C_L V(C_L)_n^2 = \beta[1 - \frac{\beta(\beta-1)^{n-1}}{(1+\beta)^n}]^2 P_0 \tag{11}$$

Define that:

$$P_0 = \frac{1}{2}C_S(V_{SMAX} - V_D)^2 \tag{12}$$

$$P_{avr}(C_L) = \frac{P(C_L)_n}{n} = \frac{1}{n}\beta[1 - \frac{\beta(\beta-1)^{n-1}}{(1+\beta)^n}]^2 P_0 \tag{13}$$

$$\alpha(P_{avr}) = \frac{1}{n}\beta[1 - \frac{\beta(\beta-1)^{n-1}}{(1+\beta)^n}]^2 \tag{14}$$

P_0 represents the maximum energy value that a single charge cycle can provide determined by the power supply, $P_{avr}(C_L)$ indicates average $P(C_L)$ in one cycle, so the parameter $\alpha(P_{avr})$ is used to characterize the average charge efficiency. As shown in Figure 2e,f, for a certain n, $\alpha(P_{avr})$ gets the maximum value corresponding to an optimal value of β, and for a certain β, $\alpha(P_{avr})$ gets the maximum value corresponding to an optimal value of n. Consider the following two points: (a) capacitor leakage or capacitance capacity is limited; (b) charging time is limited. So, according to the limitations of the actual application, select the optimal n and β.

3. Results and Discussion

As described above, we have some understanding of the output characteristics of TENG and impedance matching, in this section we focus on the interface conditioning circuit. The following key design ideas for interface conditioning circuit must be taken into account, including: (a) maximizing power extraction from TENG by using the impedance match technology; (b) storing the harvested energy; (c) conditioning output voltage to meet the power requirements of the sensor node; and (d) minimizing power consumption of the whole system.

For a non-ideal coupling inductance, it has power loss, which increases as the frequency decreases. However, the frequency of TENG output voltage that depends on the environment vibration is always low. So, in the circuit, the bi-directional switch is used to increase the frequency so that the power loss of the coupling inductances could be reduced as much as possible. The control signal of bi-directional switch is needed. An oscillation circuit that can generate a signal at a certain frequency to control the bi-directional switch is essential. When considering the primary circuit, when the circuit is turned on, the current on the inductor cannot change immediately, there will be oscillation due to the step response, it will cause the induced voltage on the secondary coil. Then, damping oscillation voltage will be observed on the storing capacitor due to the resistance of the non-ideal coupling inductance. The storing capacitor charged step by step as show in Figure 3a,b. When the circuit is turned on, the electric energy is passed to the secondary coil through the coupling inductance, and according to the secondary load, there will be different attenuation coefficient, so the turn on time is essential to make sure energy can be passed out. However, the turn-off time determines initial voltage of the primary coil. So frequency of the control circuit is also an important parameter as shown in Figure 3e,f. In Figure 3e, a 10 µf capacitor is chosen as the storing capacitor, maximum voltage of the storage capacitor $V_S(max)$ gets a maximum value as the frequency of the control circuit range from 0.1 to 100 KHz. When the load is a 10 KΩ resistor, the peak load voltage V_r and peak voltage of the primary inductance $V_i(max)$ are shown in Figure 3f.

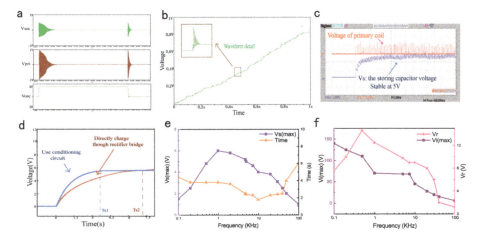

Figure 3. (a) Voltage simulation curves of the secondary inductance (*Vsec*), primary inductance (*Vpri*), the oscillator (*Vosc*). (b) Simulation curve of charging process. (c) Experiment curve of charging process. (d) Comparison to charge a capacitor via a rectifier bridge and conditioning circuit. (e) Maximum voltage of the storage capacitor and the required time. (f) When resistive load is connected, load voltage and output voltage of the primary inductance.

The experimental results show that the self-powered management circuit can meet the voltage, and power consumption needs of a wireless sensor node. In experimental test, the maximum open circuit voltage of TENG is 83.6 V, frequency is 5 Hz, when the TENG starts working, the storing capacitor is charged. After about 3.6 s, the storing capacitor voltage is basically stable at 5.5 V, as shown in Figure 3c. When compared with charging though a rectifier bridge directly, the proposed circuit greatly reduces the charging time and increases efficiency by 50%, as shown in Figure 3d.

Figure 4a shows a wireless sensor system based on environmental energy harvester by using TENG. The TENG transform environmental energy into electrical energy, then a stable DC voltage could be used though an interface conditioning circuit, so that it could power the wireless sensor node. The proposed circuit for the TENG is composed of an impedance matching circuit, a synchronous rectifier bridge, a control circuit, an energy storage device, as shown in Figure 4b. The whole PCB circuit is shown in Figure 4c. Using TENG to power a wireless sensor node which consists of a microcontroller unit (STM32, STMicroelectronics, Geneva, Swiss Confederation) via the interface conditioning circuit. The MCU (Microcontroller Unit) accesses the data, including weather information and the date, from the server through Wi-Fi and display on the screen successfully, as shown in Figure 4d.

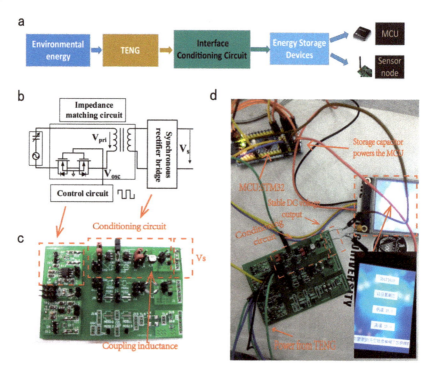

Figure 4. (**a**) An environmental energy harvesting system based on TENG. (**b**) The interface conditioning circuit for TENG. (**c**) Physical picture of the interface conditioning circuit. (**d**) An application of the environmental energy harvesting system based on TENG and the interface conditioning circuit.

4. Conclusions

This paper proposed an adaptable interface conditioning circuit, which is composed of an impedance matching circuit, a synchronous rectifier bridge, a control circuit, and an energy storage device. Especially, a novel bi-directional switch control mechanism was adopted to increase the frequency in order to reduce the energy loss of coupling inductance and increase the output efficiency of TENG. Experimental results show that, in about 3.6 s, the storing capacitor voltage was basically stable at 5.5 V by using the proposed adapted interface conditioning circuit in this paper. The charging efficiency has increased by 50%. The TENG's application in a self-powered sensor will be promoted in the future by adopted this proposed adaptable interface conditioning circuit technology.

Acknowledgments: Research was supported by the National Natural Science Foundation of China (Grant No. 61074177), Chongqing Research Program of Basic Research and Frontier Technology (Grant Nos. STC2014 jcyjA40032 and CSTC2015jcyjA40017).

Author Contributions: Yongshan Hu, Qiuqin Yue and Shan Lu contributed equally to this work. Yongshan Hu analyzed the data and wrote the paper. Qiuqin Yue wrote the paper and proposed experiment scheme. Shan Lu designed the experiment and proposed solutions for experiment. Dongchen Yang, Shuxin Shi and Xiaokun Zhang provided simulation results. Hua Yu proposed initial idea and supervised the study.

Conflicts of Interest: The authors declare no conflict of interest.

References

1. Yu, H.; Yue, Q.; Zhou, J.; Wang, W. A hybrid indoor ambient light and vibration energy harvester for wireless sensor nodes. *Sensors* **2014**, *14*, 8740–8755. [CrossRef] [PubMed]
2. Yu, H.; Zhou, J.; Deng, L.; Wen, Z. A vibration-based MEMS piezoelectric energy harvester and power conditioning circuit. *Sensors* **2014**, *14*, 3323–3341. [CrossRef] [PubMed]
3. Yu, H.; Wu, H. Design of power management ASIC for piezoelectric energy harvester. In Proceedings of the IEEE Sensors, Orlando, FL, USA, 30 October–3 November 2016; pp. 1–3.
4. Yu, H.; He, X.; Ding, W.; Hu, Y.; Yang, D.; Lu, S.; Wu, C.; Zou, H.; Liu, R.; Lu, C.; et al. A self-powered dynamic displacement monitoring system based on triboelectric accelerometer. *Adv. Energy Mater.* **2017**, 1700565. [CrossRef]
5. Perez, M.; Boisseau, S.; Gasnier, P.; Willemin, J.; Pourchier, N.; Geisler, M.; Reboud, J.L. Electret-based aeroelastic harvester and its self-starting battery-free power management circuit. In Proceedings of the IEEE 13th International New Circuits and Systems Conference (NEWCAS), Grenoble, France, 7–10 June 2015; pp. 1–4.
6. Wang, Z.L. On Maxwell's displacement current for energy and sensors: The origin of nanogenerators. *Mater. Today* **2017**, *20*, 74–82. [CrossRef]
7. Fan, F.-R.; Zhong, Q.T.; Zhong, L.W. Flexible triboelectric generator. *Nano Energy* **2012**, *1*, 328–334. [CrossRef]
8. Zi, Y.; Lin, L.; Wang, J.; Wang, S.; Chen, J.; Fan, X.; Yang, P.; Yi, F.; Wang, Z.L. Triboelectric–pyroelectric–piezoelectric hybrid cell for highefficiency energy-harvesting and self-powered sensing. *Adv. Mater.* **2015**, *27*, 2340–2347. [CrossRef] [PubMed]
9. Zi, Y.; Wang, J.; Wang, S.; Li, S.; Wen, Z.; Guo, H.; Wang, Z.L. Effective energy storage from a triboelectric nanogenerator. *Nat. Commun.* **2016**, *7*, 10987. [CrossRef] [PubMed]
10. Xi, F.; Pang, Y.; Li, W.; Jiang, T.; Zhang, L.; Guo, T.; Liu, G.; Zhang, C.; Wang, Z.L. Universal power management strategy for triboelectric nanogenerator. *Nano Energy* **2017**, *37*, 168–176. [CrossRef]
11. Cheng, X.; Miao, L.; Song, Y.; Su, Z.; Chen, X.; Zhang, J.; Zhang, H. High efficiency power management and charge boosting strategy for a triboelectric nanogenerator. *Nano Energy* **2017**, *38*, 438–446. [CrossRef]
12. Zhang, C.; Tang, W.; Han, C.; Fan, F.; Wang, Z.L. Theoretical comparison, equivalent transformation, and conjunction operations of electromagnetic induction generator and triboelectric nanogenerator for harvesting mechanical energy. *Adv. Mater.* **2014**, *26*, 3580–3591. [CrossRef] [PubMed]
13. Niu, S.; Liu, Y.; Chen, X.; Wang, S.; Zhou, Y.S.; Lin, L.; Xie, Y.; Wang, Z.L. Theory of freestanding triboelectric-layer-based nanogenerators. *Nano Energy* **2015**, *12*, 760–774. [CrossRef]
14. Zhang, J.; Li, P.; Zhang, F.; Yang, C. A Management circuit with upconversion oscillation technology for electric-field energy harvesting. *IEEE Trans. Power Electron.* **2016**, *31*, 5515–5523. [CrossRef]

Review

Recent Progress in Rapid Sintering of Nanosilver for Electronics Applications

Wei Liu [1], Rong An [1,2,*], Chunqing Wang [1,2], Zhen Zheng [1], Yanhong Tian [1], Ronglin Xu [1] and Zhongtao Wang [1]

[1]   State Key Laboratory of Advanced Welding and Joining, Harbin Institute of Technology, Harbin 150001, China; w_liu@hit.edu.cn (W.L.); wangcq@hit.edu.cn (C.W.); Zhengzhen@hit.edu.cn (Z.Z.); tianyh@hit.edu.cn (Y.T.); xuronglin123@163.com (R.X.); 14b909068@hit.edu.cn (Z.W.)

[2]   Key Laboratory of Micro-Systems and Micro-Structures Manufacturing, Ministry of Education, Harbin Institute of Technology, Harbin 150080, China

*   Correspondence: anr@hit.edu.cn; Tel.: +86-451-8641-8725

Received: 22 May 2018; Accepted: 9 July 2018; Published: 10 July 2018

Abstract: Recently, nanosilver pastes have emerged as one of the most promising high temperature bonding materials for high frequency and high power applications, which provide an effective lead-free electronic packaging solution instead of high-lead and gold-based solders. Although nanosilver pastes can be sintered at lower temperature compared to bulk silver, applications of nanosilver pastes are limited by long-term sintering time (20–30 min), relative high sintering temperature (>250 °C), and applied external pressure, which may damage chips and electronic components. Therefore, low temperature rapid sintering processes that can obtain excellent nanosilver joints are anticipated. In this regard, we present a review of recent progress in the rapid sintering of nanosilver pastes. Preparation of nanosilver particles and pastes, mechanisms of nanopastes sintering, and different rapid sintering processes are discussed. Emphasis is placed on the properties of sintered joints obtained by different sintering processes such as electric current assisted sintering, spark plasma sintering, and laser sintering, etc. Although the research on rapid sintering processes for nanosilver pastes has made a great breakthrough over the past few decades, investigations on mechanisms of rapid sintering, and the performance of joints fabricated by pastes with different compositions and morphologies are still far from enough.

Keywords: nanosilver pastes; rapid sintering; spark plasma sintering; laser sintering; electric current assisted sintering

1. Introduction

Die-attach materials play a key role in ensuring the performance and reliability of electronic devices [1–4], such as in thermal [5–8] and electrical management [9,10] for high power devices. Die-attach materials are generally classified as conductive adhesives, solder alloys, glasses, metal films, and metal pastes [5]. Nowadays, conductive adhesives [11–14] and tin (Sn) based solder alloys [15–18] are most commonly used as die-attach materials for level-1 interconnections. However, these materials are only suitable for low-temperature range applications due to a low value of performance index, M (0.1–1.8 $\times$ 10^6 W/m, $M = K/\alpha$, where K is the thermal conductivity, and α is the coefficient of thermal expansion) [5], and low melting points (<250 °C) [19]. With the transition of a microelectronic system towards high power or superpower, high density integrated circuits and nano-structure interconnections, new die-attach materials and processes, which can realize low-temperature sintering and high-temperature application, should be developed [20,21]. In addition, a lead-free packaging process for microelectronic components and micro-systems is an inevitable trend in electronics industry [22–25]. Nanosilver pastes with high thermal and electrical conductivity, low sintering temperature [9,26–30] and high operating temperature [31] have great potential to meet the requirements of the new generation of electronics [32].

Traditional hot-pressing sintering processes for nanosilver pastes needs to apply external pressure and complicated temperature profiles, and the processes are usually time-consuming and sometimes require an inert gas atmosphere [33], which severely limit the applications of nanosilver pastes [34]. In this regard, many rapid sintering processes have been proposed to overcome the drawbacks of the hot-pressing sintering processes, such as in-situ formation of nanoparticles and joints, spark plasma sintering (SPS), laser sintering, and current assisted sintering process. Nanosilver particles can be directly interconnected by in-situ generation methods. During the process, the nanosilver particles will in-situ form at the bonding interfaces, and the particles will be relatively less affected by organic carriers. As a result, sintering temperature and time of the nanoparticles can be lowered obviously. Mu et al. obtained joints with strength of 60 MPa by using the in-situ generation method, and the bonding parameters are 5 min at 250 °C with the pressure of 5 MPa [35]. SPS is a rapid sintering technology developed in recent years. The SPS technology combines the effects of hot-pressing, resistance heating, and plasma activation. Through a SPS process, joints with shear strength of 50 MPa can be obtained when the sintering temperature is 200 °C and the sintering time is as short as 1 min [36]. Laser sintering techniques have the characters of high density of energy input and rapid heating. Sintering of nanosilver pastes can be realized in 10 s by laser irradiation, and shear strength of the sintered joints can reach 10 MPa [37,38]. Current assisted sintering technology can provide enough heat to achieve the desired sintering temperature in a short sintering time. By using electric current assisted sintering processes, interconnections can be accomplished within 1.4 s and shear strength of the joints can reach 90 MPa [34]. In this review, the mechanism of nanosilver sintering, synthesis of nanosilver, and recent progresses in rapid sintering of nanosilver pastes were discussed. Emphasis was placed on the properties of sintered joints obtained by different sintering processes.

2. Sintering Mechanism of Nanosilver Particles

Nanosilver particles have attracted considerable interest as one of the most promising interconnecting materials. Therefore, sintering mechanisms of nanosilver particles have become a hot topic during last few decades [20,39–44]. Various sintering models have been developed to explain the sintering mechanisms [45–47]. The classical sphere-to-sphere model, which has been first described by Frenkel [45], reveals that the sintering process begins with rapid neck formation, and is followed by neck growth [48–50]. In the initial stage, two equal-sized spheres (with radius r) come into contact as shown in Figure 1, to form a circular neck (with radius x). Subsequently, the neck begins to grow through different mechanisms of material transportation, which consists of volume diffusion, grain boundary diffusion, surface diffusion, and viscous flow during the sintering process [45,47].

The sintering equations for different sintering mechanisms can be generally expressed as follows [47]:

$$(x/r)^n = Bt \tag{1}$$

where x/r is ratio of the neck radius to the particle radius. B is a constant which depends on the particle size, temperature, and geometric and material terms. t is the sintering time and n is a mechanism-characteristic exponent that is depend on the mass transport process (viscous flow: $n = 2$; volume diffusion: $n = 4$–5; grain boundary diffusion: $n = 6$; surface diffusion: $n = 7$).

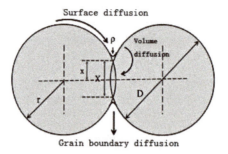

Figure 1. Schematic diagram of the sphere-to-sphere model. Reproduced with permission from [49].

In order to investigate the dominant sintering mechanism of nanosilver particles, the relationship between neck diameter and time is established. Figure 2 shows the experimental logarithm plots of the evolution of the interparticle neck size ratio x/r at different temperatures. The mechanism-characteristic exponent (the values of inverse slope) at the sintering temperatures of 160, 200, and 250 °C are 6.7, 8.8, and 8.4, respectively (the mean value is 7.9). These results indicate that surface diffusion may be the dominant diffusion mechanism at the sintering temperature range of 160–250 °C. When the sintering temperatures increase to 300–350 °C, volume diffusion is probably the prevailing diffusion mechanism [51].

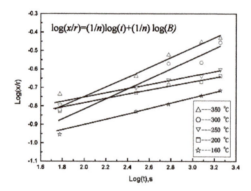

Figure 2. Neck growth kinetics during the sintering process of nanosilver particles at different temperatures. Reproduced with permission from [51].

Besides growth of the neck, the sintering mechanism also comprises the decomposition of the organic coating on the silver particles. Fourier-transform infrared spectroscopy (FTIR) analysis was performed to investigate the change of organic residues in nanosilver pastes during sintering processes [51]. The organic materials coated on silver particles play an important role in affecting the sintering mechanisms. By taking the Polyvinylpyrrolidone (PVP) as an example, as the sintering temperature is below 250 °C, the PVP still coats on the silver particles, and the surface diffusion is the dominant diffusion mechanism. When the temperature is increased above 300 °C, the PVP is destroyed, and the main sintering mechanism changes to volume diffusion. This indicates that the sintering mechanisms may be related with the decomposition of organic components in the nanosilver pastes. When alkylamine is utilized as a dispertant, the alkylamine will evaporate from 130 °C, thereby facilitating a low temperature sintering process of nanosilver particles [52].

Based on the classical sphere-to-sphere model, Yan et al. have revealed the relationship between the strength of joints and the neck growth of silver particles [51]. Basically, the strength of joints depends on the inherent strength of the material τ_o and percent of the bonding interface, which should be proportional to the ratio of the effective bond area between the adjacent particles. The bonding area between the two contacting particles (s) is calculated as follows:

$$s = \pi x^2 \tag{2}$$

where x is the neck radius and the area of the sphere section of the initial particles (S) is given as follows:

$$S = \pi r^2 \tag{3}$$

where r is the initial radius. Therefore, the ratio of effective bond area (R) in each particle is expressed as follows:

$$R = \frac{s}{S} = \frac{\pi x^2}{\pi r^2} = \left(\frac{x}{r}\right)^2 \tag{4}$$

According to the transverse rupture strength model [53], the joint strength is also related to the fractional density V_s, the effective number of bond N_c/π and the stress concentration factor K. Thus, it is suggested that the shear strength (τ) is expressed as follows:

$$\tau = V_S\left(\frac{N_C}{K\pi}\right)\tau_0 R = V_S\left(\frac{N_C}{K\pi}\right)\tau_0\left(\frac{x}{r}\right)^2 \tag{5}$$

According to the model, the strength of the sintered nanosilver joints is proportional to the ratio of effective bond areas between the adjacent particles. The ratio of effective bond areas usually increases by elevating the sintering temperature and pressure, which will help to improve the strength of the joint. Yan et al. have performed shear tests of joints sintered at different temperatures. The results confirmed that the strength of the sintered nanosilver joints is proportional to the ratio of effective bond areas between the adjacent particles [51].

3. Preparation of Nanosilver Particles and Pastes

According to the reaction conditions, preparation methods of nanosilver particles can be divided into chemical reduction methods [54–57], micro emulsion methods [58–60], template methods [61–63], electrochemical methods [64–68], light induced or photocatalytic reduction methods [69–71], microwave or ultrasonic assisted methods [72–77], radiation reduction methods [78–80], and so on. Among them, the chemical reduction method is simple, fast, and more commonly used in preparation of nanosilver particles [81,82]. Therefore, nanosilver particles (less than 20 nm) are traditionally precipitated from the silver salt solution by chemical reduction. Briefly, reducing agents such as Ascorbic Acid [83], Monohydrate Hydrazine [84], Sodium Citrate [85], Dehydrate Sodium Citrate [21,86], Polyvinyl Pyrrolidone [87–89], Ethylene Diamine Tetraacetic Acid [90–92], Sodium Sulfite [54,93] or Sodium Borohydride [57,94] are added to the silver salt solution, for instance, Silver Nitrate [95,96], Silver Chloride [97,98] or Silver Ammonia Solution [99,100], and then the chemical reduction reaction will occur in a polar solvent such as Ethanol [101,102], Methanol [103,104] or Tetrahydrofuran [105,106]. Finally, the nanoparticles and the solution are separated by the centrifugal method [107]. Research shows that ethanol that is low-cost, environmentally friendly, and easy to volatilize is favorable to form small and uniform spherical nanosilver particles. Once high-quality nanosilver particles with uniform morphology and good dispersion are obtained, nanosilver pastes can be prepared. Generally, there are approaches to prepare the nanosilver pastes preparation. One is adding the dispersant, organic carrier, and diluent to an organic solvent, such as acetone or ethanol, and then adding commercial nanosilver particles into them. The mixture should be dispersed evenly by mechanical or ultrasonic assisted mixing. Finally, the organic solvent is evaporated by vacuum heating [41,108]. In general, the nanosilver pastes obtained by this method require higher sintering temperature, longer sintering time, and also need to apply high pressure during the sintering process. This is because the sintering of nanosilver particles depend on the thermal decomposition of organic carriers. However, the organic carriers are usually a long chain polymerization whose thermal decomposition temperature is above 250 °C [109]. Notably, Lee et al. found that besides the dispersant, negative pressure aging can also effectively solve the aggregation of nanoparticles, which will promote the sintering process of nanoparticles [110].

Another method is centrifugal separation [111,112]. First, silver nanoparticles are repeatedly washed to remove impurities. Afterwards, flocculant is added to destroy the balance of a solution, and then nanosilver particles precipitate. After centrifugation, a high concentration nanosilver pastes are obtained. The nanosilver pastes usually have lower sintering temperature as compared with the nanosilver pastes with an organic carrier.

4. Rapid Sintering Processes of Nanoparticles

Lu et al. [41,113,114] are pioneers who have carried out research in the area of nanoparticle sintering. They have utilized commercial silver particles with the average diameter of 30 nm to prepare nanosilver pastes and then realized the interconnection between the SiC chip at 234 °C for about 60 min with a certain applied external pressure. Shear strength of the joints was 17–40 MPa. In order to achieve good sintering properties of joints, a long sintering time, high sintering temperature, and external pressure are usually applied on the samples, which may hinder the application of the nanosilver pastes. Therefore, new processes need to be developed to shorten the sintering time, simplify the sintering process, and improve the sintering properties of the joints. Recently, extensive studies on the rapid sintering processes for nanosilver have been carried out [34,115–117]. Processes such as discharge plasma assisted sintering, laser sintering, and current assisted sintering cannot only enhance the efficiency of sintering, but also improve the properties of the sintered joints. The related research is shown below.

4.1. In-Situ Formation of Nanoparticles and Joints

Recently, Hirose et al. and Toshiaki et al. [118,119] have proposed a novel metal-to-metal bonding process through the in-situ formation of silver nanoparticles with Ag_2O micro-particles. During the bonding process, in-situ formation of silver nanoparticles has been achieved through a reaction between the Ag_2O particles and triethylene glycol (TEG). The silver nanoparticles are relatively less affected by organic carriers. As a result, the sintering temperature of the nanoparticles can be lowered obviously to about 200 °C. Moreover, the cost of micron-sized Ag_2O particles is relatively lower than commercial Ag nanoparticles. In a word, this process can both reduce cost and decrease the sintering temperature of the silver nanoparticles [35,118,120,121]. To retard migration of the Ag ion in the joints, Cu particles or Ag coated Cu particles were added into the mixed pastes [122–125]. Micron-sized Ag_2O pastes have been successfully used in a low-temperature sintering process for the connection between silver plated copper blocks, and the sintering time can be controlled within 1 min as shown in Figure 3 [118].

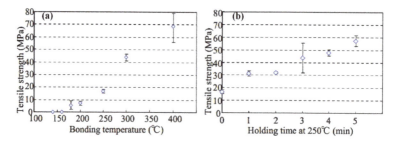

Figure 3. Relationship between bonding parameters and tensile strength of the joints: (**a**) Bonding temperature; (**b**) Holding time at 250 °C. Reproduced with permission from [118].

4.2. Spark Plasma Sintering

Spark plasma sintering (SPS) is a rapid sintering technology developed in recent years [126–128], and the technology has many extraordinary advantages such as fast heating speed (up to 500 °C/min), and short sintering time (30–300 s) [129–133]. In addition, pressure is usually applied in the SPS process to help to form a better contact between nanoparticles, thereby accelerating grain boundary diffusion, lattice diffusion, and viscous flow during the sintering process [134]. All of the mechanisms could help to control the microstructure and achieve a higher density of the sintered materials. Furthermore, SPS also has the advantages of simple operation, high reproducibility, space saving, energy saving, and low cost [131,135].

Alayli et al. [36] used nanosilver particles and the SPS process to bond power semiconductor chips with metallized substrates. Electrical and thermal properties of the samples were both better than those sintered by conventional hot pressing processes. As shown in Figure 4, the shear strength of the joints reached 100 MPa with the sintering parameters of 300 °C, 1 min, and 3 MPa. When the sintering temperature was reduced to the range of 150–200 °C, shear strength of the joints was also as high as 30–50 MPa. Munir et al. [131] systematically summarized the influence of different parameters of SPS on properties of sintered samples. It was found that the heating rate (50–700 °C/min) had little effect on the density of the sintered samples at the same sintered temperature and time. However, the heating rate could influence the size of the sintered nanoparticles. By increasing the sintering pressure, sintering temperature could be decreased, and grain growth of the joints was also restricted. Santanach et al. [136] considered that the density of the sintered samples could be increased through prolonging the sintering time. Ng et al. [137] believed that sintering temperature could also affect density of the joints. Relative density of the samples almost reached 100% when the sintering temperature was increased to 300 °C, as shown in Figure 5.

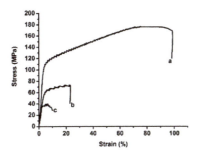

Figure 4. Compression tests on silver samples sintered by spark plasma sintering (SPS) at a low pressure (3 MPa), for a short dwell time (1 min), at a 300 °C, b 200 °C and c 150 °C. Reproduced with permission from [36].

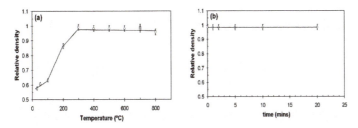

Figure 5. Relative density as a function of variable: (**a**) SPS temperature; (**b**) hold time. Reproduced with permission from [137].

4.3. Laser Sintering

Laser sintering techniques can realize fast sintering of joints with excellent properties as compared with conventional hot-pressing sintering [22,34,138,139]. At present, laser sintering techniques have been widely used in sintering processes of metal, ceramic, and composite materials [140].

Yu et al. [38] realized the bonding of a high power light-emitting diode (LED) chip (60 mil × 60 mil) with silver nanoparticles through a laser sintering process. An infrared radiation laser (30 W, d_{spot} = 600 μm, λ = 980 nm) was utilized in the study. The whole laser sintering process was 10 s after drying the organic solvent on a hot plate (230 °C, 1 min). Shear strength of the laser sintered joints could reach 9 MPa, which was higher than those fabricated by hot-pressing sintering in a convection oven (250 °C, 3 h). In addition, the LED devices showed very good performance in luminous efficiency and reliability. Liu et al. [141] have realized laser sintering dieattach processes using nanosilver pastes within 1 min. Better shear strength was obtained with increasing laser power, irradiation time, and load. Moreover, the shear strength of joints irradiated by 2–5 min of laser beam was comparable to that of the joints sintered by the hotplate for 80 min. Qin et al. [142] used a continuous wave diode pumped solid state (CWDPSS) laser to sinter thin films composed of Ag nanoparticles. The laser sintering process obtained a unique transparent conductive network structure due to the rapid heating and cooling process, whereas conventional heat treatment only formed isolated silver grains during the slow heating process, as shown in Figure 6. Liu et al. [143] successfully synthesized and transferred a transparent conductive silver film via the laser sintering process. Kunsik et al. [144] have realized laser sintering of nanosilver ink through a digital micro mirror (DMD) with high efficiency instead of the traditional printing and scanning process. Habeom Lee et al. have realized fast laser sintering of silver nanoparticle ink on plastic substrates with good properties. The laser scanning speed is 5 mm/s. In the study, the focusing lens of laser system was modified as a micro lens array or a cylindrical lens to generate multiple beamlets or an extended focal line. The modified optical settings are found to be advantageous for the creation of repetitive conducting patterns or areal sintering of the silver nanoparticle ink layer [145].

Figure 6. Scanning electron microscope (SEM) micrographs of nanosilver films: (**a**) heat treatment in air; (**b**) laser sintering. Reproduced with permission from [142].

Yu et al. [146–149] compared the effects of laser type, wavelength, and power on the electrical properties and surface morphologies of sintered nano thin film. The results showed that the picosecond pulsed laser did less damage to the substrate as compared with the nanosecond pulsed laser and continuous laser. In addition, resistivity of sintered nano thin film decreased gradually, and particle size became larger with the increase of the laser power. Cheng et al. [37] simulated the ultrafast melting and re-solidification process of nanoparticles through a one-dimensional, two-temperature model. The results obtained from the model were in good agreement with the experimental data. Huang et al. [150] studied the effects of different particle size and laser frequency on the phase changes of the particles, including melting, vaporization, and re-solidification. Choi et al. [151] measured the in-situ electrical resistance of laser sintered inkjet-printed ink to study its thermal conductivity with the Wiedemann–Franz law. It was found that thermal conductivity of the sintered inkjet-printed ink would increase with the increase of laser input energy. Moreover, the thermal conductivity was also related with surface morphologies of the aggregated nanoparticles.

Up to date, different types of laser have been used in the sintering process of silver nanoparticles. However, the mechanism of laser sintering still requires further study.

4.4. Current Assisted Sintering

Current assisted sintering technology can provide enough heat to achieve the desired sintering temperature in a short sintering time [152–157], which will restrain the coarsening of nanoparticles during the sintering process and then the fine microstructures of the joints, thereby making the joints possess good mechanical properties [158]. The shear strength of the joints fabricated by the current assisted sintering process could reach about 90 MPa with the parameters of 8.25 kA of current density for 1400 ms [159]. Mei et al. [114,160] used this technology to interconnect copper substrates with silver nanoparticles. Shear strength of the joints could reach 40 MPa within 1 s current assisted sintering. Moreover, the joints had better mechanical fatigue performance than those fabricated by traditional hot-pressing sintering methods [161]. Figure 7 shows that the shear strength of the current assisted sintered joints would increase when the current and sintering time was increased, and the maximum strength could reach 96.7 MPa. Figure 8 shows fracture surfaces of the joints. Microstructures of the joints became denser when the current was increased. Li et al. [34] found that the shear strength of the sintered joints was closely related to the peak temperature of the sintering process. Xie et al. [162] achieved robust bonding of large chips (>100 mm^2) with nanosilver by current assisted sintering within 10 s. Moreover, thermal resistance and density of the joints could reach 0.18 °C/W and 89.6%, respectively. Transmission electron microscopy (TEM) results indicated that the better performances of the chip and joints were attributed to the high density of twins in the joints formed in the current assisted sintering process. Mei et al. [163] realized a current assisted sintering of nanosilver paste within 1200 ms, and the strength of the joints could reach 50 MPa. The current assisted sintering process could be divided into three stages: rearrangement of adjacent nanosilver particles, liquid phase assisted densification, and densification by plastic deformation and elimination of crystal defects.

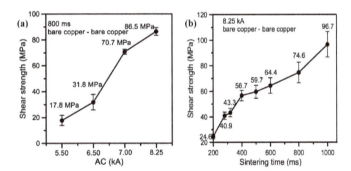

Figure 7. Comparison of shear strength: (**a**) Alternating Current (AC); (**b**) sintering time. Reproduced with permission from [161].

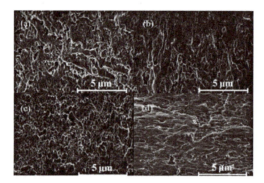

Figure 8. Fracture surfaces of samples sintered with different current: (**a**) 5.50 kA; (**b**) 6.50 kA; (**c**) 7.00 kA; (**d**) 8.25 kA. Reproduced with permission from [161].

Urbański et al. [164] also employed high frequency and high voltage (HFHV) electric energy to sinter nanoparticles, and applied the process to print a conductive pathway with nanosilver ink.

The reliability of sintered joints prepared by electric current assisted sintering and hot-pressing sintering were evaluated by cyclic shear test, respectively. The joints fabricated by electric current assisted sintering are more reliable than those by hot-pressing sintering [34].

5. Conclusions and Future Prospects

This review has summarized recent progress in the rapid sintering of nanosilver for electronics application. Emphasis is placed upon in-situ formation of nanoparticles and joints, spark plasma assisted sintering, laser sintering and electric current assisted sintering. Shear strength and microstructures of sintered joints are also discussed in terms of key process parameters, such as sintering temperature, time, current, et al. Table 1 shows the comparison of the sintering processes. The current assisted sintering could obtain relatively high shear strength in the shortest sintering time. The process of in-situ formation of nanoparticles and joints is economic because Ag_2O is used as the raw material rather than the nanosilver. Spark plasma assisted sintering can obtain joints with high density. Laser sintering has the potential in precise selective sintering, and the process is often used to sinter nanosilver inks to form conductive networks. Current assisted sintering is usually used for connection between dissimilar materials. Moreover, the joints will have excellent shear performance and anti-fatigue properties.

Table 1. Comparison of different rapid sintering methods.

Sintering Method	Sintering Time	Shear Strength	Cost	Ref.
Hot-pressing	30–90 min	30–84 MPa	Low	[22,165–167]
In-situ formation	3–5 min	50–70 MPa	Low	[35,118,120,121]
Spark Plasma	30–300 s	30–100 MPa	Medium	[36,129–132]
Laser	1–15 s	8–10 MPa	High	[38,168–170]
Current	0.1–1 s	40–97 MPa	Medium	[34,115,159–161]

Although the rapid sintering processes have many advantages as compared with conventional hot-pressing sintering processes, there are still a lot of challenges in the applications of the processes to electronic packaging. To promote the application of the rapid sintering processes, future work should focus on the following points:

(1) In some rapid sintering processes, the sintering time may be less than 1 s. The sintering mechanism of the processes may be different from that of traditional hot-pressing sintering. The

sphere-to-sphere model may not be proper to explain the sintering behavior in the rapid sintering processes. Therefore, more work needs to be done to explore the mechanism of rapid sintering.

(2)   In some rapid sintering processes, such as in-situ formation of nanoparticles and joints, high external pressure still needs to be applied on chips. The pressure may damage the chip during the sintering processes. Future work needs to focus on reducing the pressure applied on chips during the rapid sintering processes.

(3)   Generally, binder and dispersants in the nanosilver pastes can prevent the undesirable premature coalescence or agglomeration of nanosilver particles, and the metastable structure will be retained until the organic carriers have been burned out at relatively higher temperatures. It is necessary to study the burnout characteristics of the different organics systems and design nanosilver pastes with a proper processing temperature.

(4)   The bonding between different nanopaticles and metal films is a complicated process, which is related with physical, mechanical, electrostatic, diffusion, and chemical characters of the materials. Sintering parameters, such as sintering temperature, sintering time, pressure, and atmosphere will affect the bonding process and qualities of the interfaces of the materials. Future work needs to focus on the interfacial reactions and behaviors between nanoparticles and metal films during the rapid sintering processes.

(5)   Currently, studies on sintering mechanisms of nanosilver particles are usually based on the spherical particle models. However, beside nanoparticles with spherical morphology, nanomaterials with other morphologies such as wires, belts, disks, and flakes are also widely mixed in pastes. The sintering mechanism of nanomaterials with different morphologies during rapid sintering processes still needs great effort.

Funding: This research was funded by National Natural Science Foundation of China grant number 51375003.

Conflicts of Interest: The authors declare no conflict of interest.

References

1.   Siow, K.S. Mechanical properties of nano-silver joints as die attach materials. *J. Alloys Compd.* **2012**, *514*, 6–19. [CrossRef]
2.   Navarro, L.A.; Perpiñà, X.; Godignon, P.; Montserrat, J.; Banu, V.; Vellvehi, M.; Jordà, X. Thermomechanical assessment of die-attach materials for wide bandgap semiconductor devices and harsh environment applications. *IEEE Trans. Power Electron.* **2014**, *29*, 2261–2271. [CrossRef]
3.   Kong, Y.F.; Li, X.; Mei, Y.H.; Lu, G.Q. Effects of die-attach material and ambient temperature on properties of high-power COB blue LED module. *IEEE Trans. Electron. Devices* **2015**, *62*, 2251–2256. [CrossRef]
4.   Zhang, X.; Zhang, K.; Zhang, M.; Yang, C.; Sun, H.; Gao, Z.; Yuen, M.M.; Yang, S. Highly conductive die attach adhesive from percolation control and its applications in light-emitting device thermal management. *Appl. Phys. Lett.* **2013**, *102*, 1274–1301. [CrossRef]
5.   Tan, K.S.; Wong, Y.H.; Cheong, K.Y. Thermal characteristic of sintered Ag-Cu nanopaste for high-temperature die-attach application. *International J. Therm. Sci.* **2015**, *87*, 169–177. [CrossRef]
6.   Zhang, G.; Feng, S.; Zhu, H.; Li, J.; Guo, C. Determination of thermal fatigue delamination of die attach materials for high-brightness LEDs. *IEEE Photonics Technol. Lett.* **2012**, *24*, 398–400. [CrossRef]
7.   Lin, Y.C.; Hesketh, P.J.; Schuster, J.P. Finite-element analysis of thermal stresses in a silicon pressure sensor for various die-mount materials. *Sens. Actuators A Phys.* **1994**, *44*, 145–149. [CrossRef]
8.   Meyyappan, K.; Mccluskey, P.; Chen, L.Y. Thermomechanical analysis of MEMS pressure sensor die-attach for high temperature applications. *Curr. Opin. Environ. Sustain.* **2004**, *4*, 2556–2561.
9.   Shen, W.; Zhang, X.; Huang, Q.; Xu, Q.; Song, W. Preparation of solid silver nanoparticles for inkjet printed flexible electronics with high conductivity. *Nanoscale* **2014**, *6*, 1622–1628. [CrossRef] [PubMed]

10. Peng, P.; Hu, A.; Gerlich, A.P.; Zou, G.; Liu, L.; Zhou, Y.N. Joining of silver nanomaterials at low temperatures: processes, properties, and applications. *ACS Appl. Mater. Interfaces* **2015**, *7*, 12597–12618. [CrossRef] [PubMed]

11. Li, Y.; Wong, C.P. Recent advances of conductive adhesives as a lead-free alternative in electronic packaging: Materials, processing, reliability and applications. *Mater. Sci. Eng. R* **2006**, *51*, 1–35. [CrossRef]

12. Wu, H.P.; Wu, X.J.; Ge, M.Y.; Zhang, G.Q.; Wang, Y.W.; Jiang, J. Properties investigation on isotropical conductive adhesives filled with silver coated carbon nanotubes. *Compos. Sci. Technol.* **2007**, *67*, 1182–1186. [CrossRef]

13. Lin, Y.C.; Chen, X.M.; Zhang, J. Uniaxial ratchetting behavior of anisotropic conductive adhesive film under cyclic tension. *Polym. Test.* **2011**, *30*, 8–15. [CrossRef]

14. Lin, W.; Xi, X.; Yu, C. Research of silver plating nano-graphite filled conductive adhesive. *Synth. Met.* **2009**, *159*, 619–624. [CrossRef]

15. Lehman, L.P.; Xing, Y.; Bieler, T.R.; Cotts, E.J. Cyclic twin nucleation in tin-based solder alloys. *Acta Mater.* **2010**, *58*, 3546–3556. [CrossRef]

16. Wong, E.H.; Selvanayagam, C.S.; Seah, S.K.W.; Van Driel, W.D.; Caers, J.F.J.M.; Zhao, X.J.; Owens, N.; Tan, L.C.; Frear, D.R.; Leoni, M. Stress-strain characteristics of tin-based solder alloys at medium strain rate. *Mater. Lett.* **2008**, *62*, 3031–3034. [CrossRef]

17. Šebo, P.; Moser, Z.; Švec, P.; Janičkovič, D.; Dobročka, E.; Gasior, W.; Pstruś, J. Effect of indium on the microstructure of the interface between Sn3.13Ag0.74CuIn solder and Cu substrate. *J. Alloys Compd.* **2009**, *480*, 409–415. [CrossRef]

18. Yu, D.Q.; Zhao, J.; Wang, L. Improvement on the microstructure stability, mechanical and wetting properties of Sn-Ag-Cu lead-free solder with the addition of rare earth elements. *J. Alloys Compd.* **2004**, *376*, 170–175. [CrossRef]

19. Manikam, V.R.; Cheong, K.Y. Die attach materials for high temperature applications: A review. *IEEE Trans. Compon. Packag. Manuf. Technol.* **2011**, *1*, 457–478. [CrossRef]

20. Johnson, R.W.; Evans, J.L.; Jacobsen, P.; Thompson, J.R.; Christopher, M. The changing automotive environment: High-temperature electronics. *IEEE Trans. Electron. Packag. Manuf.* **2005**, *27*, 164–176. [CrossRef]

21. Alarifi, H.; Hu, A.; Yavuz, M.; Zhou, Y.N. Silver Nanoparticle Paste for Low-Temperature Bonding of Copper. *J. Electron. Mater.* **2011**, *40*, 1394–1402. [CrossRef]

22. Xiao, K.; Calata, J.N.; Zheng, H.; Ngo, K.D.; Lu, G.Q. Simplification of the nanosilver sintering process for large-area semiconductor chip bonding: reduction of hot-pressing temperature below 200/spl deg/C. *IEEE Trans. Compon. Packag. Manuf. Technol.* **2013**, *3*, 1271–1278. [CrossRef]

23. Liang, M.A.; Yin, L.M.; Xian, J.W. Research advancement of high temperature lead-free electronic packaging. *Weld. Technol.* **2009**, *5*, 003.

24. Nah, J.; Gaynes, M.A.; Feger, C.; Katsurayama, S.; Suzuki, H. Development of wafer level underfill materials and assembly processes for fine pitch Pb-free solder flip chip packaging. In Proceedings of the 2011 IEEE 61st Electronic Components and Technology Conference (ECTC), Lake Buena Vista, FL, USA, 31 May–3 June 2011; pp. 1015–1022.

25. Mustafa, M.; Suhling, J.C.; Lall, P. Experimental determination of fatigue behavior of lead free solder joints in microelectronic packaging subjected to isothermal aging. *Microelectron. Reliab.* **2016**, *56*, 136–147. [CrossRef]

26. Kosmala, A.; Wright, R.; Zhang, Q.; Kirby, P. Synthesis of silver nano particles and fabrication of aqueous Ag inks for inkjet printing. *Mater. Chem. Phys.* **2011**, *129*, 1075–1080. [CrossRef]

27. Decharat, A.; Wagle, S.; Jacobsen, S.; Melandsø, F. Using silver nano-particle ink in electrode fabrication of high frequency copolymer ultrasonic transducers: modeling and experimental investigation. *Sensors* **2015**, *15*, 9210–9227. [CrossRef] [PubMed]

28. Bell, N.B.; Diantonio, C.B.; Dimos, D.B. Development of conductivity in low conversion temperature silver pastes via addition of nanoparticles. *J. Mater. Res.* **2002**, *17*, 2423–2432. [CrossRef]

29. Huang, Q.; Shen, W.; Xu, Q.; Tan, R.; Song, W. Properties of polyacrylic acid-coated silver nanoparticle ink for inkjet printing conductive tracks on paper with high conductivity. *Mater. Chem. Phys.* **2014**, *147*, 550–556. [CrossRef]

30. Tai, Y.L.; Wang, Y.X.; Yang, Z.G.; Chai, Z.Q. Green approach to prepare silver nanoink with potentially high conductivity for printed electronics. *Surf. Interface Anal.* **2011**, *43*, 1480–1485. [CrossRef]

31. Wang, S.; Ji, H.J.; Li, M.Y.; Wang, C.Q. Pressureless low temperature sintering of Ag nanoparticles applied to electronic packaging. *Electron. Process Technol.* **2012**, *8330*, 1–4.
32. Siow, K.S. Are Sintered Silver Joints Ready for Use as Interconnect Material in Microelectronic Packaging? *J. Electron. Mater.* **2014**, *43*, 947–961. [CrossRef]
33. Zheng, H.; Berry, D.; Calata, J.N.; Ngo, K.D.; Luo, S.; Lu, G.Q. Low-pressure joining of large-area devices on copper using nanosilver paste. *IEEE Trans. Compon. Packag. Manuf. Technol.* **2013**, *3*, 915–922. [CrossRef]
34. Li, W.L. Processing and Mechanism of Electric Current Assisted Sintering Nanosilver Paste. Master's Thesis, Tianjin University, Tianjin, China, 2014.
35. Mu, F.W.; Zhao, Z.Y.; Zou, G.S.; Bai, H.; Wu, A.; Liu, L.; Zhang, D.; Zhou, Y.N. Mechanism of low temperature sintering-bonding through in-situ formation of silver nanoparticles using silver oxide microparticles. *Mater. Trans.* **2013**, *54*, 872–878. [CrossRef]
36. Alayli, N.; Schoenstein, F.; Girard, A.; Tan, K.L.; Dahoo, P.R. Spark Plasma Sintering constrained process parameters of sintered silver paste for connection in power electronic modules: Microstructure, mechanical and thermal properties. *Mater. Chem. Phys.* **2014**, *148*, 125–133. [CrossRef]
37. Cheng, C.W.; Chen, J.K. Femtosecond laser sintering of copper nanoparticles. *Appl. Phys. A* **2016**, *122*, 289. [CrossRef]
38. Yu, S.L.; Yun, C.; Kim, K.H.; Kim, W.H.; Jeon, S.W.; Lee, J.K.; Kim, J.P. Laser-sintered silver nanoparticles as a die adhesive layer for high-power light-emitting diodes. *IEEE Trans. Compon. Packag. Manuf. Technol.* **2014**, *4*, 1119–1124.
39. Hu, A.; Guo, J.Y.; Alarifi, H.; Patane, G.; Zhou, Y.; Compagnini, G.; Xu, C.X. Low temperature sintering of Ag nanoparticles for flexible electronics packaging. *Appl. Phys. Lett.* **2010**, *97*, 153117. [CrossRef]
40. Ide, E.; Angata, S.; Hirose, A.; Kobayashi, K.F. Metal-metal bonding process using Ag metallo-organic nanoparticles. *Acta Mater.* **2005**, *53*, 2385–2393. [CrossRef]
41. Bai, J.G.; Zhang, Z.Z.; Calata, J.N.; Lu, G.Q. Low-temperature sintered nanoscale silver as a novel semiconductor device-metallized substrate interconnect material. *IEEE Trans. Compon. Packag. Technol.* **2006**, *29*, 589–593. [CrossRef]
42. Yan, J.; Zou, G.; Wu, A.P.; Ren, J.; Yan, J.; Hu, A.; Zhou, Y. Pressureless bonding process using Ag nanoparticle paste for flexible electronics packaging. *Scr. Mater.* **2012**, *66*, 582–585. [CrossRef]
43. Bakhishev, T.; Subramanian, V. Investigation of gold nanoparticle inks for low-temperature lead-free packaging technology. *J. Electron. Mater.* **2009**, *38*, 2720–2725. [CrossRef]
44. Morita, T.; Ide, E.; Yasuda, Y.; Hirose, A.; Kobayashi, K. Study of bonding technology using silver nanoparticles. *Jpn. J. Appl. Phys.* **2014**, *47*, 6615–6622. [CrossRef]
45. Frenkel, J. Viscous flow of crystalline bodies under the action of surface tension. *J. Phys. USSR* **1945**, *9*, 385.
46. Shaler, A.J.; Wulff, J. Mechanism of Sintering. *Acta Metall.* **2002**, *7*, 222–223. [CrossRef]
47. Kingery, W.D.; Woulbroun, J.M.; Charvat, F.R. *Effects of Applied Pressure on Densification During Sintering in the Presence of Liquid Phase*; Sintering Key Papers; Springer: Dordrecht, The Netherlands, 1990; pp. 405–415.
48. Kang, S.J.L. Sintering: Densification, grain growth & microstructure. *J. Phys. IV* **2005**, *7*, 674–742.
49. Coble, R.L. Sintering Crystalline Solids. I. Intermediate and Final State Diffusion Models. *J. Appl. Phys.* **1961**, *32*, 787–792. [CrossRef]
50. Wu, M.; Chang, L.L.; Cui, Y.N.; Qu, X.H. Molecular dynamics simulation for the sintering process of Au nanoparticles. *J. Univ. Sci. Technol. Beijing* **2014**, *36*, 345–353.
51. Yan, J.; Zou, G.; Liu, L.; Zhang, D.; Bai, H.; Wu, A.P.; Zhou, Y.N. Sintering mechanisms and mechanical properties of joints bonded using silver nanoparticles for electronic packaging applications. *Weld. World* **2015**, *59*, 427–432. [CrossRef]
52. Wakuda, D.; Kim, K.S.; Suganuma, K. Time-dependent sintering properties of Ag nanoparticle paste for room temperature bonding. In Proceedings of the 9th IEEE Conference on Nanotechnology, Genoa, Italy, 26–30 July 2009; pp. 412–415.
53. German, R.M. Manipulation of Strength During Sintering as a Basis for Obtaining Rapid Densification without Distortion. *Mater. Trans.* **2005**, *42*, 1400–1410. [CrossRef]
54. Liu, J.; Li, X.; Zeng, X. Silver nanoparticles prepared by chemical reduction-protection method, and their application in electrically conductive silver nanopaste. *J. Alloys Compd.* **2010**, *494*, 84–87. [CrossRef]
55. Wang, C.X.; Li, Y.L.; Lei, X.U.; Zhou, S.B. Preparation of Nano-sized Silver Particles by Liquid Chemical Reduction Method. *Technol. Dev. Chem. Ind.* **2014**, *64*, 241–246.

56. Kheybari, S.; Samadi, N.; Hosseini, S.V.; Fazeli, A.; Fazeli, M.R. Synthesis and antimicrobial effects of silver nanoparticles produced by chemical reduction method. *DARU J. Pharm. Sci.* **2010**, *18*, 168–172.

57. Wang, X.Y.; Liu, J.G.; Cao, Y.; Cai, Z.X.; Li, X.Y.; Zeag, X.Y. Synthesis of Silver Nanoparticles by Chemical Reduction Method and Properties of Nano-silver Conductive Paste. *Precious Met.* **2011**, *32*, 14–19.

58. Seop, G.; Sang, U.; Chae, K.G.; Kim, S.U.; Chae, G.; Han, G.S.; Hui, B.J.; Jeong, E.; Sik, B.D. Method for Preparing Silver Nano-Sized Powder of 5–10 nm in Size by Using Micro-Emulsion Process. KR Patent KR20040093911(A), 9 November 2004.

59. Zhang, W.; Qiao, X.; Chen, J. Synthesis of nanosilver colloidal particles in water/oil microemulsion. *Colloids Surf. A Physicochem. Eng. Asp.* **2007**, *299*, 22–28. [CrossRef]

60. Solanki, J.N.; Murthy, Z.V.P. Highly monodisperse and sub-nano silver particles synthesis via microemulsion technique. *Colloids Surf. A Physicochem. Eng. Asp.* **2010**, *359*, 31–38. [CrossRef]

61. Yang, A.; Zhang, J.; Liang, S.H.; Ding, B.J. Monodisperse silver microspheres: A facile BSA template method. *Sci. China Technol. Sci.* **2013**, *56*, 2250–2258. [CrossRef]

62. Peng, G.; Zhang, M.; Hou, H.; Xiao, Q. A simple template method for hierarchical dendrites of silver nanorods and their applications in catalysis. *Mater. Res. Bull.* **2008**, *43*, 531–538.

63. Lu, Y.D.; Chen, X.X.; Chen, L.H. Synthesis of Silver Nanoparticles through the Soft Template Method and their Applications to Surface-Enhanced Raman Scattering. *Appl. Mech. Mater.* **2013**, *395–396*, 158–161. [CrossRef]

64. Khaydarov, R.A.; Khaydarov, R.R.; Gapurova, O.; Estrin, Y.; Scheper, T. Electrochemical method for the synthesis of silver nanoparticles. *J. Nanopart. Res.* **2009**, *11*, 1193–1200. [CrossRef]

65. Ma, H.; Yin, B.; Wang, S.; Jiao, Y.; Pan, W.; Huang, S.; Chen, S.; Meng, F. Synthesis of silver and gold nanoparticles by a novel electrochemical method. *ChemPhysChem* **2010**, *5*, 68–75. [CrossRef] [PubMed]

66. Zhu, J.J.; Liao, X.H.; Zhao, X.N.; Chen, H.Y. Preparation of silver nanorods by electrochemical methods. *Mater. Lett.* **2001**, *49*, 91–95. [CrossRef]

67. Reicha, F.M.; Sarhan, A.; Abdelhamid, M.I.; El-Sherbiny, I.M. Preparation of silver nanoparticles in the presence of chitosan by electrochemical method. *Carbohydr. Polym.* **2012**, *89*, 236–244. [CrossRef] [PubMed]

68. Sun, H.P.; Jin, G.S.; Lee, T.G.; Park, H.M.; ong Song, J. One-step large-scale synthesis of micrometer-sized silver nanosheets by a template-free electrochemical method. *Nanoscale Res. Lett.* **2013**, *8*, 248.

69. Krajczewski, J.; Joubert, V.; Kudelski, A. Light-induced transformation of citrate-stabilized silver nanoparticles: Photochemical method of increase of SERS activity of silver colloids. *Colloids Surf. A Physicochem. Eng. Asp.* **2014**, *456*, 41–48. [CrossRef]

70. Krajczewski, J.; Kołątaj, K.; Kudelski, A. Light-induced growth of various silver seed nanoparticles: A simple method of synthesis of different silver colloidal SERS substrates. *Chem. Phys. Lett.* **2015**, *625*, 84–90. [CrossRef]

71. Jia, H.; Xu, W.; An, J.; Li, D.; Zhao, B. A simple method to synthesize triangular silver nanoparticles by light irradiation. *Spectrochim. Acta Part A Mol. Biomol. Spectrosc.* **2006**, *64*, 956–960. [CrossRef] [PubMed]

72. Kim, K.S.; Park, B.G.; Jung, K.H.; Kim, J.W.; Jeong, M.Y.; Jung, S.B. Microwave sintering of silver nanoink for radio frequency applications. *J. Nanosc. Nanotechnol.* **2015**, *15*, 2333–2337. [CrossRef]

73. Zhu, Z.H.; Song, Y.W. Microwave method for preparing nano silver sol. *Guangzhou Chem. Ind.* **2014**, *42*, 122–123.

74. Ledrappier, F. Research of nano-silver colloids prepared by microwave-assisted synthesis method and its fresh-keeping of strawberry. *Sci. Technol. Food Ind.* **2014**, *35*, 326–327.

75. Li, Y.; Jing, H.; Han, Y.; Xu, L.; Lu, G. Microstructure and joint properties of nano-silver paste by ultrasonic-assisted pressureless sintering. *J. Electron. Mater.* **2016**, *45*, 3003–3012. [CrossRef]

76. Wani, I.A.; Ganguly, A.; Ahmed, J.; Ahmad, T. Silver nanoparticles: Ultrasonic wave assisted synthesis, optical characterization and surface area studies. *Mater. Lett.* **2011**, *65*, 520–522. [CrossRef]

77. Jiang, L.P.; Xu, S.; Zhu, J.M.; Zhang, J.R.; Zhu, J.J.; Chen, H.Y. Ultrasonic-assisted synthesis of monodisperse single-crystalline silver nanoplates and gold nanorings. *Inorg. Chem.* **2004**, *43*, 5877–5883. [CrossRef] [PubMed]

78. Cui, G. Control of morphology and size of nano-silver particles in the liquid irradiation reduction process. *J. Radiat. Res. Radiat. Process.* **2010**, *28*, 29–36.

79. Zhou, Y.; Zhao, Y.; Wang, L.; Xu, L.; Zhai, M.; Wei, S. Radiation synthesis and characterization of nanosilver/gelatin/ carboxymethyl chitosan hydrogel. *Radiat. Phys. Chem.* **2012**, *81*, 553–560. [CrossRef]

80. Singh, R. Radiation synthesis of PVP/alginate hydrogel containing nanosilver as wound dressing. *J. Mater. Sci. Mater. Med.* **2012**, *23*, 2649–2658. [CrossRef] [PubMed]

81. Zhang, W.; Qiao, X.; Qiu, X.; Chen, Q.; Cai, Y.; Chen, H. Controllable synthesis and ostwald ripening of silver nanoparticles. *Curr. Nanosci.* **2012**, *9*, 753–758. [CrossRef]

82. Zhang, W.; Zhang, W.; Qiao, X.; Qiu, X.; Chen, Q.; Cai, Y. Controllable preparation of silver nanostructures and the effects of acidity-basicity of the reaction system. *Sci. Adv. Mater.* **2014**, *6*, 304–311. [CrossRef]

83. Guan, Y.; Yu, P. The Synthesis of Nanosilver Using Gelatin as Additive. *Sci. Technol. Gelatin* **2015**, *2*, 34–39.

84. Kang, B.K.; Son, D.M.; Kim, Y.H. Preparation and Characterization of Silver Nanoparticles Embedded in Silica Sol Particles. *Bull. Korean Chem. Soc.* **2011**, *32*, 3707–3711. [CrossRef]

85. Li, Y.; Liu, X.; Zhang, J.; Dai, Z.; Li, P.; Wei, J. One-pot synthesis of Ag nanoparticle/graphene composites using sodium citrate as reducing agent. *J. Pure Appl. Microbiol.* **2013**, *7*, 105–110.

86. Wang, S.; Ji, H.; Li, M.; Wang, C. Fabrication of interconnects using pressureless low temperature sintered Ag nanoparticles. *Mater. Lett.* **2012**, *85*, 61–63. [CrossRef]

87. He, H.; Zhou, J.; Dong, H.; Song, Y. Synthesis of flower-like silver nanoparticles by polyvinyl pyrrolidone (PVP) reduction. *Gold* **2013**, *1*, 8–12.

88. Song, Y.; Zhou, J.; Lan, X. Microwave-assisted synthesis of size-controlled silver nanoparticles using polyvinyl pyrrolidone as a reducing agent. *International J. Nanomanuf.* **2014**, *10*, 33–41. [CrossRef]

89. Wang, H.; Qiao, X.; Chen, J.; Wang, X.; Ding, S. Mechanisms of PVP in the preparation of silver nanoparticles. *Mater. Chem. Phys.* **2005**, *94*, 449–453. [CrossRef]

90. Khan, M.S.; Chaudhari, V.R. Morphological Effect on Fluorescence Behavior of Silver Nanoparticles. *J. Fluoresc.* **2014**, *24*, 751–757. [CrossRef] [PubMed]

91. Gill, R.; Tian, L.; Somerville, W.R.C.; Le Ru, E.C.; van Amerongen, H.; Subramaniam, V. Silver nanoparticle aggregates as highly efficient plasmonic antennas for fluorescence enhancement. *J. Phys. Chem. C* **2017**, *116*, 16687–16693. [CrossRef]

92. Ortega, E.; Berk, D. Precipitation of Silver Powders in the Presence of Ethylenediamine Tetraacetic Acid. *Ind. Eng. Chem. Res.* **2006**, *45*, 1863–1868. [CrossRef]

93. López-Miranda, A.; López-Valdivieso, A.; Viramontes-Gamboa, G. Silver nanoparticles synthesis in aqueous solutions using sulfite as reducing agent and sodium dodecyl sulfate as stabilizer. *J. Nanopart. Res.* **2012**, *14*, 1101. [CrossRef]

94. Eltugral, N.; Simsir, H.; Karagoz, S. Preparation of nano-silver-supported activated carbon using different ligands. *Res. Chem. Intermed.* **2016**, *42*, 1663–1676. [CrossRef]

95. Lengke, M.F.; Fleet, M.E.; Southam, G. Biosynthesis of silver nanoparticles by filamentous cyanobacteria from a silver(I) nitrate complex. *Langmuir* **2007**, *23*, 2694–2699. [CrossRef] [PubMed]

96. Raut, R.W.; Mendhulkar, V.D.; Kashid, S.B. Photosensitized synthesis of silver nanoparticles using Withania somnifera, leaf powder and silver nitrate. *J. Photochem. Photobiol. B* **2014**, *132*, 45–55. [CrossRef] [PubMed]

97. Khodashenas, B.; Ghorbani, H.R. Synthesis of silver nanoparticles with different shapes. *Arabian J. Chem.* **2015**, *7*, 1–16. [CrossRef]

98. Soo, K.; Ji, H.K. One-Step Fabrication of Poly (ethylenimine)-Stabilized Silver Nanoparticles from Insoluble Silver Chloride Salt. *Bull. Korean Chem. Soc.* **2011**, *32*, 2469–2472.

99. Dubas, S.T.; Pimpan, V. Green synthesis of silver nanoparticles for ammonia sensing. *Talanta* **2008**, *76*, 29–33. [CrossRef] [PubMed]

100. Pandey, S.; Goswami, G.K.; Nanda, K.K. Green synthesis of biopolymer-silver nanoparticle nanocomposite: An optical sensor for ammonia detection. *International J. Biol. Macromol.* **2012**, *51*, 583–589. [CrossRef] [PubMed]

101. And, L.M.; Ladotouriño, I. Reduction and Stabilization of Silver Nanoparticles in Ethanol by Nonionic Surfactants. *Langmuir* **1996**, *12*, 3585–3589.

102. Pal, A.; Shah, S.; Devi, S. Microwave-assisted synthesis of silver nanoparticles using ethanol as a reducing agent. *Mater. Chem. Phys.* **2009**, *114*, 530–532. [CrossRef]

103. Hong, S.I.; Duarte, A.; Gonzalez, G.A.; Kim, N.S. Synthesis of silver nanoparticles at the liquid-liquid using ultrasonic wave. *J. Electron. Packag.* **2013**, *135*, 011005. [CrossRef]

104. Chitsazi, M.R.; Korbekandi, H.; Asghari, G.; Bahri Najafi, R.; Badii, A.; Iravani, S. Synthesis of silver nanoparticles using methanol and dichloromethane extracts of *Pulicaria gnaphalodes* (Vent.) Boiss. aerial parts. *Artif. Cells Nanomed. Biotechnol.* **2014**, *44*, 328–333. [CrossRef] [PubMed]

105. Balan, L.; Malval, J.P.; Schneider, R.; Burget, D. Silver nanoparticles: New synthesis, characterization and photophysical properties. *Mater. Chem. Phys.* **2007**, *104*, 417–421. [CrossRef]
106. Kim, M.; Byun, J.W.; Shin, D.S.; Lee, Y.S. Spontaneous formation of silver nanoparticles on polymeric supports. *Mater. Res. Bull.* **2009**, *44*, 334–338. [CrossRef]
107. Chen, Y.Y.; Chen, G.X.; Cui, Y.Y.; Chen, Q.F.; Tai, J.L.; Yang, Y. Morphology of nano silver synthesized in different solvent systems. *Packag. Eng.* **2015**, *21*, 44–47.
108. Bai, G. Low-Temperature Sintering of Nanoscale Silver Paste for Semiconductor Device Interconnection. Ph.D. Thesis, Faculty of the Virginia Polytechnic Institute and State University, Blacksburg, VA, USA, 2005.
109. Ohashi, K.; Kosaka, Y.; Suzuki, S.; Kawakami, T. Resin Composition Containing Ultrafine Silver Particles. US Patent US8921452, 30 December 2014.
110. Lee, H.S.; Yang, M.Y. The effect of negative pressure aging on the aggregation of Cu_2O nanoparticles and its application to laser induced copper electrode fabrication. *Phys. Chem. Chem. Phys.* **2015**, *17*, 4360–4366. [CrossRef] [PubMed]
111. Liu, J.F.; Yu, S.J.; Yin, Y.G.; Chao, J.B. Methods for separation, identification, characterization and quantification of silver nanoparticles. *TrAC Trends Anal. Chem.* **2012**, *33*, 95–106. [CrossRef]
112. Maheswari, P.; Prasannadevi, D.; Mohan, D. Preparation and performance of silver nanoparticle incorporated polyetherethersulfone nanofiltration membranes. *High Perform. Polym.* **2013**, *25*, 174–187. [CrossRef]
113. Bai, J.G.; Lei, T.G.; Calata, J.N.; Lu, G.Q. Control of nanosilver sintering attained through organic binder burnout. *J. Mater. Res.* **2007**, *22*, 3494–3500. [CrossRef]
114. Bai, J.G.; Lu, G.Q. Thermomechanical Reliability of Low-Temperature Sintered Silver Die Attached SiC Power Device Assembly. *IEEE Trans. Device Mater. Reliab.* **2006**, *6*, 436–441. [CrossRef]
115. Mei, Y.; Cao, Y.; Chen, G.; Li, X.; Lu, G.Q.; Chen, X. Rapid sintering nanosilver joint by pulse current for power electronics packaging. *IEEE Trans. Device Mater. Reliab.* **2013**, *13*, 258–265. [CrossRef]
116. Feng, S.T.; Mei, Y.H.; Chen, G.; Li, X.; Lu, G.Q. Characterizations of rapid sintered nanosilver joint for attaching power chips. *Materials* **2016**, *9*, 564. [CrossRef] [PubMed]
117. Ermak, O.; Zenou, M.; Toker, G.B.; Ankri, J.; Shacham-Diamand, Y.; Kotler, Z. Rapid laser sintering of metal nano-particles inks. *Nanotechnology* **2016**, *27*, 385201. [CrossRef] [PubMed]
118. Hirose, A.; Tatsumi, H.; Takeda, N.; Akada, Y.; Ogura, T.; Ide, E.; Morita, T. A novel metal-to-metal bonding process through in-situ formation of Ag nanoparticles using Ag_2O microparticles. *J. Phys. Conf. Ser.* **2009**, *165*, 012074. [CrossRef]
119. Morita, T.; Yasuda, Y.; Ide, E.; Akada, Y.; Hirose, A. Bonding technique using micro-scaled silver-oxide particles for in-situ formation of silver nanoparticles. *Mater. Trans.* **2008**, *49*, 2875–2880. [CrossRef]
120. Ogura, T.; Nishimura, M.; Tatsumi, H.; Takeda, N.; Takahara, W.; Hirose, A. Evaluation of interfacial bonding utilizing Ag2O-derived silver nanoparticles using TEM observation and molecular dynamics simulation. *Open Surf. Sci. J.* **2011**, *3*, 55–59. [CrossRef]
121. Takeda, N.; Tatsumi, H.; Akada, Y.; Ogura, T.; Ide, E.; Morita, T.; Hirose, A. Low-temperature bonding process via in-situ formation of Ag nanoparticles using Ag_2O microparticles. *Prep. Nat. Meet. JWS* **2009**, *103*.
122. Jianfeng, Y.; Guisheng, Z.; Anming, H.; Zhou, Y.N. Preparation of PVP coated Cu NPs and the application for low-temperature bonding. *J. Mater. Chem.* **2011**, *21*, 15981–15986. [CrossRef]
123. Yasuda, Y.; Ide, E.; Morita, T. Evaluation of copper oxide-based interconnecting materials. *Open Surf. Sci. J.* **2011**, *3*, 123–130. [CrossRef]
124. Morisada, Y.; Nagaoka, T.; Fukusumi, M.; Kashiwagi, Y.; Yamamoto, M.; Nakamoto, M. A Low-temperature bonding process using mixed Cu-Ag nanoparticles. *J. Electron. Mater.* **2010**, *39*, 1283–1288. [CrossRef]
125. Yan, J.; Wu, A.; Ren, J.; Hu, A.; Zhou, Y.N. Polymer-protected Cu-Ag mixed NPs for low-temperature bonding application. *J. Electron. Mater.* **2012**, *41*, 1886–1892. [CrossRef]
126. Zhang, Z.H.; Liu, Z.F.; Lu, J.F.; Shen, X.B.; Wang, F.C.; Wang, Y.D. The sintering mechanism in spark plasma sintering—Proof of the occurrence of spark discharge. *Scr. Mater.* **2014**, *81*, 56–59. [CrossRef]
127. Zhang, Z.H.; Wang, F.C.; Lee, S.K.; Liu, Y.; Cheng, J.W.; Liang, Y. Microstructure characteristic, mechanical properties and sintering mechanism of nanocrystalline copper obtained by SPS process. *Mater. Sci. Eng. A* **2009**, *523*, 134–138. [CrossRef]
128. Zhang, L.; Elwazri, A.M.; Zimmerly, T.; Brochu, M. Fabrication of bulk nanostructured silver material from nanopowders using shockwave consolidation technique. *Mater. Sci. Eng. A* **2008**, *487*, 219–227. [CrossRef]

129. Liu, Z.F.; Zhang, Z.H.; Korznikov, A.V.; Lu, J.F.; Korznikova, G.; Wang, F.C. A novel and rapid route for synthesizing nanocrystalline aluminum. *Mater. Sci. Eng. A* **2014**, *615*, 320–323. [CrossRef]
130. Sweet, G.A.; Brochu, M., Jr.; Hexemer, R.L.; Donaldson, I.W.; Bishop, D.P. Consolidation of aluminum-based metal matrix composites via spark plasma sintering. *Mater. Sci. Eng. A* **2015**, *648*, 123–133. [CrossRef]
131. Munir, Z.A.; Anselmi-Tamburini, U.; Ohyanagi, M. The effect of electric field and pressure on the synthesis and consolidation of materials: A review of the spark plasma sintering method. *J. Mater. Sci.* **2006**, *41*, 763–777. [CrossRef]
132. Sweet, G.A.; Brochu, M.; Hexemer, R.L., Jr.; Donaldson, I.W.; Bishop, D.P. Microstructure and mechanical properties of air atomized aluminum powder consolidated via spark plasma sintering. *Mater. Sci. Eng. A* **2014**, *608*, 273–282. [CrossRef]
133. Anselmi-Tamburini, U.; Garay, J.E.; Munir, Z.A.; Tacca, A.; Maglia, F.; Spinolo, G. Spark plasma sintering and characterization of bulk nanostructured fully stabilized zirconia: Part I. Densification studies. *J. Mater. Res.* **2004**, *19*, 3255–3262. [CrossRef]
134. Guillon, O.; Gonzalez-Julian, J.; Dargatz, B.; Kessel, T.; Schierning, G.; Räthel, J.; Herrmann, M. Field-assisted sintering technology/spark plasma sintering: mechanisms, materials, and technology developments. *Adv. Eng. Mater.* **2014**, *16*, 830–849. [CrossRef]
135. Ye, M.; Qiang, W.; Jia, C. Status quo of spark plasma sintering in Japan. *Powder Metall. Technol.* **2014**, *32*, 296–305.
136. Santanach, J.G.; Weibel, A.; Estournès, C.; Yang, Q.; Laurent, C.; Peigney, A. Spark plasma sintering of alumina: Study of parameters, formal sintering analysis and hypotheses on the mechanism(s) involved in densification and grain growth. *Acta Mater.* **2011**, *59*, 1400–1408. [CrossRef]
137. Ng, H.B.; Shearwood, C.; Khor, K.A. Spark plasma sintering of silver nanopowder. In Proceedings of the SPIE Microelectronics, MEMS, and Nanotechnology, Canberra, Australia, 27 December 2007.
138. Niittynen, J.; Sowade, E.; Kang, H.; Baumann, R.R.; Mäntysalo, M. Comparison of laser and intense pulsed light sintering (IPL) for inkjet-printed copper nanoparticle layers. *Sci. Rep.* **2015**, *5*, 8832. [CrossRef] [PubMed]
139. Zenou, M.; Ermak, O.; Saar, A.; Kotler, Z. Laser sintering of copper nanoparticles. *J. Phys. D Appl. Phys.* **2013**, *47*, 025501. [CrossRef]
140. Niittynen, J.; Abbel, R.; Mäntysalo, M.; Perelaer, J.; Schubert, U.S.; Lupo, D. Alternative sintering methods compared to conventional thermal sintering for inkjet printed silver nanoparticle ink. *Thin Solid Films* **2014**, *556*, 452–459. [CrossRef]
141. Liu, W.; Wang, C.; Wang, C.; Jiang, X.; Huang, X. Laser Sintering of Nano-Ag Particle Paste for High-Temperature Electronics Assembly. *IEEE Trans. Compon. Packag. Manuf. Technol.* **2017**, *7*, 1050–1057. [CrossRef]
142. Qin, G.; Watanabe, A. Conductive network structure formed by laser sintering of silver nanoparticles. *J. Nanopart. Res.* **2014**, *16*, 2684. [CrossRef]
143. Liu, Y.K.; Lee, M.T. Laser direct synthesis and patterning of silver nano/microstructures on a polymer substrate. *ACS Appl. Mater. Interfaces* **2014**, *6*, 14576–14582. [CrossRef] [PubMed]
144. An, K.; Hong, S.; Han, S.; Lee, H.; Yeo, J.; Ko, S.H. Selective sintering of metal nanoparticle ink for maskless fabrication of an electrode micropattern using a spatially modulated laser beam by a digital micromirror device. *ACS Appl. Mater. Interfaces* **2014**, *6*, 2786–2790. [CrossRef] [PubMed]
145. Lee, H.; Kwon, J.; Shin, W.S.; Kim, H.R.; Shin, J.; Cho, H.; Han, S. Large-Area Compatible Laser Sintering Schemes with a Spatially Extended Focused Beam. *Micromachines* **2017**, *8*, 153. [CrossRef]
146. Yu, J.H.; Kang, K.T.; Hwang, J.Y.; Lee, S.H.; Kang, H. Rapid sintering of copper nano ink using a laser in air. *International J. Precis. Eng. Manuf.* **2014**, *15*, 1051–1054. [CrossRef]
147. Paeng, D.; Yeo, J.; Lee, D.; Moon, S.J.; Grigoropoulos, C.P. Laser wavelength effect on laser-induced photo-thermal sintering of silver nanoparticles. *Appl. Phys. A* **2015**, *120*, 1229–1240. [CrossRef]
148. Theodorakos, I.; Zacharatos, F.; Geremia, R.; Karnakis, D.; Zergioti, I. Selective laser sintering of Ag nanoparticles ink for applications in flexible electronics. *Appl. Surf. Sci.* **2015**, *336*, 157–162. [CrossRef]
149. Yamaguchi, M.; Araga, S.; Mita, M.; Yamasaki, K.; Maekawa, K. On-demand infrared laser sintering of gold nanoparticle paste for electrical contacts. *IEEE Trans. Compon. Packag. Manuf. Technol.* **2015**, *5*, 1160–1168. [CrossRef]

150. Huang, J.; Zhang, Y.; Chen, J.K. Modeling of Ultrafast Phase Change Processes in a Thin Metal Film Irradiated by Femtosecond Laser Pulse Trains. *J. Heat Transf.* **2011**, *133*, 031003. [CrossRef]

151. Choi, J.H.; Ryu, K.; Park, K.; Moon, S.J. Thermal conductivity estimation of inkjet-printed silver nanoparticle ink during continuous wave laser sintering. *International J. Heat Mass Transf.* **2015**, *85*, 904–909. [CrossRef]

152. Munir, Z.A.; Quach, D.V.; Ohyanagi, M. Electric current activation of sintering: A review of the pulsed electric current sintering process. *J. Am. Ceram. Soc.* **2011**, *94*, 1–19. [CrossRef]

153. Gubicza, J.; Bui, H.; Fellah, F.; Dirras, G.F. Microstructure and mechanical behavior of ultrafine-grained Ni processed by different powder metallurgy methods. *J. Mater. Res.* **2009**, *24*, 217–226. [CrossRef]

154. Ritasalo, R.; Cura, M.E.; Liu, X.W.; Söderberg, O.; Ritvonen, T.; Hannula, S.P. Spark plasma sintering of submicron-sized Cu-powder-Influence of processing parameters and powder oxidization on microstructure and mechanical properties. *Mater. Sci. Eng. A* **2010**, *527*, 2733–2737. [CrossRef]

155. Kanamori, K.; Kineri, T.; Fukuda, R.; Nishio, K.; Hashimoto, M.; Mae, H. Spark plasma sintering of sol-gel derived amorphous ZrW_2O_8 nanopowder. *J. Am. Ceram. Soc.* **2010**, *92*, 32–35. [CrossRef]

156. Guo, S.Q.; Nishimura, T.; Kagawa, Y.; Yang, J.M. Spark plasma sintering of zirconium diborides. *J. Am. Ceram. Soc.* **2008**, *91*, 2848–2855. [CrossRef]

157. Musa, C.; Licheri, R.; Locci, A.M.; Orrù, R.; Cao, G.; Rodriguez, M.A.; Jaworska, L. Energy efficiency during conventional and novel sintering processes: The case of $Ti–Al_2O_3–TiC$ composites. *J. Clean. Prod.* **2009**, *17*, 877–882. [CrossRef]

158. Grasso, S.; Sakka, Y.; Maizza, G. Electric current activated/assisted sintering (ECAS): A review of patents 1906–2008. *Sci. Technol. Adv. Mater.* **2009**, *10*, 053001. [CrossRef] [PubMed]

159. Mei, Y.; Chen, G.; Cao, Y.; Li, X.; Han, D.; Chen, X. Simplification of low-temperature sintering nanosilverfor power electronics packaging. *J. Electron. Mater.* **2013**, *42*, 1209–1218. [CrossRef]

160. Mei, Y.H.; Cao, Y.; Chen, G.; Li, X.; Lu, G.Q.; Chen, X. Characterization and reliability of sintered nanosilver joints by a rapid current-assisted method for power electronics packaging. *IEEE Trans. Device Mater. Reliab.* **2014**, *14*, 262–267. [CrossRef]

161. Lu, G.Q.; Li, W.; Mei, Y.; Li, X. Measurements of electrical resistance and temperature distribution during current assisted sintering of nanosilver die-attach material. In Proceedings of the 2014 International Conference on Electronics Packaging (ICEP), Toyama, Japan, 23–25 April 2014; pp. 538–543.

162. Xie, Y.; Wang, Y.; Mei, Y.; Xie, H.; Zhang, K.; Feng, S.; Siow, K.S.; Li, X.; Lu, G.Q. Rapid sintering of nano-Ag paste at low current to bond large area (>100 mm^2) power chips for electronics packaging. *J. Mater. Process. Technol.* **2018**, *255*, 644–649. [CrossRef]

163. Mei, Y.; Li, L.; Li, X.; Li, W.; Yan, H.; Xie, Y. Electric-current-assisted sintering of nanosilver paste for copper bonding. *J. Mater. Sci. Mater. Electron.* **2017**, *28*, 9155–9166. [CrossRef]

164. Urbański, K.J.; Fałat, T.; Felba, J.; Mościcki, A.; Smolarek, A.; Bonfert, D.; Bock, K. Experimental method for low-temperature sintering of nano-Ag inks using electrical excitation. In Proceedings of the 2012 12th IEEE International Conference on Nanotechnology (IEEE-NANO), Birmingham, UK, 20–23 August 2012; pp. 1–4.

165. Khazaka, R.; Mendizabal, L.; Henry, D. Review on Joint Shear Strength of Nano-Silver Paste and Its Long-Term High Temperature Reliability. *J. Electron. Mater.* **2014**, *43*, 2459–2466. [CrossRef]

166. Pešina, Z.; Vykoukal, V.; Palcut, M.; Sopoušek, J. Shear strength of copper joints prepared by low temperature sintering of silver nanoparticles. *Electron. Mater. Lett.* **2014**, *10*, 293–298. [CrossRef]

167. Zou, G.; Yan, J.; Mu, F.; Wu, A.; Ren, J.; Hu, A.; Zhou, Y. Low temperature bonding of Cu metal through sintering of Ag nanoparticles for high temperature electronic application. *Open Surf. Sci. J.* **2011**, *3*, 70–75. [CrossRef]

168. Maekawa, K.; Yamasaki, K.; Niizeki, T.; Mita, M.; Matsuba, Y.; Terada, N.; Saito, H. Drop-on-demand laser sintering with silver nanoparticles for electronics packaging. *IEEE Trans. Compon. Packag. Manuf. Technol.* **2012**, *2*, 868–877. [CrossRef]

169. Maekawa, K.; Yamasaki, K.; Niizeki, T.; Mita, M.; Matsuba, Y.; Terada, N.; Saito, H. Laser sintering of silver nanoparticles for electronic use. *Mater. Sci. Forum* **2010**, *638–642*, 2085–2090. [CrossRef]

170. Niizeki, T.; Maekawa, K.; Mita, M.; Yamasaki, K.; Matsuba, Y.; Terada, N.; Saito, H. Laser sintering of Ag nanopaste film and its application to bond-pad formation. In Proceedings of the 2008 58th Electronic Components and Technology Conference, Lake Buena Vista, FL, USA, 27–30 May 2008; pp. 1745–1750.

MDPI

St. Alban-Anlage 66

4052 Basel

Switzerland

Tel. +41 61 683 77 34

Fax +41 61 302 89 18

www.mdpi.com

Micromachines Editorial Office

E-mail: micromachines@mdpi.com

www.mdpi.com/journal/micromachines

www.ingramcontent.com/pod-product-compliance
Lightning Source LLC
LaVergne TN
LVHW071357070326
832902LV00028B/4640